REFUGE OF MY WEARY SOUL

ANNE STEELE

SELECTED WORKS OF ANNE STEELE
FOREWORD BY KEVIN TWIT

EDITED BY ALEX J WEBSTER

REFUGE
OF MY
WEARY SOUL

Selected Works of Anne Steele

Anne Steele
Edited by Alex J. Webster

SHAZBAAR PRESS | BIRMINGHAM, AL

Publisher's Note: This work is a compilation of the works of Anne Steele taken from *Poems on Subjects Chiefly Devotional in two volumes by Theodosia* (1780), *Miscellaneous Pieces in Verse and Prose Vol. 3 (1780)* and *The Works of Anne Steele* (1808)

Book Layout © 2017 BookDesignTemplates.com

Refuge of My Weary Soul/ Anne Steele. -- 1st ed.
ISBN 978-0996988032

To J. Alan Carter

Contents

SELECTED POEMS

PSALMS, ATTEMPTED IN VERSE

Foreword

My discovery of Anne Steele and her hymns in the late 1990s has been one of the most pivotal events in my life. I will never forget first reading the hymn, "Dear Refuge of My Weary Soul." [GOD THE ONLY REFUGE OF THE TROUBLED MIND, page 124] I thought, "Can you really say this, sing this in church?" I was astonished at the honesty and vulnerability in her words. Here was a woman who invited us into her struggle, and led us to the kind of deep trust that is only forged through the struggle. When I heard that Alex Webster was going to publish a new edition of the hymns of Anne Steele, I was overjoyed. Anne's father recorded these words in his diary more than 250 years ago:

> Today Nanny sent part of her composition to London to be printed. I entreat a gracious God, who enabled and stirred her up to such a work, to direct in it and bless it for the good of many. I pray God to make it useful, and keep her humble.

I believe the Lord has answered that prayer many times over, and He's not done yet. May we all pray that this new edition will be blessed for the good of many more!

Rev. Kevin Twit
Founder, Indelible Grace Music

Editor's Preface

I first became acquainted with the writings of Anne Steele through the song, "My God, My Father Blissful Name!" by Indelible Grace Music. I was deeply moved by the lyrics and set out to discover additional Anne Steele lyrics. I was surprised to discover that they were not readily available. Facsimile copies were available, but I found the archaic typesetting distracting. Her hymns were also available on various hymn websites but were not convenient for devotional use. I therefore decided that an updated edition that was easier on the modern eye and easily available was in order.

This volume is what I initially set out to purchase for myself! I have updated the typesetting but have attempted to maintain the formatting and spelling. On some occasions, I have updated the spelling: For example, *Surprizing* has been changed to *Surprising* or *crouded* to *crowded*. I debated whether to change words that had been "apostrophed," such as,"*whene'er*" or "*ev'ry*". I decided to keep them with the understanding that their original intent was to be sung, and their placement aided in matching the text with an appropriate hymn meter.

The writings in this book were taken from *Poems on Subjects Chiefly Devotional in two volumes by Theodosia* (1780), *Miscellaneous Pieces in Verse and Prose Vol. 3 (1780);* and *The Works of Mrs. Anne Steele (1808).*

Alex J. Webster

Anne Steele

Anne Steele, born in 1717, was the daughter of Mr. William Steele, a timber merchant and lay pastor of the Particular Baptist Church at Broughton, in Hampshire in the United Kingdom. Anne's great uncle founded the Baptist church in Broughton and ministered there for 40 years. Anne's father succeeded his uncle as lay pastor. The family was prosperous, and gave cottages and a burial ground to the church. Her mother died when Anne was three years-old and devoted herself to her father and his ministry. At an early age, Anne demonstrated a taste for literature and would often entertain her friends by her poetical compositions. She spent her entire life in Broughton, devoting much of her time to writing.

The common understanding of Anne Steele's life and demeanor can be summarized by the entry for her in the 11th Edition of the *Encyclopedia Britannica*:

> The drowning of her betrothed a few hours before the time fixed for her marriage deeply affected an otherwise quiet life, and her hymns rather emphasize the less optimistic phases of Christian experience.

The effect of the entry was to portray Ms. Steele as a sort of pious Miss Havisham, who redirected her unrequited love to the composition of devotional material. However, the drowned betrothed story has now been dismissed as apocryphal, and recent research has shown her to be more active and sociable than once thought. Her personal loss and physical ailments cannot be minimized, but she transcended them, bringing encouragement and comfort to those around her. Caleb Evans, an early biographer, stated:

The duties of friendship and religion occupied her time, and the pleasures of both constituted her delight. Her heart was "apt to feel" too often to a degree too painful for her own felicity, but always with the other most tender and generous sympathies for her friends. Yet united with this exquisite sensibility, she possessed a native cheerfulness of disposition, which not even the uncommon and agonizing pains she endured in the latter part of her life to deprive her of. In every short interval of abated suffering, she would in a variety of ways, as well as by her enlivening conversation, give pleasure to all around her. Her life was a life of unaffected humility, warm benevolence, sincere friendship, and genuine devotion alive which is not easy truly to describe, or faithfully imitate.[1]

Steele's devotion to her father was described as one "united by the strongest ties of affectionate duty and gratitude."[2] She spent many years caring for her father until his death in 1769. Evans stated that her father's death greatly affected her and *"gave such a shock to her feeble frame, that she never entirely recovered it though she survived him some years."* For most of her life, she displayed symptoms consistent with malaria. As a result, she was bed ridden the final years of her life.

As a hymn writer, Anne Steele's reputation began in 1760 when she published two volumes titled, *Poems on Subjects Chiefly Devotional.* Their publication inspired John Ash of Pershore and Caleb Evans of Bristol to compile a Baptist hymn book. It was published in Bristol in 1769 and included 62 hymns by Anne Steele.

Her hymns also became popular in America. When, in 1808, the people of Trinity Church in Boston, Massachusetts

[1] The Works of Mrs. Anne Steele (1808), p.7
[2] Ibid, p.6

published their own hymn book; 59 of its 152 hymns were by Anne Steele.

The *Gadsby Hymnal* (1814) featured 27 of her hymns. The hymnal *Psalms and Hymns,* published in 1858 by The Society for Promoting Christian Knowledge, included 22 hymns by Anne Steele.

The church's familiarity with Steele's work diminished through the years as they were used less in successive hymnals. *The Baptist Church Hymnal,* published in 1900, included five hymns by Anne Steele; and *The Baptist Church Hymnal Revised,* in 1933, included only two, the same two that are in the Baptist Hymn Book of 1962.

Steele died November 11th 1778. Of her death Evans wrote:

> When the interesting hour came, she welcomed its arrival, and though her feeble body was excruciated with pain, her mind was perfectly serene. She uttered not a murmuring word, but was all resignation, peace, and holy joy. She took the most affectionate leave of her weeping friends around her, and at length, the happy moment of her dismission arising, she closed her eyes, and with these animating words on her dying lips, "I know that my Redeemer liveth," gently fell asleep in Jesus.[3]

---

[3] Ibid, p.8

HYMNS ON VARIOUS
SUBJECTS

DESIRING TO PRAISE GOD

I.

Almighty author of my frame,
   To thee my vital pow'rs belong;
Thy praise, (delightful, glorious theme!)
   Demands my heart, my life, my tongue.

II.

My heart, my life, my tongue are thine.
   Oh be thy praise their blest employ!
But may my song with angels join?
   Nor sacred awe forbid the joy?

III.

Thy glories, the seraphic lyre
   On all its strings attempts in vain;
Then how shall mortals dare aspire
   In thought, to try th' unequal strain?

IV.

Yet the great Sov'reign of the skies
   To mortals bends a gracious ear;
Nor the mean tribute will despise,
   If offer'd with a heart sincere.

V.

Great God, accept the humble praise,
   And guide my heart, and guide my tongue.
While to thy name I trembling raise
   The grateful, though unworthy song.

IMPLORING DIVINE INFLUENCES

I.

My God, whene'er my longing heart
Thy praiseful tribute would impart,
In vain my tongue with feeble aim,
    Attempts the glories of thy name.

II.

In vain my boldest thoughts arise,
    I sink to earth and lose the skies;
Yet I may still thy grace implore,
    And low in dust thy name adore.

III.

O let thy grace my heart inspire,
    And raise each languid, weak desire;
Thy grace, which condescends to meet
    The sinner prostrate at thy feet.

IV.

With humble fear let love unite,
    And mix devotion with delight;
Then shall thy name be all my joy,
    Thy praise, my constant blest employ.

V.

Thy name inspires the harps above
    With harmony, and praise, and love;
That grace, which tunes th' immortal strings,
    Looks kindly down on mortal things.

VI.

O let thy grace guide ev'ry song,
    And fill my heart and tune my tongue;
Then shall the strain harmonious flow,
    And heav'n's sweet work begin below.

MEDITATING ON CREATION AND
PROVIDENCE

I.

Lord, when my raptur'd thought surveys
Creation's beauties o'er,
All nature joins to teach thy praise,
    And bid my soul adore.

II.

Where'er I turn my gazing eyes,
    Thy radiant footsteps shine;
Ten thousand pleasing wonders rise,
    And speak their source divine.

III.

The living tribes of countless forms,
    In earth, and sea, and air;
The meanest flies, the smallest worms,
    Almighty pow'r declare.

IV.

All rose to life at thy command,
    And wait their daily food
From thy paternal, bounteous hand,
    Exhaustless spring of good!

V.

The meads, array'd in smiling green,
    With wholesome herbage crown'd;
The fields with corn, a richer scene,
    Spread thy full bounties round.

VI.

The fruitful tree, the blooming flow'r,
    In varied charms appear;
Their varied charms display thy pow'r,
    Thy goodness all declare.

3

VII.

The sun's productive quick'ning beams
   The growing verdure spread;
Refreshing rains and cooling streams
   His gentle influence aid.

VIII.

The moon and stars his absent light
   Supply with borrow'd rays,
And deck the sable veil of night,
   And speak their Maker's praise.

IX.

Thy wisdom, pow'r, and goodness, Lord,
   In all thy works appear:
And O let man thy praise record;
   Man, thy distinguish'd care.

X.

From thee the breath of life he drew;
   That breath thy pow'r maintains;
Thy tender mercy ever new,
   His brittle frame sustains.

XI

Yet nobler favors claim his praise,
   Of reason's light possest ;
By revelation's brighter rays
   Still more divinely blest.

XII.

Thy providence, his constant guard
   When threat'ning woes impend,
Or will th' impending dangers ward,
   Or timely succours lend.

XIII.

On me that providence has shone
    With gentle smiling rays;
O let my lips and life make known
    Thy goodness, and thy praise.

XIV.

All bounteous Lord, thy grace impart;
    O teach me to improve
Thy gifts with ever grateful heart,
    And crown them with thy love.

REDEEMING LOVE

I.

C ome, heav'nly love, inspire my song
    With thy immortal flame,
And teach my heart, and teach my tongue
    The Saviour's lovely name.

II.

The Saviour! O what endless charms
    Dwell in the blissful sound!
Its influence ev'ry fear disarms,
    And spreads sweet comfort round.

III.

Here pardon, life, and joys divine
    In rich effusion flow,
For guilty rebels lost in sin,
    And doom'd to endless woe.

IV.

In our first parents' crime we fell;
    Our blood, our vital breath
Deep ting'd with all the seeds of ill,
    Sad heirs to sin and death.

V.

Black o'er our wrath-devoted heads
    Avenging justice frown'd;
While hell disclos'd her deepest shades,
    And horrors rose around.

VI.

Wrapp'd in the gloom of dark despair,
    We helpless, hopeless lay:
But sov'reign mercy reach'd us there,
    And smil'd despair away.

VII.

God's only son, (stupendous grace!)
    Forsook his throne above;
And swift to save our wretched race,
    He flew on wings of love.

VIII.

Th' almighty former of the skies
    Stoop'd to our vile abode ;
While angels view'd with wond'ring eyes,
    And hail'd th' incarnate God.

IX.

The God in heav'nly strains they sung,
    Array'd in human clay:
Mysterious love! what angel tongue
    Thy wonders can display?

X.

Mysterious love, in ev'ry scene,
    Through all his life appears:
His spotless life expos'd to pain,
    And miseries and tears.

XI.

What blessings on a thankless race
    His bounteous hand bestow'd!
And from his tongue what wond'rous grace,
    What rich instruction flow'd!

XII.

The dumb, the deaf, the lame, the blind
    Confess'd his healing pow'r ;
Disease and death their prey resign'd,
    And grief complain'd no more.

XIII.

Infernal legions trembling fled,
  Aw'd by his pow'rful word:
And winds and seas his voice obey'd,
  And own'd their sov'reign Lord.

XIV.

But man, vile man, his love abus'd,
  Blind to the noblest good;
Blasphem'd his pow'r, his word refus'd,
  And sought his sacred blood.

XV.

Still his unwearied love pursued
  Salvation's glorious plan;
And firm th' approaching horrors view'd,
  Deserv'd by guilty man.

XVI.

What pain, what soul-oppressing pain,
  The great Redeemer bore;
While bloody sweat, like drops of rain,
  Distill'd from ev'ry pore!

XVII.

And ere the dreadful storm descends
  Full on his guiltless head,
See him by his familiar friends
  Deserted and betray'd!

XVIII.

While ruffian bands the Lord surround,
  Relentless, murd'rous foes;
Meek, as a lamb for slaughter bound,
  The patient suff'rer goes.

XIX.

Arraign'd at Pilate's impious bar,
  (Unparallel'd disgrace!)
See spotless innocence appear
  In guilt's detested place!

XX.

When perj'ry fails to stain his name,
  The mob's envenom'd breath
Extorts his sentence, "Public shame
  And painful lingering death."

XXI.

Patient, the cruel scourge he bore:
  The innocent, the kind!
Then to the rabble's lawless pow'r
  And rudest taunts consign'd.

XXII.

With thorns they crown that awful brow,
  Whose frown can shake the globe ',
And on their king in scorn bestow
  The reed and purple robe.

XXIII.

Ah! — see, the fatal cross appears,
  Heart-wounding, dreadful scene!
His sacred flesh rude iron tears,
  With agonizing pain.

XXIV.

Expos'd with thieves, to public view ---
  Could nature bear the sight?
The blushing sun his beams withdrew,
  And wrapt the globe in night!

XXV.

Then, Oh! what loads of wrath unknown
    The glorious suff'rer felt;
For crimes unnumber'd to atone,
    To expiate mortal guilt!

XXVI.

The Father's blissful smile withdrawn,
    In that tremendous hour;
Yet still the God sustain'd the man
    With his almighty pow'r.

XXVII.

"'Tis finish'd," now aloud he cries, "
    No more the law requires:"
And now, (amazing sacrifice!)
    The Lord of life expires.

XXVIII.

Earth's firm foundation felt the shock,
    With universal dread;
Trembled the mountain, rent the rock,
    And wak'd the sleeping dead!

XXIX.

Now breathless in the silent tomb,
    His sacred body lies:
Thither his lov'd disciples come,
    With sorrow-streaming eyes.

XXX.

But see, the promis'd morn appear!
    Their joy revives again;
The Saviour lives: adieu to fear,
    To ev'ry anxious pain.

LONGING SOULS INVITED TO THE GOSPEL FEAST

Luke 14:22.

I.

Ye wretched, hungry, starving poor,
  Behold a royal feast!
Where mercy spreads her bounteous store,
  For ev'ry humble guest.

II.

See, Jesus stands with open arms;
  He calls, he bids you come:
Guilt holds you back, and fear alarms;
  But see, there yet is room.

III.

Room in the Saviour's bleeding heart:
  There love and pity meet;
Nor will he bid the soul depart,
  That trembles at his feet.

IV.

In him, the Father reconcil'd
  Invites your souls to come;
The rebel shall be call'd a child,
  And kindly welcom'd home.

V.

O come, and with his children taste
  The blessings of his love;
While hope attends the sweet repast,
  Of nobler joys above.

VI.

There, with united heart and voice,
   Before th' eternal throne,
Ten thousand thousand souls rejoice,
   In ecstasies unknown.

VII.

And yet ten thousand thousand more,
   Are welcome still to come:
Ye longing souls, the grace adore;
   Approach, there yet is room.

LIGHT AND DELIVERANCE

I.

The weary trav'ller, lost in night,
   Breathes many a longing sigh,
And marks the welcome dawn of light,
   With rapture in his eye.

II.

Thus sweet the dawn of heav'nly day
   Lost weary sinners find;
When mercy with reviving ray,
   Beams o'er the fainting mind.

III.

To slaves oppress'd with cruel chains,
   How kind, how clear the friend,
Whose gen'rous hand relieves their pains,
   And bids their sorrows end!

IV.

Thus kind, thus dear, that friend divine
    Who ransoms captive souls,
Unbinds the cruel chains of sin,
    And all its pow'r controls.

V.

Jesus, to thy soul-cheering light,
    My dawn of hope I owe;
Once, wand'ring in the shades of night,
    And lost in hopeless woe.

VI.

'Twas thy dear hand redeem'd the slave?
And set the pris'ner free;
Be all I am, and all I have,
Devoted, Lord, to thee!

VII.

But stronger ties than nature knows,
    My grateful love confine;
And ev'n that love, thy hand bestows,
    Which wishes to be thine.

VIII.

Here, at thy feet, I wait thy will,
    And live upon thy word:
O give me warmer love and zeal,
    To serve my dearest Lord.

A MORNING HYMN

I.

LORD of my life, O may thy praise
 Employ my noblest pow'rs,
Whose goodness lengthens out my days,
 And fills the circling hours.

II.

Preserv'd by thy almighty arm,
 I pass'd the shades of night,
Serene, and safe from ev'ry harm,
 And see returning light.

III.

While many spent the night in sighs,
 And restless pains, and woes;
In gentle sleep I clos'd my eyes,
 And undisturb'd repose.

IV.

When sleep, death's 'semblance o'er me spread,
 And I unconscious lay,
Thy watchful care was round my bed,
 To guard my feeble clay.

V.

O let the same almighty care
 My waking hours attend;
From ev'ry danger, ev'ry snare,
 My heedless steps defend.

VI.

Smile on my minutes as they roll,
 And guide my future days;
And let thy goodness fill my soul
 With gratitude and praise.

AN EVENING HYMN

I.

Great God, to thee my ev'ning song
    With humble gratitude I raise:
O let thy mercy tune my tongue,
   And fill my heart with lively praise.

II.

Mercy, that rich unbounded store,
   Does my unnumber'd wants relieve;
Among thy daily, craving poor,
   On thy all-bounteous hand I live.

III.

My days unclouded, as they pass,
   And ev'ry gently rolling hour,
Are monuments of wond'rous grace,
   And witness to thy love and pow'r.

IV.

Thy love and pow'r, (celestial guard)
   Preserve me from surrounding harms:
Can danger reach me, while the Lord
   Extends his kind protecting arms?

V.

My num'rous wants are known to thee,
   Ere my slow wishes can arise;
Thy goodness measureless and free,
   Is ready still with full supplies.

VI.

And yet this thoughtless, wretched heart,
   Too oft regardless of thy love,
Ungrateful, can from thee depart,
   And fond of trifles vainly rove.

19

VII.

When calm reflection finds a place,
   How vile this wretched heart appears!
O let thy all-subduing grace
   Melt it in penitential tears.

VIII.

Seal my forgiveness in the blood
   Of Jesus: his dear name alone
I plead for pardon, gracious God,
   And kind acceptance at thy throne.

IX.

Let this blest hope my eyelids close,
   With sleep refresh my feeble frame;
Safe in thy care may I repose,
   And wake with praises to thy name.

ON A STORMY NIGHT

I.

L ORD of the earth, and seas, and skies,
All nature owns thy sovereign pow'r;
At thy command the tempests rise,
   At thy command the thunders roar.

II.

We hear, with trembling and affright,
   The voice of heav'n, (tremendous sound!)
Keen lightnings pierce the shades of night,
   And spread bright horrors all around.

III.

What mortal could sustain the stroke,
   Should wrath divine in vengeful storms,
(Which our repeated crimes provoke,)
   Descend to crush rebellious worms?

IV.

These dreadful glories of thy name
   With terror would o'erwhelm our souls;
But mercy dawns with kinder beam,
   And guilt and rising fear controls.

V.

O let thy mercy on my heart
   With cheering, healing radiance shine;
Bid ev'ry anxious fear depart,
   And gently whisper, Thou art mine.

VI.

Then safe beneath thy guardian care,
   In hope serene my soul shall rest;
Nor storms nor dangers reach me there,
   In thee, my God, my refuge, blest.

SEARCHING AFTER HAPPINESS

I.

O happiness, thou pleasing dream,
   Where is thy substance found?
Sought through the varying scenes in vain,
   Of earth's capacious round.

II.

The charms of grandeur, pomp, and shew,
   Are nought but gilded snares;
Ambition's painful steep ascent,
   Thick set with thorny cares.

III.

The busy town, the crowded street,
   Where noise and discord reign,
We gladly leave, and tir'd, retreat
   To breathe and think again.

IV.

Yet if retirement's pleasing charms
   Detain the captive mind,
The soft enchantment soon dissolves;
   'Tis empty all as wind.

V.

Religion's sacred lamp alone,
   Unerring points the way,
Where happiness forever shines
   With unpolluted ray:

VI.

To regions of eternal peace,
   Beyond the starry skies,
Where pure, sublime, and perfect joys
   In endless prospect rise.

VII.

There Jesus, source of bliss divine,
   Our glorious leader reigns;
He gives us strength to hold our way,
   And crowns the traveller's pains.

VIII.

Dear Saviour, let thy cheering smile
   My fainting soul renew;
Then shall the heav'nly Canaan yield
   A sweet, though distant view,

IX.

Be thy almighty arm my stay,
   My guide through all the road,
Till safe I reach my journey's end,
   My Saviour, and my God.

WEARY SOULS INVITED TO REST

Matthew 11:28

I.

COME weary souls with sin distress'd
The Saviour offers heav'nly rest;
The kind, the gracious call obey,
    And cast your gloomy fears away.

II.

Oppress'd with guilt, a painful load,
    O come, and spread your woes abroad;
Divine compassion, mighty love,
    Will all the painful load remove.

III.

Here mercy's boundless ocean flows,
    To cleanse your guilt and heal your woes;
Pardon, and life, and endless peace —
    How rich the gift! how free the grace!

IV.

Lord, we accept with thankful heart,
    The hope thy gracious words impart;
We come with trembling, yet rejoice,
    And bless the kind inviting voice.

V.

Dear Saviour, let thy pow'rful love
    Confirm our faith, our fears remove,
And sweetly influence ev'ry breast.
    And guide us to eternal rest.

THIRSTING AFTER GOD

Isaiah 41:17

I.

When fainting in the sultry waste,
  And parch'd with thirst extreme,
The weary pilgrim longs to taste
  The cool, refreshing stream;

II.

Should, sudden, to his hopeless eye
  A crystal spring appear,
How would th' enliv'ning sweet supply
  His drooping spirits cheer!

III.

So longs the weary fainting mind,
  Oppress'd with sins and woes,
Some soul-reviving spring to find,
  Whence heavenly comfort flows.

IV.

Thus sweet the consolations are,
  The promises impart;
Here flowing streams of life appear,
  To ease the panting heart.

V.

O may I thirst for thee, my God,
  With ardent, strong desire;
And still, through all this desert road,
  To taste thy grace aspire.

VI.

Then shall my prayer to thee ascend,
   A grateful sacrifice;
My plaintive voice thou wilt attend,
   And grant me full supplies.

THE FAVOR OF GOD THE ONLY SATISFYING GOOD

Psalm 4: 6, 7

I.

In vain the erring world inquires,
   For true substantial good:
While earth confines their low desires,
   They live on airy food.

II.

Illusive dreams of happiness,
   Their eager thoughts employ;
They wake, convinc'd their boasted bliss
   Was visionary joy.

III.

Begone, ye gilded vanities;
   I seek some solid good;
To real bliss my wishes rise,
   The favor of my God.

IV.

My God, to thee my soul aspires;
   Dispel the shades of night,
Enlarge and fill these vast desires,
   With infinite delight.

V.

Immortal joy thy smiles impart,
    Heav'n dawns in ev'ry ray;
One glimpse of thee will glad my heart,
    And turn my night to day.

VI.

Not all the good which earth bestows,
    Can fill the craving mind;
Its highest joys are mingled woes,
    And leave a sting behind.

VII.

Should boundless wealth increase my store,
    Can wealth my cares beguile?
I should be wretched still, and poor
    Without thy blissful smile.

VIII.

Grant, O my God, this one request:
    Oh, be thy love alone
My ample portion, — here I rest,
    For heav'n is in the boon.

THE TRANSFORMING VISION OF GOD

Psalm 17:15

I.

M y God, the visits of thy face
Afford superior joy,
To all the flatt'ring world can give,
  Or mortal hopes employ.

II.

But clouds and darkness intervene,
  My brightest joys decline,
And earth's gay trifles oft ensnare
  This wand'ring heart of mine.

III.

Lord, guide this wand'ring heart to thee:
  Unsatisfi'd I stray:
Break thro' the shades of sense and sin,
  With thine enlivening ray.

IV

O let thy beams resplendent shine,
  And ev'ry cloud remove;
Transform my pow'rs, and fit my soul
  For happier scenes above.

V.

There Jesus reigns! may I be cloth'd
  With his divine array;
And when I close these eyes in death,
  Awake to endless day:

VI.

To endless day! To perfect life!
   To bliss without alloy!
Where not the least faint cloud shall rise,
   To intercept the joy:

VII.

To view, unveil'd, thy radiant face,
   Thou everlasting fair!
And, chang'd to spotless purity,
   Thy glorious likeness wear:

VIII.

To feast, with ever new delight,
   On uncreated good;
And drink full satisfying draughts
   Of pleasure's sacred flood.

IX.

O bliss too high for mortal thought!
   It awes, and yet inspires:
Fain would my soul, unfetter'd, rise
   In more intense desires.

X.

Lord, raise my faith, my hope, my heart,
   To those transporting joys;
Then shall I scorn each little snare,
   Which this vain world employs:

XI.

Then, though I sink in death's cold sleep,
   I shall awake to bliss,
And in the likeness of my God,
   Find endless happiness.

THE JOYS OF HEAVEN

I.

Come, Lord, and warm each languid heart.
Inspire each lifeless tongue;
And let the joys of heav'n impart
    Their influence to our song.

II.

Then to the shining seats of bliss
    The wings of faith shall soar,
And all the charms of Paradise
    Our raptur'd thoughts explore.

III.

Pleasures, unsullied, flourish there,
    Beyond the reach of time:
Not blooming Eden smil'd so fair,
    In all her flow'ry prime.

IV.

No sun shall gild the blest abode
    With his meridian ray,
But the more radiant throne of God
    Diffuse eternal day.

V.

Sorrow, and pain, and ev'ry care,
    And discord there shall cease,
And perfect joy and love sincere
    Adorn the realms of peace.

VI.

The soul, from sin forever free,
    Shall mourn its pow'r no more;
But cloth'd in spotless purity,
    Redeeming love adore.

VII.

There on a throne, (how dazzling bright!)
    Th' exalted Saviour shines;
And beams ineffable delight
    On all the heav'nly minds.

VIII.

There shall the followers of the Lamb
    Join in immortal songs;
And endless honors to his name
    Employ their tuneful tongues.

IX.

While sweet reflection calls to mind
    The scenes of mortal care,
When God, their God, forever kind,
    Was present to their pray'r ;

X.

How will the wonders of his grace
    In their full lustre shine?
His wisdom, pow'r, and faithfulness,
    All glorious! all divine!

XI.

The Saviour, dying, rising, crown'd,
    Shall swell the lofty strains,
Seraph and saint his praise resound,
    Through all th' ethereal plains.

XII.

But oh! their transports, oh! their songs,
    What mortal thought can paint?
Transcendent glory awes our tongues,
    And all our notes are faint.

XIII.

Lord, tune our hearts to praise and love,
   Our feeble notes inspire;
Till in thy blissful courts above,
   We join the heav'nly choir.

HUMBLE WORSHIP

I.

Great King of kings, eternal God,
   Shall mortal creatures dare to raise
Their songs to thy supreme abode,
   And join with angels in thy praise?

II.

The brightest Seraph veils his face;
   And low before thy dazzling throne,
With prostrate homage all confess
   Thou art the infinite unknown.

III.

Man, ah how far remov'd below,
   Wrapt in the shades of gloomy night:
His brightest day can only show
   A few faint streaks of distant light.

IV.

But see, the bright, the morning-star!
   His beams shall chase the shades away;
His beams, resplendent from afar,
   Sweet promise of immortal day!

V.

To him, our longing eyes we raise,
    Our guide to thee, the great unknown,
Through him, O may our humble praise
    Accepted rise before thy throne.

PRAISE FOR NATIONAL PEACE

Psalm 46:9

I.

G reat Ruler of the earth and skies,
    A word of thy almighty breath
Can sink the world, or bid it rise:
    Thy smile is life, thy frown is death.

II.

When angry nations rush to arms,
    And rage and noise, and tumult reign,
And war resounds its dire alarms,
    And slaughter spreads the hostile plain;

III.

Thy sov'reign eye looks calmly down,
    And marks their course, and bounds their pow'r;
Thy word the angry nations own,
    And noise and war are heard no more.

IV.

Then peace returns with balmy wing,
    (Sweet peace! with her what blessings fled!)
Glad plenty laughs, the valleys sing,
    Reviving commerce lifts her head.

V.

Thou good, and wise, and righteous Lord,
 All move subservient to thy will ;
And peace and war await thy word,
 And thy sublime decrees fulfil.

VI.

To thee we pay our grateful songs,
 Thy kind protection still implore:
O may our hearts, and lives, and tongues
 Confess thy goodness and adore.

THE VOICE OF THE CREATURES

I.

There is a God, all nature speaks,
 Through earth, and air, and seas, and skies:
See, from the clouds his glory breaks,
 When the first beams of morning rise:

II.

The rising sun, serenely bright,
 O'er the wide world's extended frame,
Inscribes, in characters of light,
 His mighty Maker's glorious name.

III.

Diffusing life, his influence spreads,
 And health and plenty smile around,
And fruitful fields, and verdant meads,
 Are with a thousand blessings crown'd.

IV.

Almighty goodness, pow'r divine,
  The fields and verdant meads display;
And bless the hand which made them shine
  With various charms profusely gay.

V.

For man and beast, here daily food
  In wide diffusive plenty grows;
And there, for drink, the crystal flood
  In streams sweet winding, gently flows.

VI.

By cooling streams, and soft'ning show'rs,
  The vegetable race are fed,
And trees, and plants, and herbs, and flow'rs,
  Their Maker's bounty smiling spread.

VII.

The flow'ry tribes, all blooming, rise
Above the faint attempts of art:
Their bright, inimitable dyes
  Speak sweet conviction to the heart.

VIII.

Ye curious minds, who roam abroad,
And trace creation's wonders o'er,
Confess the footsteps of the God,
And bow before him, and adore.

ANNE STEELE

A RURAL HYMN

I.

To your creator God,
   Your great preserver, raise,
Ye creatures of his hand,
   Your highest notes of praise:
      Let ev'ry voice
      Proclaim his pow'r,
      His name adore,
      And loud rejoice.

II.

Let all creation join
   To pay the tribute due;
Ye meaner ranks begin,
   And man shall learn of you:
      Let nature raise
      From ev'ry tongue,
      A gen'ral song
      Of grateful praise.

III.

Ye num'rous fleecy flocks,
   Far spreading o'er the plain,
With gentle artless voice,
   Assist the humble strain :
      To give you food,
      He bids the field
      Its verdure yield ;
      Extensive good.

IV.

Ye herds of larger size,
   Who feed in meads below,
Resound your Maker's praise
   In each responsive low:

You wait his hand;
The herbage grows,
The riv'let flows,
At his command.

V.

Ye feather'd warblers come,
And bring your sweetest lays,
And tune the sprightly song
To your Creator's praise:
His work you are;
He tun'd your voice,
And you rejoice
Beneath his care.

VI.

Ye trees, which form the shade,
Or bend the loaded bough
With fruits of various kinds,
Your Maker's bounty shew:
From him you rose,
Your vernal suits,
And autumn fruits,
His hand bestows.

VII.

Ye lovely, verdant fields,
In all your green array,
Though silent, speak his praise,
Who makes you bright and gay:
While we in you,
With future bread
Profusely spread,
His goodness view.

VIII.

Ye flow'rs, which blooming shew
  A thousand beauteous dyes,
Your sweetest odors breathe,
  A fragrant sacrifice,
      To him, whose word
      Gave all your bloom,
      And sweet perfume;
      All-bounteous Lord!

IX.

Ye rivers, as you flow,
  Convey your Maker's name,
(Where'er you winding rove)
  On ev'ry silver stream:
      Your cooling flood,
      His hand ordains
      To bless the plains;
      Great spring of good!

X.

Ye winds, that shake the world
  With tempests on your wing,
Or breathe in gentler gales,
  To waft the smiling spring;
      Proclaim abroad,
      (As you fulfil
      His sov'reign will)
      The pow'rful God.

XI.

Ye clouds, or fraught with show'rs,
  Or ting'd with beauteous dyes,
That pour your blessings down,
  Or charm our gazing eyes ;
      His goodness speak,
      His praise declare.
      As through the air
      You shine or break.

XII.

Thou source of light and heat,
  Bright sovereign of the day,
Dispensing blessings round,
  With all-diffusive ray ;
      From morn to night,
      With ev'ry beam,
      Record his name,
      Who made thee bright.

XIII

Fair regent of the night,
  With all thy starry train,
Which rise in shining hosts,
  To gild the azure plain;
      With countless rays
      Declare his name,
      Prolong the theme,
      Reflect his praise.

XIV.

Let ev'ry creature join
   To celebrate his name,
And all their various pow'rs
   Assist th' exalted theme.
      Let nature raise
      From ev'ry tongue,
      A gen'ral song
      Of grateful praise.

XV.

But oh! from human tongues
   Should nobler praises flow;
And ev'ry thankful heart,
   With warm devotion glow:
      Your voices raise,
      Ye highly blest
      Above the rest;
      Declare his praise.

XVI.

Assist me, gracious God,
   My heart, my voice inspire;
Then shall I grateful join
   The universal choir:
      Thy grace can raise
      My heart, my tongue,
      And tune my song
      To lively praise.

GOD MY CREATOR AND BENEFACTOR

I.

My Maker, and my King,
  To thee my all I owe;
Thy sov'reign bounty is the spring
  From whence my blessings flow.

II.

Thou ever good, and kind,
  A thousand reasons move,
A thousand obligations bind,
  My heart to grateful love.

III.

The creature of thy hand,
  On thee alone I live:
My God, thy benefits demand
  More praise than life can give.

IV.

Oh! what can I impart,
  When all is thine before?
Thy love demands a thankful heart,
  The gift, alas, how poor!

V.

Shall I withhold thy due?
And shall my passions rove?
  Lord, form this wretched heart anew.
And fill it with thy love.

VI.

O let thy grace inspire
  My soul with strength divine;
Let all my pow'rs to thee aspire,
  And all my days be thine,

PRAISE TO GOD FOR THE BLESSINGS OF PROVIDENCE AND GRACE

I.

Almighty Father, gracious Lord,
   Kind guardian of my days,
Thy mercies, let my heart record
   In songs of grateful praise.

II.

In life's first dawn, my tender frame
   Was thy indulgent care,
Long ere I could pronounce thy name,
   Or breathe the infant pray'r.

III.

When reason with my stature grew,
   How weak her brightest ray!
How little of my God I knew!
   How apt from thee to stray!

IV.

Around my path what dangers rose!
   What snares spread all my road!
No pow'r could guard me from my foes
   But my preserver, God.

V.

When life hung trembling on a breath,
   'Twas thy almighty love
That sav'd me from impending death,
And bade my fears remove.

VI.

How many blessings round me shone,
   Where'er I turn'd my eye!
How many pass'd almost unknown,
   Or unregarded, by.

VII.

Each rolling year new favors brought
 From thy exhaustless store:
But ah! in vain my lab'ring thought
 Would count thy mercies o'er.

VIII.

While sweet reflection, through my days
 Thy bounteous hand would trace;
Still dearer blessings claim my praise,
 The blessings of thy grace.

IX.

Yes, I adore thee, gracious Lord,
 For favors more divine;
That I have known thy sacred word,
 Where all thy glories shine.

X.

'Tis here, I view with pleasing pain,
 How Jesus left the sky,
(Almighty love! surprising scene!)
 For man, lost man, to die.

XI.

When blest with that transporting view,
 That Jesus died for me,
For this sweet hope what praise is due,
 O God of grace, to thee!

XII

And may I hope that Christ is mine?
 That source of ev'ry bliss,
That noblest gift of love divine —
 What wond'rous grace is this!

XIII.

My highest praise, alas, how poor!
  How cold my warmest love!
Dear Saviour, teach me to adore
  As angels do above.

XIV.

But frail mortality in vain
  Attempts the blissful song;
The high, the vast, the boundless strain,
  Claims an immortal tongue.

XV.

Lord, when this mortal frame decays,
  And ev'ry weakness dies,
Complete the wonders of thy grace,
  And raise me to the skies.

XVI.

Then shall my joyful pow'rs unite,
  In more exalted lays,
And join the happy sons of light,
  In everlasting praise.

CHRIST THE WAY TO HEAVEN

I.

Jesus, the spring of joys divine.
   Whence all my hopes and comforts flow;
Jesus, no other name but thine
   Can save me from eternal woe.

II.

In vain would boasting reason find
   The way to happiness and God;
Her weak directions leave the mind
   Bewilder'd in a dubious road.

III.

No other name will heav'n approve;
   Thou art the true, the living way,
(Ordain'd by everlasting love,)
   To the bright realms of endless day.

IV.

Here let my constant feet abide,
   Nor from the heav'nly path depart;
O let thy spirit, gracious guide,
   Direct my steps, and cheer my heart.

V.

Safe lead me through this world of night,
   And bring me to the blissful plains,
The regions of unclouded light,
   Where perfect joy forever reigns.

LIFE AND SAFETY IN CHRIST ALONE

John 6:68

I.

Thou only sovereign of my heart,
   My refuge, my almighty friend, —
And can my soul from thee depart,
   On whom alone my hopes depend?

II.

Whither, ah! whither shall I go,
   A wretched wand'rer from my Lord?
Can this dark world of sin and woe
   One glimpse of happiness afford?

III.

Eternal life thy words impart,
   On these my fainting spirit lives;
Here sweeter comforts cheer my heart,
   Than all the round of nature gives.

IV.

Let earth's alluring joys combine,
   While thou art near, in vain they call;
One smile, one blissful smile of thine,
   My dearest Lord, outweighs them all.

V.

Thy name my inmost pow'rs adore,
   Thou art my life, my joy, my care:
Depart from thee — 'tis death, — 'tis more,
   Tis endless ruin, deep despair.

VI.

Low at thy feet my soul would lie,
  Here safety dwells, and peace divine;
Still let me live beneath thine eye,
  For life, eternal life is thine.

AN EVENING REFLECTION

I.

Another day is past,
  The hours forever fled,
And time is bearing me in haste,
  To mingle with the dead.

II.

Perhaps my closing eyes
  No more may hail the light,
Seal'd up, before the morning rise.
  In everlasting night.

III.

But I've a part to live,
  A never dying ray,
The soul, immortal, will survive
  The ruins of her clay.

IV.

This mortal frame must lie
  Unconscious in the tomb,
But oh! where will my spirit fly,
  And what will be her doom?

V.

On the tremendous brink
    Of vast eternity,
Where souls with strange amazement shrink,
    What will my prospect be?

VI.

When the dark gulf below,
    With death and horror fraught,
Reveals its scenes of endless woe —
    Oh dreadful, dreadful thought!

VII.

But lo! yon shining skies
    Beam down a cheerful ray,
And bid my drooping hopes arise
    To glorious realms of day.

VIII.

'Tis there my Saviour lives,
    My Lord, my life, my light;
His blissful name my soul revives —
    Adieu to death and night.

IX.

He conquer'd death and hell,
    And his victorious love
Shall bear his ransom'd friends, to dwell
    In his bright courts above.

X.

Jesus! and art thou mine?
    O let thy heav'nly voice
Confirm my hope with pow'r divine,
    And bid my soul rejoice.

XI.

Then shall my closing eyes,
    Contented, sink to rest;
For if tonight this body dies,
    My spirit shall be blest.

THE EXCELLENCY OF THE HOLY SCRIPTURES

I.

Father of mercies, in thy word
    What endless glory shines;
Forever be thy name ador'd
    For these celestial lines.

II.

Here, mines of heav'nly wealth disclose
    Their bright, unbounded store:
The glitt'ring gem no longer glows,
    And India boasts no more.

III.

Here, may the wretched sons of want
    Exhaustless riches find:
Riches, above what earth can grant,
    And lasting as the mind.

IV.

Here, the fair tree of knowledge grows,
    And yields a free repast;
Sublimer sweets than nature knows,
    Invite the longing taste.

V.

Here may the blind and hungry come,
    And light, and food receive;
Here, shall the meanest guest have room.
    And taste, and see, and live.

VI.

Amidst these gloomy wilds below,
    When dark and sad we stray;
Here, beams of heav'n relieve our woe
    And guide to endless day.

VII.

Here, springs of consolation rise,
    To cheer the fainting mind;
And thirsty souls receive supplies,
    And sweet refreshment find.

VIII

When guilt and terror, pain and grief,
    United rend the heart,
Here, sinners meet divine relief,
    And cool the raging smart.

IX.

Here, the Redeemer's welcome voice,
    Spreads heav'nly peace around;
And life, and everlasting joys
    Attend the blissful sound.

X.

But when his painful sufferings rise,
    (Delightful, dreadful scene!)
Angels may read with wond'ring eyes,
    That Jesus died for men.

XI.

O may these heav'nly pages be
    My ever dear delight,
And still new beauties may I see,
    And still increasing light.

XII.

Divine instructor, gracious Lord,
    Be thou forever near,
Teach me to love thy sacred word,
    And view my Saviour there.

THE INFLUENCES OF THE SPIRIT OF GOD
IN THE HEART

John 14:16, 17

I.

Dear Lord, and shall thy Spirit rest
    In such a wretched heart as mine?
Unworthy dwelling! glorious guest!
    Favor astonishing, divine!

II.

When sin prevails, and gloomy fear,
    And hope almost expires in night,
Lord, can thy Spirit then be here,
    Great spring of comfort, life, and light?

III.

Sure the blest Comforter is nigh,
   'Tis he sustains my fainting heart;
Else would my hopes forever die,
   And ev'ry cheering ray depart.

IV.

When some kind promise glads my soul,
   Do I not find his healing voice
The tempest of my fears control,
   And bid my drooping pow'rs rejoice?

V.

Whene'er to call the Saviour mine,
   With ardent wish my heart aspires,
Can it be less than pow'r divine,
   Which animates these strong desires?

VI.

What less than thy almighty word,
   Can raise my heart from earth and dust,
And bid me cleave to thee, my Lord,
   My life, my treasure, and my trust?

VII.

And when my cheerful hope can say
   I love my God, and taste his grace,
Lord, is it not thy blissful ray,
   Which brings this dawn of sacred peace!

VIII.

Let thy kind Spirit in my heart
   Forever dwell, O God of love,
And light and heav'nly peace impart,
   Sweet earnest of the joys above.

CHRIST THE PHYSICIAN OF SOULS

Jeremiah 8:22

I.

Deep are the wounds which sin hath made;
  Where shall the sinner find a cure?
In vain, alas, is nature's aid,
  The work exceeds all nature's pow'r.

II.

Sin like a raging fever reigns,
  With fatal strength in ev'ry part;
The dire contagion fills the veins,
  And spreads its poison to the heart.

III.

And can no sov'reign balm be found,
  And is no kind physician nigh,
To ease the pain, and heal the wound,
  Ere life and hope forever fly?

IV.

There is a great Physician near,
  Look up, O fainting soul, and live;
See, in his heav'nly smiles, appear
  Such ease as nature cannot give!

V.

See, in the Saviour's dying blood,
  Life, health, and bliss, abundant flow!
'Tis only this dear, sacred flood
  Can ease thy pain, and heal thy woe.

VI.

Sin throws in vain its pointed dart.
  For here a sov'reign cure is found;
A cordial for the fainting heart,
  A balm for ev'ry painful wound.

THE INTERCESSION OF CHRIST

Hebrews 7:2

I.

He lives, the great Redeemer lives,
  (What joy the blest assurance gives!)
And now before his Father God,
  Pleads the full merits of his blood.

II.

Repeated crimes awake our fears,
  And justice, arm'd with frowns, appears;
But in the Saviour's lovely face
  Sweet mercy smiles, and all is peace.

III.

Hence then, ye black despairing thoughts;
  Above our fears, above our faults,
His pow'rful intercessions rise,
  And guilt recedes, and terror dies.

IV.

In ev'ry dark distressful hour,
  When sin and Satan join their pow'r;
Let this dear hope repel the dart,
  That Jesus bears us on his heart.

V.

Great advocate, almighty friend —
   On him our humble hopes depend;
Our cause can never, never fail,
   For Jesus pleads, and must prevail.

THE CONDESCENSION OF GOD

1 Kings 8:27

I.

Eternal pow'r, almighty God,
   Who can approach thy throne?
Accessless light is thy abode,
   To angel-eyes unknown.

II.

Before the radiance of thine eye
   The heav'ns no longer shine,
And all the glories of the sky
   Are but the shade of thine.

III.

Great God, and wilt thou condescend
   To cast a look below,
To this vile world thy notice bend,
   These seats of sin and woe?

IV.

But oh! to shew thy smiling face,
　To bring thy glories near-
Amazing and transporting grace
　To dwell with mortals here!

V.

How strange! how awful is thy love!
　With trembling we adore:
Not all th' exalted minds above
　Its wonders can explore.

VI.

While golden harps, and angel tongues
　Resound immortal lays,
Great God, permit our humble songs
　To rise and mean thy praise.

THE HEAVENLY GUEST

Revelation 3:20

I.

And will the Lord thus condescend
　　To visit sinful worms?
Thus at the door shall mercy stand
　　In all her winning forms?

II.

Surprising grace! — and shall my heart
　　Unmov'd and cold remain?
Has this hard rock no tender part?
　　Must mercy plead in vain?

III.

Shall Jesus for admission sue,
　　His charming voice unheard?
And this vile heart, his rightful due,
　　Remain forever barr'd?

IV.

'Tis sin, alas, with tyrant pow'r
　　The lodging has possest;
And crowds of traitors bar the door
　　Against the heav'nly guest.

V.

Lord, rise in thy all-conqu'ring grace,
　　Thy mighty pow'r display;
One beam of glory from thy face
　　Can drive my foes away.

VI.

Ye dang'rous inmates, hence depart;
  Dear Saviour, enter in,
And guard the passage to my heart,
  And keep out ev'ry sin.

GOD THE SOUL'S ONLY PORTION

Lamentations 3:24

I.

In vain the world's alluring smile
Would my unwary heart beguile:
Deluding world! its brightest day,
  Dream of a moment, fleets away!

II.

Earth's highest pleasures, could they last,
  Would pall and languish on the taste;
Such airy chaff was ne'er design'd
  To feed th' immortal, craving mind.

III.

To nobler bliss my soul aspires,
  Come, Lord, and fill these vast desires;
Be thou my portion, here I rest,
  Since of my utmost wish possest.

IV.

O let thy sacred word impart
   Its sealing influence to my heart;
With pow'r, and light, and love divine,
   Assure my soul that thou art mine.

V.

The blissful word, with joy replete,
   Shall bid my gloomy fears retreat,
And heav'n-born hope, serenely bright,
   Shine cheerful through this mortal night.

VI.

Then shall my joyful spirit rise
   On wings of faith above the skies;
And when these transient scenes are o'er,
   And this vain world shall tempt no more:

VII.

O may I reach the blissful plains,
   Where thy unclouded glory reigns,
And dwell forever near thy throne
   In joys to mortal thought unknown.

FAITH IN THE JOYS OF HEAVEN

2 Corinthians. 5:7

I.

Faith leads to joys beyond the sky;
    Why then is this weak mind
Afraid to raise a cheerful eye
    To more than sense can find?

II.

Sense can but furnish scenes of woe,
    In this low vale of tears;
No groves of heav'nly pleasures grow,
    No paradise appears.

III.

Ah! why should this mistaken mind
    Still rove with restless pain?
Delight on earth expect to find,
    Yet still expect in vain?

IV.

Faith, rising upward, points her view
    To regions in the skies;
There lovelier scenes than Eden knew,
    In bright perspective rise.

V.

Oh! if this heav'n-born grace were mine.
    Would not my spirit soar,
Transported gaze on joys divine,
    And cleave to earth no more?

VI.

If in my heart true faith appears,
  How weak the sacred ray!
Feebly aspiring, press'd with fears,
  Almost it dies away.

VII.

O thou, from whose almighty breath
  It first began to rise,
Purge off these mists, these dregs of earth,
  And bid it reach the skies.

VIII.

Let this weak, erring mind no more,
  On earth bewilder'd rove,
But with celestial ardour soar
  To endless joys above.

STRENGTH AND SAFETY IN GOD ALONE

Psalm 105: 4

I

Permit me, Lord, to seek thy face,
   Obedient to thy call,
To seek the presence of thy grace,
   My strength, my life, my all.

II.

All I can wish is thine to give;
   My God, I ask thy love,
That greatest bliss I can receive,
   That bliss of heav'n above.

III.

In these dark scenes of pain and woe,
   What can my spirit find?
No happiness can dwell below,
   To fill th' immortal mind.

IV.

To heav'n my restless heart aspires:
   O for a quick'ning ray,
T' invigorate my faint desires,
   And cheer the tiresome way.

V.

The path to thy divine abode,
   Through a wild desert lies;
A thousand snares beset the road,
   A thousand terrors rise.

VI.

Satan and sin unite their art,
    To keep me from my Lord:
Dear Saviour, guard my trembling heart,
    And guide me by thy word.

VII.

Whene'er the tempting foe alarms,
    Or spreads the fatal snare,
I'll fly to my Redeemer's arms,
    For safety must be there.

VIII.

My guardian, my almighty friend,
    On thee, my soul would rest;
On thee alone, my hopes depend,
    Be near, and I am blest.

ANNE STEELE

A FUNERAL HYMN

I.

While to the grave our friends are borne,
    Around their cold remains
How all the tender passions mourn,
    And each fond heart complains!

II.

But down to earth, alas, in vain
    We bend our weeping eyes;
Ah! let us leave these seats of pain,
    And upward learn to rise.

III.

Hope cheerful smiles amid the gloom,
    And beams a healing ray,
And guides us from the darksome tomb,
    To realms of endless day.

IV.

Jesus, who left his blest abode,
    (Amazing grace!) to die,
Mark'd, when he rose, the shining road
    To his bright courts on high.

V.

To those bright courts, when hope ascends,
    The tears forget to flow;
Hope views our absent happy friends,
    And calms the swelling woe:

VI.

Then let our hearts repine no more,
    That earthly comfort dies,
But lasting happiness explore,
    And ask it from the skies.

SIN THE CAUSE OF SORROW

I.

The pains that wait our fleeting breath.
Too oft my mournful thoughts employ;
Amid the gloomy shades of death,
The hope of heav'n is life, is joy.

II.

But ah! how soon the blissful ray
With guilt o'ershaded, disappears:
'Tis sin alone, that clouds my day,
'Tis sin alone, deserves my tears.

III.

Yes, I have cause indeed to mourn,
When God conceals his radiant face;
And pray and long till he return,
With smiles of sweet forgiving grace.

IV.

Then weep my eyes, complain my heart,
But mourn not, hopeless of relief!
For sov'reign mercy will impart
Its healing beams, to ease my grief.

V.

The Saviour pleads his dying blood,
Awake my hope, away my fears;
Through him I'll seek my absent God,
Till his returning smile appears.

ENTREATING THE PRESENCE OF CHRIST
IN HIS CHURCHES

Haggiah. 2:7

I.

Come, thou desire of all thy saints,
  Our humble strains attend,
While with our praises and complaints
  Low at thy feet we bend.

II.

When we thy wond'rous glories hear,
  And all thy suff 'rings trace,
What sweetly awful scenes appear!
  What rich unbounded grace!

III.

How should our songs, like those above,
  With warm devotion rise!
How should our souls, on wings of love,
  Mount upward to the skies!

IV.

But ah! the song, how cold it flows!
  How languid our desire!
How faint the sacred passion glows,
  Till thou the heart inspire!

V.

Come, Lord, thy love alone can raise
  In us the heav'nly flame;
Then shall our lips resound thy praise,
  Our hearts adore thy name.

VI.

Dear Saviour, let thy glory shine,
   And fill thy dwellings here,
Till life, and love, and joy divine
   A heav'n on earth appear.

VII.

Then shall our hearts enraptur'd say,
   Come, great Redeemer, come,
And bring the bright, the glorious day,
   That calls thy children home.

DESIRING TO TRUST IN GOD

Isaiah. 26:4.

I.

Great source of boundless pow'r and grace,
   Attend my mournful cry;
In the dark hour of deep distress,
   To thee, to thee I fly.

II.

Thou art my strength, my life, my stay,
   Assist my feeble trust;
Drive these distressing fears away,
   And raise me from the dust.

III.

O let mc call thy grace to mind,
   And trust thy glorious name;
Jehovah, pow'rful, wise, and kind,
   Forever is the same.

IV.

Here let me rest, on thee depend,
   My God, my hope, my all;
Be thou my everlasting- friend,
   And I can never fall.

WATCHFULNESS AND PRAYER

Matthew 26:41

I.

Alas, what hourly dangers rise!
   What snares beset my way!
To heav'n O let me lift my eyes,
   And hourly watch and pray.

II.

How oft my mournful thoughts complain,
   And melt in flowing tears!
My weak resistance, ah, how vain!
   How strong my foes and fears?

III.

O gracious God, in whom I live,
    My feeble efforts aid,
Help me to watch, and pray, and strive,
    Tho' trembling and afraid.

IV.

Increase my faith, increase my hope,
    When foes and fears prevail;
And bear my fainting spirit up,
    Or soon my strength will fail.

V.

Whene'er temptations fright my heart,
    Or lure my feet aside,
My God, thy pow'rful aid impart,
    My guardian and my guide.

VI.

O keep me in thy heav'nly way,
    And bid the tempter flee;
And let me never, never stray
    From happiness and thee.

DIVINE COMPASSION

Isaiah 49:14-16

I.

The Lord forgets his wonted grace,
   Afflicted Zion said;
My God withdraws his smiling face,
   Withdraws his heav'nly aid.

II.

Shall the kind mother's gentle breast
   No soft emotions share;
But, ev'ry tender thought suppress'd,
   Forget her infant care?

III.

The helpless child, that oft her eyes
   Have watch'd with anxious thought,
While her fond breast appeas'd his cries —
   And can he be forgot?

IV.

Strange as it is, yet this may be,
   For creature -love is frail;
But thy Creator's love to thee,
   O Zion, cannot fail.

V.

No, thy dear name engraven stands,
   In characters of love,
On thy almighty Father's hands;
   And never shall remove.

VI.

Before his ever-watchful eye
  Thy mournful state appears,
And ev'ry groan, and ev'ry sigh
  Divine compassion hears.

VII.

These anxious doubts indulge no more,
  Be ev'ry fear suppress'd;
Unchanging truth, and love, and pow'r,
  Command thy cares to rest.

DESIRING ASSURANCE OF THE FAVOR OF GOD

I.

Eternal source of joys divine,
  To thee my soul aspires;
O could I say " The Lord is mine!"
  'Tis all my soul desires.

II.

Thy smile can give me real joy,
  Unmingled and refin'd,
Substantial bliss, without alloy,
  And lasting as the mind.

III.

Thy smile can gild the shades of woe,
  Bid stormy trouble cease,
Spread the fair dawn of heav'n below,
  And sweeten pain to peace.

IV.

My hope, my trust, my life, my Lord,
  Assure me of thy love;
O speak the kind transporting word,
  And bid my fears remove.

V.

Then shall my thankful pow'rs rejoice,
  And triumph in my God,
Till heav'nly rapture tune my voice
  To spread thy praise abroad.

HOPE ENCOURAGED IN THE CONTEMPLATION
OF THE DIVINE PERFECTIONS

I.

Why sinks my -weak desponding mind?
  Why heaves my heart the anxious sigh?
Can sov'reign goodness be unkind?
  Am I not safe, if God is nigh?

II.

He holds all nature in his hand:
  That gracious hand on which I live,
Does life, and time, and death command,
  And has immortal joys to give.

III.

'Tis he supports this fainting frame,
  On him alone my hopes recline;
The wond'rous glories of his name,
  How wide they spread! how bright they shine!

IV.

Infinite wisdom! boundless pow'r!
    Unchanging faithfulness and love!
Here let me trust, while I adore,
    Nor from thy refuge e'er remove.

V.

My God, if thou art mine indeed,
    Then I have all my heart can crave;
A present help in times of need,
    Still kind to hear, and strong to save,

VI.

Forgive my doubts, O gracious Lord,
    And ease the sorrows of my breast;
Speak to my heart the healing word,
    That thou art mine, — and I am blest.

THE INCARNATE SAVIOUR

John 1:14

I.

A wake, awake the sacred song,
To our incarnate Lord:
Let ev'ry heart and ev'ry tongue
  Adore th' eternal Word.

II.

That awful Word, that sov'reign pow'r,
  By whom the worlds were made;
(O happy morn! illustrious hour!)
  Was once in flesh array'd;

III.

Then shone almighty pow'r and love,
  In all their glorious forms,
When Jesus left his throne above,
  To dwell with sinful worms.

IV.

To dwell with misery below,
  The Saviour left the skies;
And sunk to wretchedness and woe.
  That worthless man might rise.

V.

Adoring angels tun'd their songs
  To hail the joyful day:
With rapture then, let mortal tongues
  Their grateful worship pay.

VI.

What glory, Lord, to thee is due?
　　With wonder we adore;
But could we sing as angels do,
　　Our highest praise were poor.

FAITH IN GOD IN TIME OF DISTRESS

Habakkuk 3:17,18

I.

S hould famine o'er the mourning field
　Extend her desolating reign,
Nor spring her blooming beauties yield.
　　Nor autumn swell the foodful grain.

II.

Should lowing herds and bleating sheep
　　Around their famish'd master die;
And hope itself despairing weep,
　　While life deplores its last supply:

III.

Amid the dark, and deathful scene,
　　If I can say, The Lord is mine,
The joy shall triumph o'er the pain,
　　And glory dawn, though life decline

IV.

The God of my salvation lives
   My nobler life he will sustain;
His word immortal vigour gives.
   Nor shall my glorious hopes be vain.

V.

Thy presence, Lord, can cheer my heart,
   Though ev'ry earthly comfort die;
Thy smile can bid my pains depart,
   And raise my sacred pleasures high,

VI.

O let me hear thy blissful voice,
   Inspiring life and joys divine!
The barren desert shall rejoice,
   'Tis paradise, if thou art mine.

PARDONING LOVE

Jeremiah 3:22; Hosea 14:4.

I.

How oft, alas, this wretched heart
  Has wander'd from the Lord!
How oft my roving thoughts depart,
  Forgetful of his word.

II.

Yet sov'reign mercy calls, Return:
  Dear Lord, and may I come?
My vile ingratitude I mourn;
  Oh take the wand'rer home.

III.

And canst thou, wilt thou yet forgive,
  And bid my crimes remove?
And shall a pardon'd rebel live
  To speak thy wond'rous love?

IV.

Almighty grace, thy healing pow'r
  How glorious, how divine!
That can to bliss and life restore
  So vile a heart as mine.

V.

Thy pardoning love, so free, so sweet,
  Dear Saviour, I adore;
O keep me at thy sacred feet,
  And let me rove no more.

THE GOODNESS OF GOD

Nahum 1:7

I.

Ye humble souls, approach your God
 With songs of sacred praise;
For he is good, immensely good,
 And kind are all his ways.

II.

All nature owns his guardian care.
 In him we live and move;
But nobler benefits declare
 The wonders of his love.

III.

He gave his son, his only son,
 To ransom rebel worms;
'Tis here he makes his goodness known
 In its divinest forms.

IV.

To this dear refuge, Lord, we come,
 'Tis here our hope relies;
A safe defence, a peaceful home,
 When storms of trouble rise.

V.

Thy eye beholds, with kind regard,
 The souls who trust in thee;
Their humble hope thou wilt reward,
 With bliss divinely free.

VI.

Great God, to thy almighty love,
 What honors shall we raise?
Not all the raptur'd songs above
 Can render equal praise.

TRUE HONOR

Daniel 12:3

I.

There is a glorious world on high,
　Resplendent with eternal day;
Faith views the blissful prospect nigh,
　　While God's own word reveals the way.

II.

There shall the fav'rites of the Lord
　With never-fading- lustre shine;
Surprising honor! vast reward
　　Conferred on man, by love divine!

III.

How blest are those, how truly wise,
　Who learn and keep the sacred road!
Happy the men, whom heav'n employs
　　To turn rebellious hearts to God!

IV.

To win them from the fatal way,
　Where erring folly thoughtless roves;
And that blest righteousness display,
　　Which Jesus wrought, and God approves.

V.

The shining firmament shall fade,
　And sparkling stars resign their light;
But these shall know nor change, nor shade?
　　Forever fair, forever bright!

VI.

No fancy'd joy beyond the sky,
   No fair delusion is reveal'd;
'Tis God that speaks, who cannot lie,
   And all his word must be fulfill'd.

VII.

And shall not these cold hearts of ours
   Be kindled at the glorious view?
Come, Lord, awake our active pow'rs,
   Our feeble, dying strength renew.

VIII.

On wings of faith and strong desire,
   O may our spirits daily rise;
And reach at last the shining choir,
   In the bright mansions of the skies.

DIVINE BOUNTY

Colossians 1:19

I.

Lord, we adore thy boundless grace,
   The heights and depths unknown,
Of pardon, life, and joy, and peace,
   In thy beloved son.

II.

O wond'rous gift of love divine,
    Dear source of ev'ry good!
Jesus, in thee what glories shine!
    How rich thy flowing blood!

III.

Come all ye pining, hungry poor.
    The Saviour's bounty taste;
Behold a never-failing store,
    For ev'ry willing guest.

IV.

Here shall your num'rous wants receive
    A free, a full supply:
He has unmeasur'd bliss to give,
    And joys that never die.

V.

Can those, who hear the Saviour's voice,
    Prefer earth's empty toys,
(Ah, wretched souls! ah, fatal choice!)
    To everlasting joys?

VI.

Lord, bring unwilling souls to thee,
    With sweet resistless pow'r;
Thy boundless grace, let rebels see,
    And at thy feet adore.

THE HEAVENLY CONQUEROR

Revelation 3:21.

I.

To Jesus, our victorious Lord,
   The praises of our lives belong;
Forever be his name ador'd:
   Sweet theme of ev'ry thankful song.

II.

Lost in despair, beset with foes,
   Undone, and perishing we lay;
His pity melted o'er our woes,
   And sav'd the trembling, dying prey.

III.

He fought, he conquer'd, though he fell,
   While with his last expiring breath,
He triumph'd o'er the pow'rs of hell,
   And by his dying vanquish 'd death.

IV.

Now on his Father's throne he reigns,
   And all the tuneful choir above
Resound in high immortal strains,
   The praises of victorious love.

V.

Though still reviving foes arise,
   Temptation, sin, and doubts appear,
And pain our hearts, and fill our eyes
   With many a groan, and many a tear:

VI.

Still shall we fight, and still prevail,
    In our almighty leader's name;
His strength, whene'er our spirits fail,
    Shall all our active pow'rs inflame.

VII.

Immortal honors wait above,
    To crown the dying conqu'ror's brow;
And endless peace, and joy, and love,
    For the short war sustain'd below.

VIII.

Exalted near their Saviour's seat,
    His saints shall dwell, their dangers o'er.
And cast their crowns beneath his feet,
    And love, and wonder, and adore.

LONGING AFTER UNSEEN PLEASURES

2 Corinthians 4:18.

I.

How long shall earth's alluring toys
　　Detain our hearts and eyes;
Regardless of immortal joys,
　　And strangers to the skies?

II.

These transient scenes will soon decay,
　　They fade upon the sight;
And quickly will their brightest day
　　Be lost in endless night.

III.

Their brightest day, alas, how vain!
　　With conscious sighs we own;
While clouds of sorrow, care and pain,
　　O'ershade the smiling noon.

IV.

O could our thoughts and wishes fly,
　　Above these gloomy shades,
To those bright worlds beyond the sky
　　Which sorrow ne'er invades.

V.

There joys unseen by mortal eyes
　　Or reason's feeble ray,
In ever-blooming prospect rise,
　　Unconscious of decay.

VI.

Lord, send a beam of light divine,
  To guide our upward aim;
With one reviving touch of thine,
  Our languid hearts inflame.

VII.

Then shall on faith's sublimest wing
  Our ardent wishes rise
To those bright scenes, where pleasures spring
  Immortal in the skies.

THE CHRISTIAN'S PROSPECT

I.

Happy the soul, whose wishes climb
  To mansions in the skies!
He looks on all the joys of time,
  With undesiring eyes.

II.

In vain soft pleasure spreads her charms,
  And throws her silken chain;
And wealth and fame invite his arms,
  And tempt his ear in vain.

III.

He knows that all these glitt'ring things
  Must yield to sure decay;
And sees on time's extended wings,
  How swift they fleet away!

IV.

Nor low to earth in sorrow bends,
　　When pains and cares invade;
With cheerful wing his faith ascends
　　Above the gloomy shade.

V.

To things unseen by mortal eyes,
　　A beam of sacred light
Directs his view, his prospects rise,
　　All permanent and bright.

VI.

His hopes are fix'd on joys to come;
　　Those blissful scenes on high
Shall flourish in immortal bloom,
　　When time and nature die.

VII.

O were these heavenly prospects mine,
　　These pleasures could I prove,
Earth's fleeting views I would resign,
　　And raise my hopes above.

LIFE A JOURNEY

I.

Life is a journey, heav'n my home,
　　And shall I negligently stray?
In paths of danger heedless roam,
　　Forget my guide, forget my way?

II.

Think, O my soul, each flying hour
　　Thy folly chides, thy speed alarms;
And shall an insect, or a flow'r
　　Amuse thee with their painted charms?

III.

Such are the objects earth displays,
　　To tempt my stay, and gain my heart!
And shall I fondly, vainly gaze!
　　Ye shining trifles, hence depart.

IV.

O think what glorious scenes above,
　　In bright unbounded prospect rise!
Nor let one vagrant passion rove,
　　Nor leave a wish below the skies.

V.

But ah! how weak my best desires,
　　My warmest ardours soon decay;
My fainting soul, till grace inspires,
　　Can ne'er pursue the heav'nly way.

VI.

On thee I lean, all-gracious God,
　　O breathe new life through all my pow'rs,
Teach me to keep thy sacred road,
　　And well improve my remnant hours.

TRUE HAPPINESS TO BE FOUND ONLY IN GOD

I.

When fancy spreads her boldest wings,
 And wanders unconfin'd,
Amid the unbounded scene of things
 Which entertain the mind:

II.

In vain I trace creation o'er,
 In search of sacred rest;
The whole creation is too poor,
 Too mean, to make me blest.

III.

In vain would this low world employ
 Each flatt'ring, specious wile;
There's nought can yield a real joy,
 But my Creator's smile.

IV

Let earth and all her charms depart,
 Unworthy of the mind;
In God alone, this restless heart
 An equal bliss can find.

V.

Great spring of all felicity,
 To whom my wishes tend,
Do not these wishes rise from thee,
 And in thy favor end?

VI.

Thy favor, Lord, is all I want,
 Here would my spirit rest;
O seal the rich, the boundless grant,
 And make me fully blest.

LASTING HAPPINESS

I.

In vain my roving thoughts would find
A portion worthy of the mind;
On earth my soul can never rest,
  For earth can never make me blest.

II.

Can lasting happiness be found
  Where seasons roll their hasty round,
And days and hours with rapid flight
  Sweep cares and pleasures out of sight?

III.

Arise my thoughts, my heart arise,
  Leave this low world, and seek the skies
There joys forever, ever last,
  When seasons, days, and hours are past.

IV.

Come, Lord, thy powerful grace impart,
  Thy grace can raise my wand'ring heart
To pleasure perfect and sublime,
  Unmeasur'd by the wings of time.

V.

Let those bright worlds of endless joy
  My thoughts, my hopes, my cares employ,
No more, ye restless passions, roam,
  God is my bliss, and heav'n my home.

BIDDING ADIEU TO EARTHLY PLEASURES

I.

Ye gay deceivers of the mind,
  Ye dreams of happiness, adieu;
No more your soft enchantments bind,
  This heart was never made for you.

II.

The brightest joy your smile can boast,
  Is but a moment's glitt'ring light;
It sparkles now, and now 'tis lost,
  Extinguish'd in the shades of night.

III.

Begone, with all your soothing charms;
  Pleasure on earth! — O empty name!
Superior joy my bosom warms,
  And heav'n approves the sacred flame.

IV.

To perfect bliss my soul aspires,
  That shines with never-fading ray;
No less can satiate my desires,
  Than full delight, and endless day.

V.

Blest be the kind, the gracious pow'r,
  That gently call'd and bade me rise;
And taught my nobler thoughts to soar
  To happiness beyond the skies.

LONGING FOR IMMORTALITY

2 Corinthians 5:4

I.

Sad pris'ners in a house of clay,
With sins, and griefs, and pains oppress'd
We groan the ling'ring hours away,
And wish, and long to be releas'd,

II.

Nor is it liberty alone,
Which prompts our restless ardent sighs;
For immortality we groan,
For robes and mansions in the skies.

III.

Eternal mansions! bright array!
O blest exchange! transporting thought!
Free from th' approaches of decay,
Or the least shadow of a spot!

IV.

There shall mortality no more
Its wide extended empire boast,
Forgotten all its dreadful pow'r,
In life's unbounded ocean lost.

V.

Bright world of bliss! O could I see
One shining glimpse, one cheerful ray
(Fair dawn of immortality!)
Break through these tott'ring walls of clay.

VI.

Jesus, in thy dear name I trust,
   My light, my life, my Saviour God;
When this frail house dissolves in dust,
   O raise me to thy bright abode.

AT THE FUNERAL OF A YOUNG PERSON

I.

When blooming youth is snatch'd away
   By death's resistless hand,
Our hearts the mournful tribute pay,
   Which pity must demand.

II.

While pity prompts the rising sigh,
   O may this truth, impress'd
With awful pow'r — I too must die —
   Sink deep in ev'ry breast,

III.

Let this vain world engage no more;
   Behold the gaping tomb!
It bids us sieze the present hour,
   Tomorrow, death may come,

IV.

The voice of this alarming scene
   May ev'ry heart obey,
Nor be the heavenly warning vain,
   Which calls to watch and pray.

V.

O let us fly, to Jesus fly,
　　Whose pow'rful arm can save;
Then shall our hopes ascend on high,
　　And triumph o'er the grave.

VI.

Great God, thy sov'reign grace impart,
　　With cleansing, healing pow'r ;
This only can prepare the heart
　　For death's surprising hour.

SIN THE STING OF DEATH

I.

Death! 'tis a name with terror fraught;
　　It rends the guilty heart,
When conscience wakes remorseful thought,
　　With agonizing smart.

II.

'Tis guilt alone provokes that frown
　　Which all the soul alarms;
Gives terror to the monarch's crown.
　　And conquest to his arms!

III.

Dear Saviour, thy victorious love
　　Can all his force control,
Can bid the pangs of guilt remove,
　　And cheer the trembling soul.

IV.

Victorious love! thy wond'rous pow'r
　From sin and death can raise;
Can gild the dark departing hour,
　And tune its groans to praise,

V.

Then shall the joyful spirit soar
　To life beyond the skies,
Where gloomy death can frown no more,
　And guilt and terror dies.

VI.

No more, O pale destroyer, boast
　Thy universal sway;
To heav'n-born souls thy sting is lost,
　Thy night, the gates of day.

THE PRESENCE OF CHRIST THE JOY
OF HIS PEOPLE

I.

The wond'ring nations have beheld
　The sacred prophesy fulfilled,
And angels hail'd the glorious morn
　That saw the great Messiah born:

II.

The prince! the Saviour! long desir'd,
　Whom prophets taught, by heav'n inspir'd,
And shew'd far off the blissful day;
　Rise o'er the world with healing ray.

III.

Oft in the temples of his grace
   His saints behold his smiling face,
And oft have seen his glory shine,
   With pow'r and majesty divine :

IV.

But soon, alas! his absence mourn,
   And pray and wish his kind return;
Without his life-inspiring light,
   'Tis all a scene of gloomy night.

V.

Come, dearest Lord, thy children cry,
   Our graces droop, our comforts die;
Return, and let thy glories rise,
   Again to our admiring eyes:

VI.

Till fill'd with light, and joy, and love,
   Thy courts below, like those above,
Triumphant hallelujahs raise,
   And heav'n and earth resound thy praise.

ABSENCE FROM GOD

I.

O thou, whose tender mercy hears
    Contrition's humble sigh;
Whose hand, indulgent, wipes the tears
    From sorrow's weeping eye:

II.

See! low before thy throne of grace,
    A wretched wand'rer mourn;
Hast thou not bid me seek thy face?
    Hast thou not said, Return?

III.

And shall my guilty fears prevail
    To drive me from thy feet?
O let not this dear refuge fail,
    This only safe retreat.

IV.

Absent from thee, my guide, my light,
    Without one cheering ray,
Through dangers, fears, and gloomy night,
    How desolate my way!

V.

O shine on this benighted heart,
    With beams of mercy shine;
And let thy healing voice impart
    A taste of joys divine.

VI.

Thy presence only can bestow
    Delights which never cloy;
Be this my solace, here below,
    And my eternal joy.

DESIRING A TASTE OF REAL JOY

I.

Why should my spirit cleave to earth,
  This nest of worms, this vile abode?
Why thus forget her nobler birth,
  Nor wish to trace the heav'nly road?

II.

How barren of sincere delight
  Are all the fairest scenes below!
Though beauteous colours charm the sight,
  They only varnish real woe.

III.

Were I to mount the flying wind,
  And search the wide creation round,
There's nothing here to suit the mind;
  On earth no solid joy is found.

IV.

Oh! could my weary spirit rise,
  And, panting with intense desire,
Reach the bright mansions in the skies,
  And mix among the blissful choir:

V.

How should I look, with pitying eye,
  On this low world of gloomy care,
And wonder, how my soul could lie
  Wrapp'd up in shades and darkness there!

VI.

Say, happy natives of the sky,
  What is it makes your heav'n above?
You dwell beneath your father's eye,
  And feast forever on his love.

VII.

My God, thy presence can impart
 A glimpse of heav'n to earth and night;
O smile, and bless my mournful heart,
 Sweet foretaste of sincere delight.

VIII.

Then shall my soul contented stay
 Till my Redeemer calls me home:
Yet let me oft with transport say,
 "Come, O my Lord, my Saviour, come."

HUMBLE RELIANCE

I.

My God, my Father, blissful name!
 O may I call thee mine,
May I with sweet assurance claim
 A portion so divine?

II.

This only can my fears control,
 And bid my sorrows fly;
What harm can ever reach my soul
 Beneath my Father's eye?

III.

Whate'er thy providence denies,
 I calmly would resign,
For thou art just, and good, and wise;
 O bend my will to thine.

IV.

Whate'er thy sacred will ordains,
　O give me strength to bear;
And let me know my Father reigns,
　And trust his tender care.

V.

If pain and sickness rend this frame,
　And life almost depart,
Is not thy mercy still the same,
　To cheer my drooping heart?

VI.

If cares and sorrows me surround,
　Their pow'r why should I fear?
My inward peace they cannot wound,
　If thou, my God, art near.

VII.

Thy sov'reign ways are all unknown
　To my weak, erring sight;
Yet let my soul, adoring, own
　That all thy ways are right.

VIII.

My God, my Father, be thy name
　My solace and my stay;
O wilt thou seal my humble claim,
　And drive my fears away.

THE PRESENCE OF GOD THE LIFE AND LIGHT
OF THE SOUL

I.

My God, my hope, if thou art mine,
 Why should my soul with sorrow pine?
On thee alone I cast my care;
 O leave me not in dark despair.

II.

Though ev'ry comfort should depart,
 And life forsake this drooping heart;
One smile from thee, one blissful ray,
 Can chase the shades of death away.

III.

My God, my life, if thou appear,
 Not death itself can make me fear;
Thy presence cheers the sable gloom?
 And gilds the horrors of the tomb.

IV.

Not all its horrors can affright,
 If thou appear, my God, my light;
Thy love shall all my fears control,
 And glory dawn around my soul.

V.

Should all created blessings fade,
 And mourning nature, disarrayed,
Deplore her ev'ry charm withdrawn,
 Light, hope, and joy, forever gone;

VI.

Though nought remain below the sky,
 To please my taste, my ear, my eye,
Be thou my hope, my life, my light,
 Amid the universal night.

VII.

My God, be thou forever nigh;
   Beneath the radiance of thine eye,
My hope, my joy, shall ever rise,
   Nor terminate below the skies.

RESIGNING THE HEART TO GOD

Psalm 119:94

I.

Thee, dearest Lord, my soul adores,
   I would be thine, and only thine;
To thee, my heart and all its pow'rs,
   With full consent, I would resign.

II.

But, ah! this weak inconstant mind,
   How frail, how apt from thee to stray!
Trifles, as empty as the wind,
   Can tempt my roving thoughts away.

III.

Sure I am thine — or why this load
   When earthly vanities beguile?
Why do I mourn my absent God,
   And languish for thy cheering smile?

IV.

If thou return, how sweet the joy,
　　Though mix'd with penitential smart!
Then I despise each tempting toy,
　　And long to give thee all my heart.

V.

Come, Lord, thy saving pow'r display,
　　(Resistless pow'r of love divine!)
And drive thy hated foes away,
　　And make mc thine, and only thine.

THE INCONSTANT HEART

I.

Ah! wretched, vile, ungrateful heart,
　　That can from Jesus thus depart,
Thus fond of trifles vainly rove,
　　Forgetful of a Saviour's love!

II.

In vain I charge my thoughts to stay,
　　And chide each vanity away;
In vain, alas! resolve to bind
　　This rebel heart, this wandering mind.

III.

Through all resolves, how soon it flies,
　　And mocks the weak, the slender ties!
There's nought beneath a pow'r divine,
　　That can this roving heart confine.

IV.

Jesus, to thee I would return,
 At thy dear feet repentant mourn;
There let me view thy pard'ning love,
 And never from thy sight remove.

V.

O let thy love with sweet control,
 Bind all the passions of my soul,
Bid ev'ry vanity depart,
 And dwell forever in my heart.

COLD AFFECTIONS

I.

Sure I must love the Saviour's name—
Or is the heav'n-born passion dead,
Extinguish'd the celestial flame,
 And all my joys forever fled?

II.

At the sweet mention of his love,
 How should the sacred ardour rise!
And ev'ry thought, transported, move
 In grateful joy, and glad surprise!

III.

Jesus demands this heart of mine,
 Demands my wish, my joy, my care;
But ah! how dead to things divine,
 How cold my best affections are!

IV.

What death-like lethargy detains
   My captive pow'rs with fatal art,
And spreads its unrelenting chains
   Heavy and cold, around my heart!

V.

'Tis sin, alas! with dreadful pow'r
   Divides my Saviour from my sight;
O for one happy, shining hour
   Of sacred freedom, sweet delight!

VI.

See, dearest Lord, my wretched state,
   And thy almighty pow'r employ;
To thee I seek, on thee I wait,
   For life, and liberty, and joy.

VI.

O let thy love shine forth, and raise
   My captive pow'rs from sin and death;
And fill my heart and life with praise,
   And tune my last expiring breath.

VIII.

Then bear me to the blissful seats
   Of perfect freedom, life, and light,
Where thy redeem'd assembly meets,
   To love and praise with full delight.

IX.

There shall my thoughts transported trace
   And all my soul forever prove,
The boundless riches of thy grace,
   The endless wonders of thy love.

THE EXAMPLE OF CHRIST

I.

And is the gospel, peace and love?
  Such let our conversation be;
The serpent blended with the dove,
  Wisdom and meek simplicity,

II.

Whene'er the angry passions rise,
  And tempt our thoughts or tongues to strife,
To Jesus let us lift our eyes,
  Bright pattern of the Christian life!

III.

O how benevolent and kind!
  How mild! how ready to forgive!
Be this the temper of our mind,
  And these the rules by which we live.

IV.

To do his heav'nly Father's will,
  Was his employment and delight;
Humility and holy zeal
  Shone through his life, divinely bright.

V.

Dispensing good where'er he came,
  The labours of his life were love;
O, if we love the Saviour's name,
  Let his divine example move.

VI.

But ah, how blind! how weak we are!
  How frail! how apt to turn aside!
Lord, we depend upon thy care,
  And ask thy spirit for our guide.

VII.

Thy fair example may we trace,
    To teach us what Ave ought to be;
Make us by thy transforming grace,
    Dear Saviour, daily more like thee.

RETIREMENT AND REFLECTION

I.

Hence, vain, intruding world, depart,
No more allure nor vex my heart;
Let ev'ry vanity begone,
    I would be peaceful and alone.

II.

Here let me search my inmost mind,
    And try its real state to find,
The secret springs of thought explore,
    And call my words and actions o'er.

III.

Reflect how soon my life will end,
    And think on what my hopes depend,
What aim my busy thoughts pursue,
    What work is done, and what to do.

IV.

Eternity is just at hand;
    And shall I waste my ebbing sand,
And careless view departing day,
    And throw my inch of time away?

V.

Eternity, tremendous sound!
   To guilty souls, a dreadful wound!
But, oh! if Christ and heav'n be mine,
   How sweet the accents! How divine!

VI.

Be this my chief, my only care,
   My high pursuit, my ardent pray'r,
An int'rest in the Saviour's blood,
   My pardon seal'd, and peace with God.

VII.

But should my brightest hopes be vain,
   The rising doubt, how sharp its pain!
My fears, O gracious God, remove,
   Confirm my title to thy love.

VIII.

Search, Lord, O search my inmost heart
   And light, and hope, and joy impart;
From guilt and error set me free,
   And guide me safe to heav'n and thee.

HOPE IN DARKNESS.

I.

God is my sun, his blissful rays
    Irradiate, warm, and guide my heart!
How dark, how mournful, are my days,
    If his enlivening beams depart!

II.

Scarce through the shades, a glimpse of day
    Appears to these desiring eyes;
But shall my drooping spirit say,
    The cheerful morn will never rise?

III.

O let me not despairing mourn,
    Though gloomy darkness spreads the sky;
My glorious sun will yet return,
    And night with all its horrors fly.

IV.

Hope, in the absence of my Lord,
    Shall be my taper; sacred light,
Kindled at his celestial word,
    To cheer the melancholy night!

V.

O for the bright the joyful day,
    When hope shall in assurance die!
So tapers lose their feeble ray,
    Beneath the sun's refulgent eye.

DEATH AND HEAVEN

I.

Oft have I said, with inward sighs,
    I find no solid good below;
Earth's fairest scenes but cheat my eyes,
    Her pleasure is but painted woe.

II.

Then why, my soul, so loth to leave
    These seats of vanity and care?
Why do I thus to trifles cleave,
    And feed on chaff, and grasp the air?

III.

There is a world all fair and bright;
    But clouds and darkness dwell between,
The sable veil obstructs my sight,
    And hides the lovely, distant scene.

IV.

Whene'er I look with frighted eyes
    On death's impenetrable shade,
Alas! what gloomy horrors rise,
    And all my trembling frame invade!

V.

O death, frail nature's dreaded foe,
    Thy frown with terror fills my heart;
How shall I bear the fatal blow,
    Which must my soul and body part?

VI.

'Tis sin which arms his dreadful frown,
    This only points his deadly sting;
My sins which throw this gloom around,
    And all these shocking terrors briny.

VII.

O could I know my sins forgiv'n,
   Soon would these terrors disappear;
Then should I see a glimpse of heav'n.
   And look on death without a fear.

VIII.

Jesus, my Saviour, and my God,
   To thee my trembling spirit flies;
Thy merits, thy atoning- blood,
   On this alone my soul relies.

IX.

O let thy love's all-pow'rful ray
   With pleasing force, divine control,
Arise, and chase these clouds away,
   And shine around my doubting soul.

X.

Then shall I change the mournful strain,
   And bid my thoughts and hopes arise,
Above these gloomy seats of pain,
   To glorious worlds beyond the skies.

XI.

With cheerful heart I then shall sing,
   And triumph o'er my vanquish'd foe —
O death, where is thy pointed sting?
   My Saviour wards the fatal blow.

XII.

O when will that illustrious day,
   When will that blissful moment come?
That shall my weary soul convey
   Safe to her everlasting home?

XIII.

Then shall I leave these fetters here,
    And upward rise to joys unknown;
And call, without an anxious fear,
    The fair inheritance my own.

XIV.

Adieu to all terrestrial things;
    Come, bear me through the starry road,
Bright Seraphs, on your soaring wings,
    To see my Saviour, and my God.

REDEMPTION BY CHRIST ALONE

1 Peter 1:18, 19

I.

E nslav'd by sin, and bound in chains,
Beneath its dreadful tyrant sway,
And doom'd to everlasting pains,
   We wretched, guilty captives lay.

II.

Nor gold nor gems could buy our peace;
   Nor the whole world's collected store
Suffice to purchase our release;
   A thousand worlds were all too poor.

III.

Jesus the Lord, the mighty God,
   An all-sufficient ransom paid;
In valued price, his precious blood,
   For vile rebellious traitors shed.

IV.

Jesus the sacrifice became,
   To rescue guilty souls from hell;
The spotless, bleeding, dying Lamb
   Beneath avenging justice fell.

V.

Amazing goodness! love divine!
   O may our grateful hearts adore
The matchless grace, nor yield to sin,
   Nor wear its cruel fetters more!

VI.

Dear Saviour, let thy love pursue
  The glorious work it has begun,
Each secret, lurking foe subdue,
  And let our hearts be thine alone.

※ ※ ※

THE MYSTERIES OF PROVIDENCE

I.

LORD, how mysterious are thy ways!
How blind are we! How mean our praise!
Thy steps can mortal eyes explore?
  'Tis ours, to wonder and adore.

II.

Thy deep decrees from creature sight
  Are hid in shades of awful night;
Amid the lines, with curious eye,
  Not angel minds presume to pry.

III.

Great God, I would not ask to see
  What in futurity shall be;
If light and bliss attend my days,
  Then let my future hours be praise.

IV.

Is darkness and distress my share?
  Then let me trust thy guardian care;
Enough for me, if love divine,
  At length through ev'ry cloud shall shine.

V.

Yet this my soul desires to know,
    Be this my only wish below,
"That Christ is mine!" — this great request
    Grant, bounteous God, — and I am blest.

REFUGE AND STRENGTH IN THE MERCY OF GOD

I.

My God, 'tis to thy mercy-seat
    My soul for shelter flies;
'Tis here, I find a safe retreat,
    When storms and tempests rise.

II.

'Tis here, my faith resolves to dwell,
    Nor shall I be afraid
Of all the pow'rs of earth or hell,
    If thou vouchsafe thy aid.

III.

My cheerful hope can never die,
    If thou my God art near;
Thy grace can raise my comforts high,
    And banish ev'ry fear.

IV.

Against thy all-supporting grace
    My foes can ne'er prevail;
But oh! if frowns becloud thy face,
    Faith, hope, and life will fail.

V.

My great protector, and my Lord,
    Thy constant aid impart,
And let thy kind, thy gracious word
    Sustain my trembling heart.

VI.

O never let my soul remove,
    From this divine retreat;
Still let me trust thy pow'r and love,
    And dwell beneath thy feet.

DESIRING RESIGNATION AND THANKFULNESS

I.

When I survey life's varied scene,
    Amid the darkest hours,
Sweet rays of comfort shine between,
    And thorns are mix'd with flow'rs.

II.

Lord, teach me to adore thy hand,
    From whence my comforts flow;
And let me in this desert land
    A glimpse of Canaan know.

III.

Is health and ease my happy share?
    O may I bless my God;
Thy kindness let my songs declare,
    And spread thy praise abroad.

IV.

While such delightful gifts as these
   Are kindly dealt to me,
Be all my hours of health and ease
   Devoted, Lord, to thee.

V.

In griefs and pains thy sacred word,
   (Dear solace of my soul!)
Celestial comforts can afford,
   And all their pow'r control.

VI.

When present suff'rings pain my heart
   Or future terrors rise,
And light and hope almost depart
   From these dejected eyes:

VII.

Thy pow'rful word supports my hope,
   Sweet cordial of the mind!
And bears my fainting spirit up,
   And bids me wait resign'd.

VIII.

And O, whatever of earthly bliss
   Thy sov'reign hand denies,
Accepted at thy throne of grace.
   Let this petition rise:

IX.

"Give me a calm, a thankful heart,
   "From ev'ry murmur free;
"The blessings of thy grace impart,
   "And let me live to thee.

X.

"Let the sweet hope that thou art mine,
   "My path of life attend;
"Thy presence through my journey shine,
   "And bless its happy end."

DESIRING THE PRESENCE OF GOD

Isaiah 50:10

I.

Hear, gracious God, my humble moan,
   To thee I breathe my sighs,
When will the mournful night be gone?
   And when my joys arise?

II.

My God — O could I make the claim —
   My father and my friend—
And call thee mine, by ev'ry name,
   On which thy saints depend!

III.

By ev'ry name of pow'r and love,
   I would thy grace entreat;
Nor should my humble hopes remove,
   Nor leave thy sacred seat.

IV.

Yet though my soul in darkness mourns,
　　Thy word is all my stay;
Here I would rest till light returns,
　　Thy presence makes my day.

V.

Speak, Lord, and bid celestial peace
　　Relieve my aching heart;
O smile, and bid my sorrows cease,
　　And all the gloom depart.

VI

Then shall my drooping spirit rise,
　　And bless thy healing rays,
And change these deep complaining sighs,
　　For songs of sacred praise.

CHRIST THE LIFE OF THE SOUL

John 14:39

I.

When sins and fears prevailing rise,
　　And fainting hope almost expires;
Jesus, to thee I lift my eyes,
　　To thee I breathe my soul's desires.

II.

Art thou not mine, my living Lord?
　　And can my hope, my comfort die,
Fix'd on thy everlasting word,
　　That word which built the earth and sky?

III.

If my immortal Saviour lives,
    Then my immortal life is sure;
His word a firm foundation gives,
    Here, let me build, and rest secure.

IV.

Here, let my faith unshaken dwell,
    Immoveable the promise stands j
Nor all the pow'rs of earth or hell,
    Can e'er dissolve the sacred bands.

V.

Here, O my soul, thy trust repose;
    If Jesus is forever mine,
Not death itself, that last of foes,
    Shall break a union so divine,

ASPIRING TOWARDS HEAVEN

I.

Vain world, be gone, nor vex my heart
    With thy deluding wiles;
Hence, empty promiser, depart
    With all thy soothing smiles.

II.

Superior bliss invites my eyes,
    Delight unmix'd with woe;
Now let my nobler thoughts arise,
    To joys unknown below.

III.

Yon starry plains, how bright they shine,
    With radiant specks of light ;
Fair pavement of the courts divine,
    That sparkles on the sight!

IV.

'Tis distance lessens ev'ry star;
    Could I behold them nigh,
Bright worlds of wonder would appear
    To my astonish'd eye!

V.

Thus heav'nly joys attract my eyes,
    My heart the lustre warms;
But could I reach those upper skies,
    How infinite their charms!

VI.

Come, heav'n-born faith, and aid my flight,
    And guide my rising thought,
Till earth, still lessening to my sight,
    Shall vanish, quite forgot.

VII.

But when to reach those blissful plains
    Her utmost ardour tries,
And almost hears the charming strains
    Of hymning angels rise:

VIII;

Mortality, with painful load,
    Forbids the raptur'd flight;
In vain she means heav'n's bright abode.
    And sinks to earth and night.

IX.

O let thy love, my God, my King,
  My hope, my heart, inspire;
And teach my faith with stronger wing
  To rise, and warm desire.

X.

Oft let thy shining visits cheer
  This dark abode of clay,
Till I shall leave these fetters here,
  And rise to endless day.

GOD MY ONLY HAPPINESS

I.

When fill'd with grief, my anxious heart
  To thee, my God, complains,
Sweet pleasure mingles with the smart,
  And softens all my pains.

II.

Earth flies with all her soothing charms,
  Nor I the loss deplore;
No more, ye phantoms, mock my arms,
  Nor tease my spirit more.

III.

I languish for superior joy
  To all that earth bestows;
For pleasure which can never cloy,
  Nor change, nor period knows.

IV.

Still, must the scenes of bliss remain
   Conceal'd from mortal eyes?
And must my wishes rise in vain,
   And never reach the skies?

V.

My God, O could I call thee mine
   Without a wav'ring fear,
This would be happiness divine,
   A heav'n of pleasure here!

VI.

This joy, my wishes long to find,
   To this my heart aspires,
A bliss, immortal as the mind,
   And vast as its desires!

MOURNING THE ABSENCE OF GOD, AND LONGING
FOR HIS GRACIOUS PRESENCE

I.

My God, to thee I call-
   Must I forever mourn?
So far from thee, my life, my all?
   O when wilt thou return?

II.

Dark as the shades of night
   My gloomy sorrows rise,
And hide thy soul-reviving light
   From these desiring eyes.

III.

My comforts all decay,
   My inward foes prevail;
If thou withhold thy healing ray,
   Expiring hope will fail.

IV.

Away, distressing fears,
   My gracious God is nigh,
And heav'nly pity sees my tears,
   And marks each rising sigh.

V.

Dear source of all my joys,
   And solace of my care,
O wilt thou hear my plaintive voice
   And grant my humble pray'r!

VI.

These envious clouds remove,
   Thy cheering light restore,
Confirm my int'rest in thy love
   Till I can doubt no more,

VII.

Then if my troubles rise,
   To thee, my God, I'll flee,
And raise my hopes above the skies.
   And cast my cares on thee.

ANNE STEELE

GOD THE ONLY REFUGE OF THE TROUBLED MIND

I.

Dear refuge of my weary soul,
  On thee, when sorrows rise;
On thee, when waves of trouble roll,
  My fainting hope relies.

II.

While hope revives, though press'd with fears,
  And I can say, my God,
Beneath thy feet I spread my cares,
  And pour my woes abroad.

III.

To thee I tell each rising grief,
  For thou alone canst heal;
Thy word can bring a sweet relief
  For ev'ry pain I feel.

IV.

But oh! when gloomy doubts prevail,
  I fear to call thee mine;
The springs of comfort seem to fail,
  And all my hopes decline.

V.

Yet, gracious God, where shall I flee?
  Thou art my only trust,
And still my soul would cleave to thee,
  Though prostrate in the dust.

VI.

Hast thou not bid me seek thy face?
  And shall I seek in vain?
And can the ear of sov'reign grace
  Be deaf when I complain?

VII.

No, still the ear of sov'reign grace
   Attends the mourner's pray'r ;
O may I ever find access,
   To breathe my sorrows there.

VIII.

Thy mercy-seat is open still;
   Here let my soul retreat,
With humble hope attend thy will,
   And wait beneath thy feet.

COMPLAINING AT THE THRONE OF GRACE

I.

O'erwhelm'd with restless griefs and fears,
   Lord, I approach thy mercy-seat,
With aching heart and flowing tears,
   To pour my sorrows at thy feet.

II.

Can mournful penitence and pray'r
   Address thy mercy-seat in vain?
Unnotic'd by thy gracious ear,
   Can sorrow and distress complain?

III.

Thy promises are large and free,
   To humble souls who seek thy face;
O where for refuge can I flee,
   My God! — but to the throne of grace?

IV.

My God, for yet my trembling heart
   Would fain rely upon thy word;
Fain would I bid my fears depart,
   And cast my burthen on the Lord.

V.

Thou see'st the tempest of my soul,
   These restless waves of fear and sin;
Thy voice can all their rage control.
   And make a sacred calm within,

VI.

Amid the gloomy shades of night,
   To thee, I lift my longing eyes;
My Saviour God, my life, my light,
   When will thy cheering beams arise?

VII.

My thoughts recall thy favors past,
   In many a dark distressing hour,
Thy kind support my heart confess'd,
   And own'd thy wisdom, love, and pow'r

VIII.

And still these bright perfections shine,
   Eternal their unclouded rays;
Unchanging faithfulness is thine,
   And just, and right, are all thy ways.

IX.

And can my vile ungrateful heart
   Still harbour black distrust and fear?
O bid these heavy clouds depart,
   Bright sun of righteousness, appear.

X.

Let thy enliv'ning healing voice,
  The kind assurance of thy love,
Relieve my heart, revive my joys,
  And all my sins and fears remove.

SUBMISSION TO GOD UNDER AFFLICTION

I.

Peace, my complaining, doubting heart,
  Ye busy cares, be still;
Adore the just, the sov'reign Lord,
  Nor murmur at his will.

II.

Unerring wisdom guides his hand;
  Nor dares my guilty fear,
Amid the sharpest pains I feel,
  Pronounce his hand severe.

III.

To soften ev'ry painful stroke,
  Indulgent mercy bends;
And unrepining when I plead,
  His gracious ear attends.

IV.

Let me reflect with humble awe
  Whene'er my heart complains,
Compar'd with what my sins deserve,
  How easy are my pains!

V.

Yes, Lord, I own thy sovereign hand,
   Thou just, and wise, and kind;
Be ev'ry anxious thought suppress'd,
   And all my soul resign'd.

VI.

But oh! indulge this only wish,
   This boon I must implore;
Assure my soul, that thou art mine,
   My God, I ask no more.

TRUSTING IN THE DIVINE VERACITY

I.

When sin and sorrow, fear and pain,
   My trembling heart dismay,
My feeble strength, alas, how vain!
   It sinks and dies away.

II.

My spirit asks a firmer prop,
   I lean upon the Lord;
My God, the pillar of my hope
   Is thy unchanging word.

III.

On this are built the brightest joys,
   Celestial beings know,
And 'tis the same almighty voice
   Supports the saints below.

IV.

'Tis this upholds the rolling spheres,
  And heav'n's immortal frame;
Then, O my soul, suppress thy fears.
  Thy basis is the same.

V.

The sacred word, the solemn oath,
  Forever must remain;
I trust in everlasting truth,
  Nor can my trust be vain.

TIME FLYING, AND DEATH APPROACHING

I.

Awake, my soul, nor slumb'ring lie
  Amid the gloomy haunts of death;
Perhaps the awful hour is nigh,
  Commission 'd for my parting breath.

II.

That awful hour will soon appear,
  Swift on the wings of time it flies,
When all that pains or pleases here,
  Will vanish from my closing eyes.

III.

Death calls my friends, my neighbors hence
  And none resist the fatal dart;
Continual warnings strike my sense,
  And shall they fail to reach my heart?

IV.

Shall gay amusements rise between,
　　When scenes of horror spread around?
Death's pointed arrows fly unseen,
　　But ah, how sure, how deep they wound!

V.

Think, O my soul, how much depends
　　On the short period of a day;
Shall time, which heav'n in mercy lends,
　　Be negligently thrown away?

VI.

Thy remnant minutes strive to use,
　　Awake! rouse ev'ry active pow'r!
And not in dreams and trifles lose
　　This little now! this precious hour!

VII.

Lord of my life, inspire my heart
　　With heav'nly ardour, grace divine;
Nor let thy presence e'er depart,
　　For strength, and life, and death are thine.

VIII.

O teach me the celestial skill,
　　Each awful warning to improve;
And while my days are short'ning still,
　　Prepare me for the joys above.

IX.

Insure my nobler life on high,
　　Life, from a dying Saviour's blood!
Then though my minutes swiftly fly,
　　They bear me nearer to my God.

VICTORY OVER DEATH THROUGH CHRIST

1 Corinthians 15:57

I.

When death appears before my sight,
   In all his dire array,
Unequal to the dreadful fight,
   My courage dies away.

II.

How shall I meet this potent foe,
   Whose frown my soul alarms?
Dark horror sits upon his brow,
   And vict'ry waits his arms.

III.

But see, my glorious Leader nigh!
   My Lord, my Saviour lives;
Before him death's pale terrors fly,
   And my faint heart revives.

IV.

Jesus, be thou my sure defense,
   My guard forever near;
And faith shall triumph over sense,
   And never yield to fear.

V.

O may I meet the dreadful hour,
   With fortitude divine;
Sustain'd by thy almighty pow'r,
   The conquest must be mine.

VI.

What though subdued this body lies,
    Slain in the mortal strife,
My spirit shall unconquer'd rise
    To a diviner life.

VII.

Lord, I commit my soul to thee,
    Accept the sacred trust,
Receive this nobler part of me,
    And watch my sleeping dust:

VIII.

Till that illustrious morning come,
    When all thy saints shall rise,
And cloth'd in full, immortal bloom,
    Attend thee to the skies.

IX.

When thy triumphant armies sing
    The honors of'thy name,
And heav'ns eternal arches ring,
    With glory to the Lamb:

X.

O let me join the raptur'd lays,
    And, with the blissful throng,
Resound salvation, pow'r, and praise,
    In everlasting song.

CHRIST THE SUPREME BEAUTY

Isaiah 33:17

I.

Should nature's charms, to please the eye,
  In sweet assemblage join,
All nature's charms would droop and die,
  Jesus, compared with thine.

II.

Vain were her fairest beams display'd,
  And vain her blooming store;
Ev'n brightness languishes to shade,
  And beauty is no more.

III.

But ah, how far from mortal sight,
  The Lord of glory dwells!
A veil of interposing night
  His radiant face conceals.

IV.

O could my longing spirit rise
  On strong immortal wing,
And reach thy palace in the skies,
  My Saviour, and my king!

V.

There myriads worship at thy feet,
  And there, (divine employ!)
The triumphs of thy love repeat,
  In songs of endless joy.

VI.

Thy presence beams eternal day,
  O'er all the blissful place;
Who would not drop this load of clay,
  And die to see thy face?

THE PROMISED LAND

Isaiah 33:17

I.

Far from these narrow scenes of night
  Unbounded glories rise,
And realms of infinite delight,
  Unknown to mortal eyes.

II.

Fair distant land! — could mortal eyes
  But half its joys explore,
How would our spirits long to rise,
  And dwell on earth no more!

III.

There pain and sickness never come,
  And grief no more complains;
Health triumphs in immortal bloom,
  And endless pleasure reigns!

IV.

From discord free, and war's alarms,
    And want, and pining care,
Plenty and peace unite their charms,
    And smile unchanging there.

V.

There rich varieties of joy
    Continual feast the mind;
Pleasures which fill, but never cloy,
    Immortal and refin'd!

VI.

No factious strife, no envy there,
    The sons of peace molest,
But harmony and love sincere
    Fill every happy breast.

VII.

No clouds those blissful regions know.
    Forever bright and fair!
For sin, the source of mortal woe,
    Can never enter there.

VIII.

There no alternate night is known,
    Nor sun's faint sickly ray;
But glory from the sacred throne
    Spreads everlasting day.

IX.

The glorious monarch there displays
    His beams of wond'rous grace;
His happy subjects sing his praise,
    And bow before his face.

X.

O may the heav'nly prospect fire
   Our hearts with ardent love,
Till wings of faith and strong desire
   Bear ev'ry thought above.

XI.

Prepare us, Lord, by grace divine,
   For thy bright courts on high;
Then bid our spirits rise and join
   The chorus of the sky.

THE HEAVENLY SHEPHERD

Psalm 23: 1, 2, 3

I.

While my Redeemer's near,
   My shepherd and my guide,
I bid farewel to anxious fear,
   My wants are all supply'd.

II.

To ever-fragrant meads,
   Where rich abundance grows.
His gracious hand indulgent leads,
   And guards my sweet repose.

III.

Along the lovely scene,
  Cool waters gently roll,
And kind refreshment smiles serene;
  To cheer my fainting soul.

IV.

Here let my spirit rest;
  How sweet a lot is mine!
With pleasure, food, and safety blest;
  Beneficence divine!

V.

Dear shepherd, if I stray,
  My wand'ring feet restore,
To thy fair pastures guide my way,
  And let me rove no more.

VI.

Unworthy, as I am,
  Of thy protecting care,
Jesus, I plead thy gracious name,
  For all my hopes are there.

ANNE STEELE

THE CHRISTIAN'S NOBLEST RESOLUTION

Joshua 24:15

I.

Ah, wretched souls, who strive in vain,
  Slaves to the world, and slaves to sin!
A nobler toil may I sustain,
  A nobler satisfaction win.

II.

May I resolve with all my heart,
  With all my pow'rs, to serve the Lord.
Nor from his precepts e'er depart,
  Whose service is a rich reward.

III.

O be his service all my joy,
  Around let my example shine,
Till others love the blest employ.
  And join in labours so divine.

IV.

Be this the purpose of my soul,
  My solemn, my determin'd choice,
To yield to his supreme control,
  And in his kind commands rejoice.

V.

O may I never faint nor tire,
  Nor wandering leave his sacred ways;
Great God, accept my soul's desire,
  And give me strength to live thy praise.

THE SAVIOUR'S INVITATION

John 7:37

I.

The Saviour calls — let ev'ry ear
  Attend the heav'nly sound;
Ye doubting souls, dismiss your fear,
  Hope smiles reviving round.

II.

For ev'ry thirsty, longing heart,
  Here streams of bounty flow,
And life, and health, and bliss impart.
  To banish mortal woe.

III.

Here, springs of sacred pleasure rise,
  To ease your every pain,
(Immortal fountain! full supplies!)
  Nor shall you thirst in vain.

IV.

Ye sinners, come, 'tis mercy's voice,
  The gracious call obey;
Mercy invites to heav'nly joys —
  And can you yet delay?

V.

Dear Saviour, draw reluctant hearts,
  To thee let sinners fly,
And take the bliss thy love imparts,
  And drink and never die.

JESUS THE BEST BELOVED

I.

Dear centre of my best desires,
  And sov'reign of my heart,
What sweet delight thy name inspires!
  What bliss thy smiles impart!

II.

Jesus — O loveliest, dearest name!
  And wilt thou condescend
To own the bold, yet humble claim,
  My everlasting friend?

III.

Too oft, alas, my passions rove,
  In search of meaner charms;
Trifles unworthy of my love
  Divide me from thy arms.

IV.

Ye teasing vanities depart,
  I seek my absent Lord;
No balm to ease my aching heart,
  Can all your joys afford.

V.

Come, dearest Lord, with pow'r divine,
  And drive thy foes away;
be my heart, my passions thine,
  And never, never stray.

DESIRING TO KNOW AND LOVE HIM MORE

I.

Thou lovely source of true delight,
　Whom I unseen adore,
Unveil thy beauties to my sight,
　That I may love thee more.

II.

Thy glory o'er creation shines;
　But in thy sacred word
I read, in fairer, brighter lines,
　My bleeding, dying Lord.

III.

'Tis here, whene'er my comforts droop,
　And sins and sorrows rise,
Thy love, with cheerful beams of hope,
　My fainting heart supplies.

IV.

But ah, too soon, the pleasing scene
Is clouded o'er with pain;
My gloomy fears rise dark between,
And I again complain.

V.

Jesus, my Lord, my life, my light,
　O come with blissful ray,
Break radiant through the shades of night,
　And chase my fears away.

VI.

Then shall my soul with rapture trace
The wonders of thy love;
But the full glories of thy face
　Are only known above.

ANNE STEELE

THE GLORIOUS PRESENCE OF CHRIST IN HEAVEN
John 17:24

I.
O for a sweet inspiring ray,
  To animate our feeble strains,
From the bright realms of endless day,
  The blissful realms, where Jesus reigns!

II.
There low before his glorious throne
  Adoring saints and angels fall,
And with delightful worship own
  His smile their bliss, their heav'n, their all

III.
Immortal glories crown his head,
  While tuneful hallelujahs rise,
And love, and joy, and triumph spread
  Through all th' assemblies of the skies.

IV.
He smiles, and seraphs tune their songs
  To boundless rapture while they gaze;
Ten thousand thousand joyful tongues
  Resound his everlasting praise.

V.
There all the fav'rites of the Lamb
  Shall join at last the heav'nly choir;
O may the joy-inspiring theme
  Awake our faith and warm desire.

VI.

Dear Saviour, let thy spirit seal
   Our int'rest in that blissful place;
Till death remove this mortal veil,
   And we behold thy lovely face.

THE HAPPINESS OF THE SAINTS ABOVE

John 17:24

I.

O could we read our int'rest here,
   Jesus, in these dear words of thine,
A heav'n of pleasure would appear,
   A blissful view of joys divine.

II.

Dear Saviour, let thy boundless grace
   Remove our guilt, our fears remove;
Then shall our thoughts with rapture trace
   The radiant mansions of thy love.

III.

There shall our hearts no more complain,
   Nor sin prevail, nor grace decay;
But perfect joy forever reign,
   One glorious, undeclining day.

IV.

No darkness there shall cloud our sight;
   These now dejected, feeble eyes,
Shall gaze, with infinite delight,
   On the full glories of the skies.

V.

There shall we see thy lovely face,
   And, chang'd to purity divine,
Partake the splendors of the place,
   And in thy glorious likeness shine.

VI.

Yes, dearest Lord, to dwell with thee,
   Thy praise our endless, sweet employ,
Must be immense felicity,
   A full infinitude of joy!

VII.

O let thy spirit now impart,
   The kind assurance of thy love,
With sealing pow'r to ev'ry heart.
   Sweet earnest of the joys above.

HYMN TO JESUS

I.

Jesus, in thy transporting name
  What blissful glories rise!
Jesus, the angel's sweetest theme!
  The wonder of the skies!

II.

Well might the skies with wonder view
  A love so strange as thine!
No thought of angels ever knew
  Compassion so divine!

III.

Didst thou forsake thy radiant crown,
  And boundless realms of day,
(Aside thy robes of glory thrown,)
  To dwell in feeble clay?

IV.

Jesus, — and didst thou leave the sky
  For miseries and woes?
And didst thou bleed, and groan and die,
  For vile rebellious foes?

V.

Through the deep horrors of thy pain
  Then love triumphant smil'd;
Earth trembled at the dreadful scene,
  And heav'n was reconcil'd.

VI.

Victorious love! can language tell
  The wonders of thy pow'r,
Which conquer'd all the force of hell,
  In that tremendous hour?

145

VII.

Is there a heart that will not bend
   To thy divine control?
Descend, O sov'reign love, descend,
   And melt the stubborn soul.

VIII.

O may our willing hearts confess
   Thy sweet, thy gentle sway;
Glad captives of resistless grace,
   Thy pleasing rule obey.

IX.

Come, dearest Lord, extend thy reign,
   Till rebels rise no more;
Thy praise all nature then shall join,
   And heav'n and earth adore.

PRAISE TO THE REDEEMER

I.

To our Redeemer's glorious name,
　Awake the sacred song!
O may his love, (immortal flame!)
　Tune ev'ry heart and tongue.

II.

His love, what mortal thought can reach?
　What mortal tongue display?
Imagination's utmost stretch
　In wonder dies away.

III.

Let wonder still with love unite,
　And gratitude and joy;
Be Jesus our supreme delight,
　His praise, our best employ.

IV.

Jesus, who left his throne on high,
　Left the bright realms of bliss,
And came on earth to bleed and die —.
　Was ever love like this?

V.

Dear Lord, while we adoring pay
　Our humble thanks to thee,
May ev'ry heart with rapture say,
　The Saviour dy'd for me.

VI.

O may the sweet, the blissful theme
　Fill ev'ry heart and tongue,
Till strangers love thy charming name.
　And join the sacred song.

DESIRING TO LOVE CHRIST
WITHOUT WANDERING

I.

Ye earthly vanities, depart,
   Forever hence remove;
Jesus alone deserves my heart,
   And ev'ry thought of love.

II.

His heart, where love and pity dwelt
   In all their softest forms,
Sustain'd the heavy load of guilt,
   For lost rebellious worms:

III.

His heart, whence love abundant fiow'd
   To wash the stains of sin,
In precious streams of vital blood—
   Here, all my hopes begin.

IV.

Can I my bleeding Saviour view.
   And yet ungrateful prove,
And pierce his wounded heart anew,
And grieve his injur'd love?

V.

Forbid it, Lord, O bind this heart,
   This rebel heart of mine,
So firm, that it may ne'er depart,
   In chains of love divine.

THE EXALTED SAVIOUR

I.

Now let us raise our cheerful strains,
   And join the blissful choir above;
There our exalted Saviour reigns,
   And there they sing his wond'rous love.

II.

While seraphs tune th' immortal song,
   O may we feel the sacred flame;
And ev'ry heart and ev'ry tongue
   Adore the Saviour's glorious name.

III.

Jesus, who once upon the tree
   In agonizing pains expir'd,
Who dy'd for rebels — yes, 'tis he!
   How bright! how lovely! how admir'd!

IV.

Jesus, who dy'd that we might live,
   Dy'd in the wretched traitor's place—
O what returns can mortals give,
   For such immeasurable grace?

V.

Were universal nature ours,
   And art with all her boasted store,
Nature and art with all their pow'rs
   Would still confess the off'rer poor!

VI.

Yet though for bounty so divine
   We ne'er can equal honors raise,
Jesus, may all our hearts be thine,
   And all our tongues proclaim thy praise.

ANNE STEELE

THE WONDERS OF REDEMPTION

1 Peter 3:18

I.

A nd did the holy and the just,
    The sov'reign of the skies,
Stoop down to wretchedness and dust,
    That guilty worms might rise?

II.

Yes, the Redeemer left his throne,
    His radiant throne on high,
(Surprising mercy! love unknown!)
    To suffer, bleed, and die.

III.

He took the dying traitor's place,
    And suffer'd in his stead;
For man, (O miracle of grace!)
    For man the Saviour bled!

IV.

Dear Lord, what heav'nly wonders dwell
    In thy atoning blood?
By this are sinners snatch'd from hell,
    And rebels brought to God.

V.

Jesus, my soul, adoring, bends
    To love so full, so free;
And may I hope that love extends
    Its sacred power to me?

VI.

What glad return can I impart,
    For favors so divine?
O take my all, — this worthless heart.
    And make it only thine.

COMMUNION WITH CHRIST AT HIS TABLE

I.

To Jesus, our exalted Lord,
    (Dear name, by heav'n and earth ador'd!)
Fain would our hearts and voices raise
    A cheerful song of sacred praise.

II.

But all the notes which mortals know,
    Are weak, and languishing, and low;
Far, far above our humble songs,
    The theme demands immortal tongues.

III.

Yet while around his board we meet.
    And worship at his glorious feet;
O let our warm affections move
    In glad returns of grateful love.

IV.

Yes, Lord, we love and we adore,
    But long to know and love thee more;
And while we taste the bread and wine,
    Desire to feed on joys divine.

V.

Let faith our feeble senses aid,
  To see thy wond'rous love display'd,
Thy broken flesh, thy bleeding veins,
  Thy dreadful agonizing pains.

VI.

Let humble penitential woe,
  With painful, pleasing anguish flow,
And thy forgiving smiles impart
  Life, hope, and joy, to ev'ry heart.

FAITH IN A REDEEMER'S SUFFERINGS

I.

LORD, when my thoughts delighted rove
  Amid the wonders of thy love,
Sweet hope revives my drooping heart,
  And bids intruding fears depart.

II.

But while thy sufferings I survey,
  And faith enjoys a heav'nly ray,
These dear memorials of thy pain
  Present anew the dreadful scene,

III.

I hear thy groans with deep surprise,
  And view thy wounds with weeping eyes,
Each bleeding wound, each dying groan,
  With anguish fraught, and pains unknown.

IV.

For mortal crimes a sacrifice,
 The Lord of life, the Saviour dies:
What love, what mercy, how divine! —
 Jesus, and can I call thee mine? —

V.

Repentant sorrow fills my heart,
 But mingling joy allays the smart:
O may my future life declare
 The sorrow and the joy sincere.

VI.

Be all my heart, and all my days
 Devoted to my Saviour's praise;
And let my glad obedience prove
 How much I owe, how much I love.

ANNE STEELE

A DYING SAVIOUR

I.

Stretch'd on the cross the Saviour dies;
Hark! his expiring groans arise!
See, from his hands, his feet, his side,
   Runs down the sacred crimson tide!

II.

But life attends the deathful sound,
   And flows from ev'ry bleeding wound:
The vital stream, how free it flows,
   To save and cleanse his rebel foes!

III.

To suffer in the traitor's place,
   To die for man, surprising grace!
Yet pass rebellious angels by —
   O why for man, dear Saviour, why!

IV.

And didst thou bleed, for sinners bleed?
   And could the sun behold the deed?
No, he withdrew his sick'ning ray,
   And darkness veil'd the mourning day.

V.

Can I survey this scene of woe,
   Where mingling grief and wonder flow;
And yet my heart unmov'd remain,
   Insensible to love or pain!

VI.

Come, dearest Lord, thy pow'r impart,
   To warm this cold, this stupid heart;
Till all its pow'rs and passions move,
   In melting grief and ardent love.

MEDITATING ON THE REDEEMER'S SUFFERINGS

I.

R ecall, my heart, that dreadful hour,
    When Jesus on the cursed tree
Infinite pains and sorrows bore —
    Think, O my soul, was this for thee?

II.

See, crown'd with thorns that sacred head,
    With beams of glory once adorn'd!
That voice, which heav'n and earth obey'd,
    Is now by traitors mock'd and scorn'd.

III.

And see those lovely melting eyes,
    Whence kind compassion often flow'd,
Now rais'd imploring to the skies,
    For harden'd souls athirst for blood!

IV.

Those healing hands with blessings fraught,
    Nail'd to the cross with pungent smart!
Inhuman deed! could no kind thought
    To pity move the ruthless heart?

V.

But oh! what agonies unknown,
    His soul sustain'd beneath the load
Of mortal crimes! how deep the groan
    Which calm'd the vengeance of a God!

VI.

He groan'd! he dy'd! the awful scene
    Of wonder, grief, surprising love,
Forever let my heart retain,
    Nor from my Saviour's feet remove.

155

VII.

Jesus, accept this wretched heart,
    Which trembling, mourning, comes to thee
The blessing of thy death impart,
    And tell my soul, 'tis all for me.

⟨✦⟩⟨✦⟩⟨✦⟩

SIN THE CAUSE OF CHRIST'S DEATH

I.

Was it for sin, for mortal guilt,
    The Saviour gave his vital blood?
For sin amazing anguish felt,
    The wrath of an offended God?

II.

When bleeding, groaning, on the tree,
    He breath'd such agonizing cries,
When nature suffer'd, Lord, with thee,
    And darkness cloth'd the mourning skies,

III.

And shall I harbour in my breast
    (Tremble my soul at such a deed)
This dreadful foe, this fatal guest?
    'Twas sin that made my Saviour bleed.

IV.

'Tis sin that would my ruin prove,
    And sink me down to endless woe;
But O forbid it, heavenly love,
    And save me from the cursed foe.

V.

Ye sins, ye cruel sins, depart,
 Your tyrant sway I cannot bear;
My rightful sov'reign claims my heart,
 Jesus alone shall govern here.

VI.

Come, glorious conqu'ror, gracious Lord,
 Thy all-prevailing pow'r employ;
O come, with thy resistless word,
 These hateful enemies destroy.

VII.

Guilty and weak to thee I fly,
 My Lord, my Saviour, and my friend,
On thy almighty arm rely,
 On thy atoning blood depend.

VIII.

My all of hope is fix'd on thee,
 For thou alone hast pow'r divine;
O come, and conquer, Lord, for me,
 And all the glory shall be thine.

CHRIST DYING AND RISING

I.

Come tune, ye saints, your noblest strains,
  Your dying, rising Lord to sing,
And echo to the heav'nly plains
    The triumphs of your Saviour-King.

II.

In songs of grateful rapture tell
    How he subdu'd your potent foes,
Subdu'd the pow'rs of death and hell,
    And, dying, finish'd all your woes.

III.

Then to his glorious throne on high
    Return 'd, while hymning angels round,
Through the bright arches of the sky,
    The God, the conqu'ring God, resound.

IV.

Almighty love! victorious pow'r!
    Not angel-tongues can e'er display
The wonders of that dreadful hour,
    The joys of that illustrious day.

V.

Then well may mortals try in vain,
    In vain their feeble voices raise;
Yet Jesus hears the humble strain,
    And kindly owns our wish to praise.

VI.

Dear Saviour, let thy wond'rous grace
    Fill ev'ry heart and ev'ry tongue,
Till the full glories of thy face
    Inspire a sweeter, nobler song.

SELECTED POEMS

TO LYSANDER

I.

A muse, in learning's arduous toil unskill'd,
  That sung her wild notes to the silent shade,
Collected blossoms from her native field,
And o'er the rural scenes delighted stray'd:
Though unambitious of the wreath of fame,
Yet glow'd her bosom with a nobler flame.

II.

Nor kings nor heroes grac'd her artless lay,
For peaceful themes to sylvan shades belong
Alike unknown among the great and gay,
Soft adulation flow'd not in her song.
To heav'n that gave them, oft her notes aspire.
Or friendship wakes the sympathizing lyre.

III.

Indulgent Friendship, listening, caught the strain,
And fondly fancy'd it was tun'd to move;
Then, smiling, bore it to the distant plain,
Far, ah how far beyond its native grove;
But say, Lysander, can such notes as these
Amid politer scenes expect to please?

IV.

Say, can these untaught airs acceptance find
Where Milton, wond'rous bard! divinely sung?
Or yield a taste of pleasure to the mind
That raptur'd soars with Hervey or with Young?
In minds of polish'd frame can friendship dwell
Plain, unadorn'd, as in the rural cell?

V.

Yet friendship dwells with piety sincere,
Or in the cottage, or the stately dome,
Whether detain'd in crowded scenes of care,
Or in the village fix'd, her peaceful home:
Where these reside, though artless be her strain,
O may the muse a kind admission gain.

VI.

If minds, where piety and friendship glow,
Approving smile, and own the kindred theme;
That smile a nobler pleasure will bestow,
Than all the laurell'd wreaths of boasting fame:
Blest minds! to these the Muse devotes her lays;
If these approve, she seeks no other praise

AN EVENING MEDITATION

When Phoebus had withdrawn his radiant beams,
And evening spread her sable curtains round;
In that soft hour when to the list'ning grove
Her pleasing, soothing, melancholy airs
Poor Philomel begins — (the kindly dews
Shed their soft influence on the fragrant herb,
And gave fresh odors to the flow'ry shrub,
Refreshing to the sense) — the charming scene
Alluring call'd to taste the evening air,
Amid the verdure of the lonely shade;
The lonely shade indulgent to the Muse.

Here may I stretch my wond'ring eyes around
O'er all the beauteous landscape, and behold
Almighty pow'r and wisdom plain impress'd
On ev'ry tree, on ev'ry plant and flower.
All own the sov'reign Architect divine,
And in their different language speak his praise.
The gentle zephyrs with harmonious breath,
Brush through the grove, and play along the stream,
And in soft whispers to the silver wave,
Speak their Creator's name, and die away.
The silver wave retains the pleasing theme,
Laves her glad banks, and gently murm'ring on,
Bears to the neighb'ring trees the welcome sound;

They bend their wav'ring tops, adore, and praise.
The lofty mountains rear their tow'ring heads,
Tall and majestic, to the fleecy clouds;
With awful pride confess their Maker God,
How great his pow'r, how wide his dread command.
Dress'd in a thousand charms, the flow'ry vale
Displays his goodness in her cheerful bloom,
And smiling owns beneficence divine.
Harmonious all and fair! whole nature joins
To speak the wonders of creating skill;
Bids us in all his works confess the God,
And bend our souls adoring at his feet.

Whether with pleasing rapture I survey
The smiling green in rich embroid'ry drest,
Or the more solemn grove in shady state,
Or contemplate the smoothly flowing stream;
Or if I raise my wand'ring eyes to gaze
On yonder azure plain, unnumberd beauties
Inspire my breast with wonder and delight.

Serenely bright ascends the silver moon
Attended by th' innumerable train
Of sparkling stars, with rich profusion pour'd
O'er all the vast expanse; and ev'ry star,
In ev'ry beam, proclaims his Maker's praise.

O Thou, both nature's author and her lord,
Whose pow'r and skill, in all thy works confess'd,
Demand the tribute of my noblest song;

Instruct my heart, and raise my humble thoughts
To trace thy forming hand in ev'ry scene,
And in thy works to meditate thy praise:
Till, led by these, my raptur'd soul ascends,
On heav'nly contemplation's soaring wing,
To thee, the sacred source of all perfection.

HAPPINESS

I.

O Happiness, by all admir'd, pursu'd,
How oft defin'd, how seldom understood,
And always at a painful distance view'd!

II.

Thy charms, alluring, in fair prospect rise;
They court our eager arms and longing eyes,
And prompt our fond desires and restless sighs

III.

If thou art but a dream, an empty name,
Then why this active pow'r, this quenchless flame;
By heav'n implanted in the human frame?

IV.

The great Creator, just, and good, and wise,
The wants of all his creatures well supplies,
Nor blessings to the lowest rank denies.

V.

Shall man, alone, unsatisfy'd remain?
And doom'd to ceaseless unavailing pain,
Must all his ardent wishes rise in vain?

VI.

No, there is nobler bliss for man design'd,
A happiness of an immortal kind,
Wide as his wishes, ample as his mind.

VII.

Earth never can bestow the sov'reign good;
The sacred word, unerring, points the road,
To happiness, to glory, and to God.

VIII.

But foolish mortals oft mistake the way,
In search of bliss on earth, we anxious stray,
And take a meteor for the lamp of day.

IX.

Phantoms of pleasure rise, and smiling fair,
They tempt our feet through labyrinths of care,
Till catching at the prize we grasp the air.

X.

Almighty goodness, call our hearts and eyes
From these deluding, tempting vanities,
And upward bid our ardent wishes rise.

XI

O bid each fatal, fair illusion flee,
Mark out our path from ev'ry error free,
And let us seek for bliss, alone, in thee.

PRIDE AND HUMILITY

Mark, how the stately tree disdainful rears
His tow'ring head, and mingles with the clouds;
But by his fatal height, the more expos'd
To all the fury of the raging storm:
His honors fly, the sport of angry winds;
Till the loud blast with direful stroke descends:
Torn from his basis, low on earth he lies,
And the hills echo to the sounding fall.
So pride, with haughty port, defies in vain.
The force of rough adversity, which rends
With double violence the stubborn heart.

But, like a tender plant, humility
Bends low before the threat'ning blast unhurt,
Eludes its rage, and lives through all the storm.
Pride is the liv'ry of the prince of darkness,
Worn by his slaves, who glory in their shame;
A gaudy dress, but tarnish'd, rent and foul,
And loathsome to the holy eye of heav'n.
But sweet humility, a shining robe,
Bestow'd by heav'n upon its fav'rite sons:
The robe which God approves, and angels wear
Fair semblance of the glorious Prince of light,
Who stoop'd to dwell (divine humility!)
With sinful worms, and poverty, and scorn.

Pride is the source of discord, strife, and war.
And all the endless train of heavy woes,
Which wait on wretched man; the direful sting
Of envy, and the dreaded frowns of scorn,
And gloomy discontent, and black despair.
But sweet humility, the source of peace,
Of amity and love, content and joy;
Where she resides, a thousand blessings wait,
To gild our lives, and form a heav'n below.
Pride leads her wretched vot'ries to contempt,
To certain ruin, infamy, and death.
But sweet humility points out the way
To happiness, and life, and lasting honors.
Humility how glorious! how divine!
Thus cloth'd, and thus enrich'd, O may I shine,
Be mine this treasure, this celestial robe,
And let the sons of pride possess the globe.

IMITATION OF MR. POPE'S ODE ON SOLITUDE

I.

Is there on earth a solitude
Which anxious care can ne'er invade;
Where pains nor sorrows e'er intrude?
A hallow'd shade?

II.

Where peace extends her halcyon wing,
To guard and bless the soft retreat;
Content sweet breathes eternal Spring
Around her seat?

III.

Some gentle spirit aid my flight
To this delightful, blissful spot,
From human converse, human sight;
Blest, and forgot.

IV.

Illusive dream! it fleets in air!
No paradise is found below,
No solitude secludes from care,
Or shuts out woe.

V.

Happy the man, and he alone,
To whom the easy lot is giv'n,
Cheerful to wait, and thankful own
The hand of heav'n.

VI.

Then solitude, or social joy,
Can please, yet not engage his heart;
Nor sorrow, pain, nor care annoy
His nobler part.

VII.

His wish, his hope, his soul aspires
To a fair paradise above;
Yet patient waits, till heav'n requires
His blest remove.

VIII.

Thus may my hopes and wishes rise,
Be mine serenity like this,
Till death's kind sleep shall close my eyes;
Then wake to bliss.

ON FRIENDSHIP

How fondly those mistake who seek for joys
In crowds, and mirth, and never ceasing noise:
Their mirth, how empty! and their joys, how vain!
Reflection ever flies the laughing train.
Stunn'd with the din, thought sickens; and the mind
No true delight, no taste of bliss can find.

   Alike they err, who leave the world to dwell
With gloomy sadness in a lonely cell:
Heavy and dull, the joyless hours move on,
To all the sweets of social life unknown.

   If pleasure smiles sincere below the skies,
That pleasure must from sacred friendship rise;
Of all which animates the human frame,
The noblest ardour, and the purest flame:
Offspring of heav'n! — there friendship all refin'd,

Immortal glows in each seraphic mind:
Mix'd with the streams of bliss forever flows,
Nor change, decay, nor interruption knows:
A glorious native of the realms of love,
And only, in perfection, known above:
Yet is the blessing, by indulgent heav'n,
Though in a less degree, to mortals giv'n:
Its pleasing pow'r by providence design'd
To soften human cares, and mend the mind;
To calm our passions by its gentle sway,
And bid them reason's sacred laws obey.
Friendship can often o'er the heart prevail,
When philosophic rules and maxims fail:
It turns to mutual tenderness the thought,
And views with kind indulgence ev'ry fault.
And where corrosives ought to be apply'd,
The gentle hand soft love and pity guide:
While each can bear reproof, and each reprove,
(All proud resentment lost in grateful love,)
Point out each fault, and blame yet not offend,
And free from nauseous flatt'ry, can commend,
To merit its proportion'd honors raise;
Alike exact the censure and the praise.

   Friendship communicates our joys and pains,
And in each breast rejoices, or complains;
Divides our weight of woe, relieves our cares,
And ev'ry pleasure heightens, as it shares.

   While sacred virtue lights the holy fire,
By time uninjur'd, it will ne'er expire:
No force of rough adversity can part,
Can tear the gen'rous passion from the heart.
   O friendship, what sincere delights are thine!

Fair miniature of happiness divine;
Propitious, pleasing, heav'n-descended guest,
Who only with the virtuous few canst rest:
May thy kind influence smooth my path of life,
Still calm and peaceful, free from noisy strife,
Be virtue, sweet content, and friendship mine,
I at my humble lot shall ne'er repine.
From these alone more real pleasures flow,
Than the gay round of mirth or gaudy show,
Or all the charms of greatness can bestow.

ON THE SAME

True friendship is the noblest earthly gift
    Which heav'n on man bestows; the cordial drop,
That mingling with the bitter cup of woe,
Gives a kind tincture to the deadly draught.
Not mines afford a gem of equal worth;
But ah, how rarely found! amid the crowd
Though glitt'ring counterfeits may oft appear
And many a phantom borrow friendship's name.

Smooth complaisance, and well-dissembled kindness.
And flatt'ry, hid beneath the specious mask
Of humble admiration and esteem,
Are often seen; they wear a fair appearance,
And dress'd in friendship's garb may please a while;
But cheat th' unwary heart, that trusts too far
Their seeming innocence, and honest face.
Self-interest is the secret spring that guides them;

171

This stopp'd, or broken, the machine stands still,
Or falls, and shivers into worthless fragments.

   Happy the mind of nobler texture fram'd,
Sincere, benevolent, above disguise,
Dress'd in the plain unborrow'd robe of truth.
These virtues make her fav'rite residence;
With virtue only, real friendship dwells,
And friendship loves for virtue's sake alone.

   While the frail scenes of momentary life
Bound the low narrow view of vulgar minds,
Ambition, envy, pride, and restless rage
Emit their baleful sparks; but soon, ah! soon,
The blaze expires, and all is dark forever.

   But friendship, kindled by fair piety,
(And thus she claims relation to the skies,)
Sheds her kind lustre o'er the path of life,
And guides the feet through many a thorny brake
Unhurt: she points with upward aim to heaven;
To heaven, from whence the sacred ardour came,
And guardian angels own the kindred flame.

ODE TO CONTENT

I.

Come, charming guest, divine Content,
  And chase my cares away;
The sweetest bliss to mortals lent,
  Is thy kind healing ray.

II.

Thy presence smooths the face of woe,
  And softens ev'ry pain;
From thee a thousand pleasures flow,
  A guiltless, lovely train.

III.

Humility thy steps attends;
  Her sweetly pensive eyes
To earth in peaceful thought she bends,
  Without a wish to rise.

IV.

With cheerful air and look sedate,
  See gentle Patience nigh,
And Hope, fair sister, smiling wait,
  With heav'n-erected eye:

V.

While Faith, (kind seraph!) points her view
  Beyond the starry plain,
To the bright worlds where, ever new,
Immortal pleasures reign.

VI.

Thy comforts, O divine Content,
  From those fair regions flow;
For bliss sincere was never meant
  On earth's low soil to grow.

VII.

In cold affliction's dreary shade,
  Fresh-blooming joys are thine!
Can wintry storms the heart invade
  When vernal sun-beams shine?

VIII.

Come then, thou dear delightful guest.
  Thy lov'd companions bring;
Come, take possession of my breast,
  And winter shall be spring.

ON REASON

Reason, the glory of the human frame,
Eye of the mind, the stamp of heav'n impressed
On man alone, of all the various ranks
Of being, which the great Creator form'd,
To people numberless this earthly globe,
To man alone he gave this ray divine,
This emanation of the deity:
A gift of countless value! rais'd by this
Above his fellow worms, and taught to view
His maker's hand in all his wondrous works;
To trace his glories, his divine perfections,
And worship with accepted adoration:
Fitted by this for converse with his God.
Amazing thought! the distance, how immense,
Betwixt infinity, and humble clay!

Yet, thus exalted, man, ungrateful man
Rebell'd, and spurn'd his Maker's righteous law;
And, in his just resentment, God withdrew
His blissful presence from his wretched offspring.
Then reason, heav'nly flame, with faded lustre
Glow'd faintly, its primeval brightness gone,
Sullied and clouded with surrounding guilt;
And, feebly glimm'ring with uncertain light,
No more it mounts sublime, to earth confin'd.
Weak, erring guide, no more it points the way
To happiness, but leaves the mind bewilder'd,
And lost in paths of danger, guilt, and death.

But light divine breaks from the sacred word,
And cheers the darksome gloom; while heav'n-born faith
The dawning glory views, and soars aloft.
Borne on her wings, Hope cheerful smiles; and lo
The clouds disperse, the prospect brightens round;
A glimpse of heav'n appears, of bliss immortal
Reserv'd for mortal man; and joys unknown,
Blest fruit of the Redeemer's dying pains,
Pardon, and peace, and life, laid up in him
For guilty rebels! Reconcil'd through him,
With his bright presence God revisits earth!
Transporting view! lost happiness restor'd!

Weak-sighted reason upward rises too,
Thus aided, and pursues the shining tract
With cheerful wing, though slow; and glad adores
The dazzling glories, which she cannot reach
With steady light: yet with delightful toil
By gradual steps ascends, and joyful sees
The bright perfections of the Deity,

175

In humbler scenes display'd, where'er she turns
Her raptur'd eye; and blest employment finds
For never-ceasing praise and grateful homage.

   Rekindled now from heav'n, her dying lamp
Glows with increasing lustre: Grace assisting.
Her empire o'er the mind she now resumes;
Her gentle sway the warring passions own;
Her voice their wilder tumults can control,
And tune them all to harmony and peace.

   Nor is her pow'r to single minds confin'd;
Senates and nations own her sov'reign rule,
And boast their different governments and laws
Inspir'd by her, and founded on her dictates.
The bliss of civil and of social life
Depends on her; without her all would sink
To discord, anarchy, and wild confusion.
Each individual, through the various ranks,
Whether of public or of private life,
To her his safety, peace and pleasure owes.
Her influence soothes the cares of life, and shews
The use and value of its num'rous blessings.

   Robb'd of her cheering light, what woes attend
On helpless wretched man! self-preservation.
By gracious heav'n implanted in his frame,
Oft in the hand of providence a guard
Amid surrounding dangers, then forsakes him.

Were reason's beam withdrawn, life would be death.
Existence a mere blank; — the sweets of life
Be tasteless, and its blessings unenjoy'd;
Fame, pleasure, riches, useless all, and vain;
And health and friends, (dearest of comforts!) sink
O'erwhelm'd in dark oblivion: dreadful state,
Recoiling nature trembles at the thought!

O may my soul with gratitude sincere,
And constant praise, adore the God of mercy,
Who gives this blessing still to shine on me.
Lord, raise my gratitude, and tune my praise
To thy almighty goodness, which bestows
On me this gift of reason, and continues
Its cheering ray; and may thy pow'rful grace
Assist me, O my God, still to devote
Reason, and life, and all my pow'rs to thee,
Till this frail transient scene shall close in death,
Then may I rise, by angel-guards convoy'd,
To the bright mansions of eternal bliss.
There nobler praise, and worship all refin'd,
Unnumber'd hearts, unnumber'd tongues employ;
And joys unknown to mortals. — Reason there
Shall shine with perfect and unclouded lustre j
And all my pow'rs, exalted and renew'd,
Glow with immortal vigour. — There my voice?
Tun'd to the strains of paradise, shall join
With saints and seraphs, in transporting songs
To thee, the source of everlasting joy.

ON READING MR. HERVEY'S MEDITATIONS

Happy the man, whom grace divine has taught
To raise to nobler scenes the flying thought;
Beyond the bounds of sense and time to soar,
And awful immortality explore.
Amid the chill of death's tremendous gloom,
And all the dreary horrors of the tomb,
He walks serene — 'tis heav'n with sacred ray
Darts through the sable shade a glimpse of day;
Faith views the dawning bliss with raptur'd eye,
And bears his thoughts and hopes above the sky.

Yet, o'er the ruins of mankind he weeps,
O'er mortal hope which here in silence sleeps;
But from the pitying tear, the pious woe,
Celestial truths with soft persuasion flow.
He from these silent teachers bids us learn
Our certain fate, our infinite concern.
To realms of life he points the radiant way,
Where death resigns his universal sway;
And this frail, dying frame, renew'd, shall shine,
Safe from decay in splendors all divine.

Thus Hervey mourns; his kind instructive page,
Full of compassion for a thoughtless age,
In all the charms of eloquence appears,
And wakes our pleasure, while it steals our tears.

Now rising from the dark retreats of death,
Soft as the morning Zephyr's gentle breath,
His language flows, and cheers our fainting pow'rs
With all the sweetness of the op'ning flow'rs;
Displays the beauties of the blooming race:

Their various beauties, though with matchless grace
They scorn the pencil's art, yet flourish here,
In bright description all their charms appear;
Charms, which the heedless, unobserving eye,
Or slightly views, or wholly passes by:
But to the heav'n-taught mind, how bright they shine,
Mark'd with the traces of the hand divine!
Their sweets collected with engaging art,
At once regale the sense, and cheer the heart.

  While all our pow'rs obey the soft control,
To beauty's source he leads th' enraptur'd soul;
To Jesus leads, the everlasting Fair:
In the dear name ten thousand charms appear;
Beneath the heav'nly radiance of his eye,
Created beauties droop, and fade, and die.

  Thou Sun of righteousness, thy beams impart,
And bless my eyes, and warm my languid heart;
O let me dwell beneath thy light divine,
And nature's charms contented I resign.

But oh! what mortal eye can bear the ray,
When thy full glories beam ethereal day?
The brightest seraphs, veil'd before thy throne,
Adoring low, the dazzling splendors own
Too strong for finite natures to sustain,
Thy praise too lofty for their noblest strain.

Come, gentle ev'ning, cheer my fainting sense,
Pain'd and oppress'd with glories too intense.
The ev'ning comes — all mild, and sweet, and fair;
The dusk how grateful! how serene the air? —
Yet still my soul would see her Saviour God,

The living source of all that's fair and good;
His beauties, though at humble distance, view
And trace him in the scenes his pencil drew.
His bright perfections round me are display'd,
The morn, the noon, the grateful ev'ning shade,
Present his different glories to the sight,
Or strike with wonder, or inspire delight.
His pow'r and love, in plenty's smiling form,
O'er the wide fields each grateful bosom warm.
From him, the gentle ev'ning breezes spring,
And waft refreshment on their balmy wing.
His beauty glitters in the pearly dew,
And smiles amid the bright ethereal blue
Which paints yon spacious arch; and charms our eyes
In clouds of gold, which streak the western skies.
And now the shining lamps of heav'n advance,
Rang'd in bright order o'er the fair expanse;
Like lamps they sparkle on th' unaided sight;
But nearer view'd in philosophic light,
Prodigious orbs, unnumber'd worlds arise!
New scenes of wonder meet our gazing eyes!

Jesus, thy glory beaming from afar,
Great source of light, illumines ev'ry star.
Thy word inform'd the planets where to roll,
And station'd ev'ry orb that gilds the pole.
To thee, 'midst all the glories of the skies,
To thee alone I raise my longing eyes:
"Bright morning star, arise with healing ray,
"Arise, and chase the shades of night away,
"Sweet harbinger of everlasting day."

A SIMILE

Oft have I view'd the flow'rs while bright and gay,
They gave their beauties to the noon-tide ray.
But short, alas! their bloom, and soon they fade,
Unbless'd with cooling show'rs, or friendly shade.
See the clouds blacken, heavy show'rs descend,
The weak, soft race o'erladen, droop and bend,
Recline their languid heads, and seem to mourn,
Till the storm cease, and sunny beams return:
Then smiling, rise more lovely, bright and fair,
And with new sweets perfume the ambient air.

 Thus, to the soul affliction oft supplies
New life, and bids declining virtue rise.
The storm, which seem'd a while t' oppress, revives
Each fading grace, and strength and beauty gives.
Their drooping pow'rs, by heavVs kind influence fed,
A fairer bloom, and sweeter fragrance spread.
Prest with affliction, let me then conclude,
That storms and sunshine, (kind vicissitude!)
Are mingled blessings, meant to work my good

A MEDITATION ON DEATH

Come, bid adieu, my soul, to earthly pleasures. -
Illusive phantoms! distant how they smile,
Fair as the colours of the radiant bow!
But nearer fade upon the cheated eye,
Lose all their lustre, or dissolve in air.
Ah, think how soon these dreams will flit away;
How soon these gaily tempting forms will sink
In death's eternal shade — Death onward comes
With hasty step, though unperceiv'd and silent.
Perhaps (alarming thought!) perhaps he aims
E'en now the fatal blow that ends my life.
O let me then, arous'd, reflect in time,
And make this awful, this important theme
Familiar to my thoughts! Awake, my soul,
Nor, careless, slumber on the brink of fate.
With constant warnings, with loud admonitions,
Can I be unconcern'd? At length my eyes,
Long held in mists, or cheated with false visions,
Begin to open on the awful scene.
Let idle-active fancy, now no more
Spread her gay, flatt'ring colours to my view;
But aid my better thoughts, and represent
Important truths in all their striking forms.

Behold the gaping tomb! it seems to speak,
With silent horror, to my shiv'ring heart;
Bids me survey my swift approaching doom,
And view the dark retreat which waits my coming.

O death, thou king of terrors! dreadful name!
What tongue can e'er describe, what thought can image
The scenes of horror that surround thy throne?
From thy wide-wasting hand, what vast destruction
Is pour'd on all the tribes of wretched mortals?
Behold, on ev'ry side the scatter'd bones
Pave all the dreary mansion, and impart
Chill melancholy to the sinking spirits,
While all aghast I stand, and fix mine eyes
On the dire prospect! O thou gloomy Monarch,
Are these the trophies of thy conqu'ring arms?

Nor rev'rend hoary age, nor blooming youth,
Nor boasted strength escape thy fatal dart.
Not the persuasive pow'r of beauty's charms,
Nor the soft moving tears of innocence
Can stay thy hand: nor can the miser's gold,
Nor all the treasures of the eastern shore
Buy one short moment of relentless death.

Not ev'n the good man's virtues ought avail
To ward the direful stroke; nor all the pray'rs
And ardent wishes of the grateful poor,
Fed from his table, and who daily knew
The blessings of his charitable hand.
See, his sad relatives, his mournful friends
Around his dying bed! what silent sorrow
Sits on each visage, while their streaming eyes
And wringing hands confess their inward anguish!
Who can describe th' unutterable woe
Which fills their hearts, to see a father, brother,
A friend, in whom their all of earthly bliss
Was center'd, gasping on the verge of life?
And ev'n the sad remains of hope are lost.

183

His ev'ry dying groan augments their tears,
And the cold sweats declare his exit nigh;
Till the last breath consigns them to despair.
Heart-rending pain! Inexorable death!

Then, O my soul, since this deluding world,
With all her boasted stores, has nought to give
That can procure an hour's, a moment's pause,
When death commission'd aims the parting stroke;
Nor this weak frame, this mortal tenement
Of feeble texture, long sustain th' assault
Of his attendants, sickness, pain, and sorrow;
Seek, timely seek, while mercy points the way,
A firm, clear title to those blest abodes,
Prepar'd on high, unconscious of decay:
That when this totaling frame, (not built to last)
Frail house of clay, which shakes with ev'ry wind,
Dissolves, and falls a heap of dust and ruin;
In realms of light I may forever dwell,
In mansions never form'd by mortal hands,
Beyond the reach of sorrow, pain, or death.

O may my name but find some humble place
In the bright records of the court of heav'n,
Sign'd with th' atoning blood of my Redeemer!
May his almighty love cheer my last hours,
Shew me my sins all cancell'd by his death,
And smiling open endless joy before me!
Then shall I triumph o'er my mortal foe,
And with exulting, heav'nly transport say,
O death, where is thy sting? and where, O grave,
Insatiate grave, is thy victorious pow'r?
Then shall my last expiring accents breathe
His blissful name, who, dying, vanquish'd death.

And purchas'd life, immortal life, for me —
Jesus, my Lord, my Saviour, and my all!

TO DELIA

I.

The gifts indulgent heav'n bestows,
  Are variously convey 'd;
The human mind, like nature, knows
  Alternate light and shade.

II.

While changing aspects all things wear,
  Can we expect to find
Unclouded sunshine all the year,
  Or constant peace of mind?

III.

More gaily smiles the blooming spring,
  When wintry storms are o'er;
Retreating sorrows thus may bring
  Delights unknown before.

IV.

Then, Delia, send four fears away,
  Nor sink in gloomy care,
Though clouds o'erspread the scene today,
  Tomorrow may be fair.

TO AMIRA ON HER MARRIAGE

While round you hourly gratulations rise,
  And joy and happiness, (gay soothing sounds)
Salute your ear; accept the artless wish
That friendship dictates, breathing from the heart.

May gracious heav'n the happy union crown,
Propitious still and kind, with all the bliss
Which mortals can enjoy; may health, and peace,
And love, and friendship, guide the circling hours.
Soft roll the circling hours, serene and fair,
Still bright'ning as they roll: may true content
With kindly mixture sweeten ev'ry care,
Till scarce th' unpleasing tincture can be found.

But earthly bliss is ever mix'd with pain,
And thorns among its flow'ry pleasures grow.
May all the joys, the nobler, purer joys
Religion yields be yours; to fairer scenes,
And brighter prospects, may your hopes ascend;
While heav'n-born faith presents a charming glimpse
Of that immortal paradise on high,
Where pleasure blooms without a thorny care,
And friendship smiles beyond the reach of pain.

THE PLEASURES OF SPRING

Now reigns the lovely spring in all her pride,
And spreads her verdant robe, adorn'd with fiow'rs,
Around the fields and meads; they cheerful smile
In her gay livery drest ; the whisp'ring winds
Breathe soft, and on their balmy wings convey
Reviving sweets; the feather'd choir awake
Their artless songs, and all th' enchanting scene
Is harmony and beauty: nature's charms
Subdue the heart, and ev'ry sense is fill'd!

But while the eye roves o'er the blooming mead
With careless pleasure, or the list'ning ear
Attends the soothing music of the grove;
Think, whither does the soft enchantment tend?
Are nature's various beauties lent for this,
Only to please the sense? For nobler ends
The God of nature gave them. Nature spreads
An open volume, where in ev'ry page
We read the wonders of almighty pow'r!
Infinite wisdom, and unbounded love.
Here sweet instruction, entertaining truths
Reward the searching mind, and onward lead
Enquiring thought; new beauties still unfold
And op'ning wonders rise upon the view.
The mind, rejoicing, comments as she reads;
While through th' inspiring page, conviction glows,
And warms to praise her animated pow'rs.

187

How great, how glorious, is the sov'reign hand,
Which forms so beauteous ev'ry plant and flow'r,
And on the vegetable world inscribes,
In lively characters, his wond'rous name?
While active life speaks in a thousand forms,
Pow'r, wisdom, and beneficence divine,
The parts of nature in their just proportion,
Uniting, harmonizing, blend to form
One perfect system; truth and beauty smile,
Inviting contemplation upward still,
From step to step, till at their glorious source
Arriv'd, the soul in low prostration bends,
Adoring, with submissive, silent awe,
The great Unsearchable, the wond'rous name,
Which creature praise can never, never reach?

ON THE SICKNESS OF A FRIEND

I.

Shall fond expectance lean on earthly friends,
Since earthly friends, alas! are born to die;
And disappointment waits, and grief attends
The best, the dearest joys below the sky?

II.

Why will this wretched, this deluded heart
So fast to earth's uncertain comforts cleave?
'Tis but to cherish pain, to treasure smart,
And teach the unavailing sigh to heave.

III.

Great source of good, attend my plaintive cries,
My weakness with indulgent pity see,
And teach this restless, anxious heart to rise,
And centre all its hopes and joys in thee.

IV.

Then, should my dearest earthly comforts die,
Should ev'ry friend (distressing thought!) depart,
My refuge, my unfailing friend on high,
Will never, never leave this trembling heart.

V.

Should sorrow like a whelming deluge roll,
And gloomy death appear on ev'ry wave;
Then hope, blest anchor, shall sustain my soul
And faith shall rise and triumph o'er the grave,

VI.

Then shall I meet my much-lov'd friends above.
Safe landed on the ever-peaceful shore,
The blissful regions of immortal love,
Where happiness and friendship part no more,

THE FETTERED MIND

I.

A h! why should this immortal mind,
Enslav'd by sense, be thus confin'd,
And never, never rise?
  Why thus amus'd with empty toys,
And sooth'd with visionary joys,
  Forget her native skies?

II.

The mind was form'd to mount sublime,
Beyond the narrow bounds of time,
  To everlasting things;
But earthly vapours cloud her sight,
And hang with cold oppressive weight
  Upon her drooping wings.

III.

The world employs its various snares,
Of hopes and pleasures, pains and cares,
  And chain'd to earth I lie:
When shall my fetter'd pow'rs be free,
And leave these seats of vanity,
  And upward learn to fly.

IV.

Bright scenes of bliss, unclouded skies,
Invite my soul: O could I rise,
  Nor leave a thought below;
I'd bid farewell to anxious care,
  And say to ev'ry tempting snare,
Heav'n calls, and I must go.

V.

Heav'n calls! and can I yet delay?
Can aught on earth engage my stay?
   Ah wretched, ling'ring heart!
Come, Lord, with strength, and life, and light,
   Assist, and guide my upward flight,
And bid the world depart.

VI.

One word of thy resistless pow'r
Can bid my joyful spirit soar,
   And scorn the feeble chain:
Come, bear my raptur'd thoughts above,
   On pinions of seraphic love;
And earth shall tempt in vain.

VII.

In vain, her siren voice may try,
To lure me downward from the sky,
   To this dark vale of tears;
How will her transient glories fade,
   And unregarded sink in shade,
When heav'n's bright dawn appears?

VIII.

So, wand'ring meteors of the night,
Amuse the weary traveler's sight,
   With fair deceitful ray;
But all their glimm'ring lustre flies,
   And ev'ry gay delusion dies,
When Phoebus wakes the day.

ANNE STEELE

TO A FRIEND IN TROUBLE

If when the tender sympathizing sigh
Swells the full heart, or melts the pitying eye,
The soft compassion could convey relief,
This heart should lessen, while it shar'd your grief.
Unchecked the sigh should rise, the sorrow flow,
And pleasure mingle with the kindred woe.
But this is vain, 'tis not in nature's pow'r
To cheer, with lightsome rays, the gloomy hour.
The soothing voice of friendship may beguile
Our cares, and sorrow wear a transient smile.
Poor solace; soon the spreading gloom returns,
The heart that fain would comfort, only mourns.
Ah, wretched state! must friendship ever share,
Yet never hope to ease the load of care,
Partake the anguish of infectious grief,
And wish, in vain, to bring a kind relief?
Ah, wretched state! each aching heart replies,
Till fainting, dying, hope begins to rise:
Hope, heav'n-born comforter, with cheerful air,
Sheds her kind lustre o'er the scenes of care;
Her gentle whisper calms the rising sigh,
And weeping sorrow lifts her tearful eye;
Nor lifts in vain, at his supreme command,
Who holds our welfare in his gracious hand:
His gracious hand alone has pow'r to heal,
Who pities, while he deals the pains we feel.
The springs of life are his; and cares and pains
Fulfil whate'er his sacred will ordains.
He knows what most we need: when skill divine
Presents a bitter draught, shall we repine?
While mercy mingles all with lenient art,
To ease the anguish of the throbbing heart.

The steps of providence, though we in vain
Attempt to trace, while clouds o'erspread the scene:
Its dealings all are just, and wise, and kind;
Our lesson this — « Be humble and resign'd!"
Through wild and thorny paths, our journey lies,
And darkness terrifies, and dangers rise.
O may our heav'nly Father's guardian care,
Preserve our steps from ev'ry fatal snare:
Be his almighty arm our guide, our stay,
Through all the toils and terrors of the way.
No dangers can affright if God is near,
A present God can banish ev'ry fear;
His gracious smile can make the darkness fly,
Smooth all the road, and brighten all the sky.
"He is our sun:" his soul-reviving light,
Alone, can chase the horrors of the night.
"He is our shield:" when darts fly thick around,
They fall repell'd, and fix no deadly wound.
Our God, our Guide! O may we never stray,
But trust his care, and keep the heav'nly way;
Till safe we reach the happy seats of peace,
And darkness, grief, and pain, and danger cease.

THE ABSENT MUSE

I.

How soft roll'd the hours, how serene was my heart,
  When the Muse my companion, and friend,
Unknown to ambition, a stranger to art,
   Deign'd oft on my call to attend!

II.

While she sooth'd all my cares, and my passions to rest,
   (Sweet moments, why would you not stay!)
Delighted and easy I thought myself blest,
   Nor envy'd the great, nor the gay.

III.

Ye gentle delusions! ye dreams of delight!
   And will ye approach me no more?
Shall the scene be a desert, o'ershaded with night,
   Which was sunshine and Eden before?

IV.

No, the pleasures were real, though soon they withdrew;
   And my cares I will call a long dream,
If the Muse will return, and present to my view
   The scenes which were once my glad theme.

V.

When Urania appears, o'er the field and the grave
   New verdure and beauty shall rise;
The prospect shall brighten wherever I rove,
   And Eden again meet my eyes.

VI.

How vain the dear hope! — She despises the lays
   Which I once fondly thought she inspir'd;
Unfetter'd, transported, with Hervey she strays,
   Applauded, belov'd, and admir'd.

THE WASTE OF TIME.
OCCASIONED BY HEARING THESE LINES REPEATED

"Another, and another, and the last,
"Are copies of the dull, defective past."

"*T*he dull, defective!" 'tis too faint a name,
    For vile ingratitude, for guilt, and shame! —
Such is my conduct, when I waste away
In trifles, or in indolence, a day.
Each future minute is beyond my power:
Can India's mines procure a single hour?
O much-neglected time, thy worth how high?
Not thy least particle, the world can buy.
When heaven bestows this boon, it bids employ,
(O blest command!) in seeking endless joy.
And shall my thoughtless heart, ungrateful, waste
The present hour, as I have done the past?
Forbid it, gracious God! O let my soul
Obey reflection's strict, but kind control;
And humbly bend before that awful eye,
Which marks my squander'd minutes as they fly;
With deep contrition bend, and ardent pray-
That love may turn his angry frown away:
Indulgent love, through that atoning blood.
In which alone I can approach to God.

    To thee, great Advocate, to thee I fly,
And on thy righteousness alone rely.
O may thy spirit cleanse this guilty heart,
My pardon seal, and strength divine impart;
And may my hours, if future hours are lent,
To nobler, higher purposes be spent.

THE DEATH-WATCH

A death-watch! how distinct it beats! — in vain
It beats to me, nor brings one anxious pain.
Thou gloomy insect, oft inspiring fear,
Dreadful to superstition's list'ning ear;
How many start to hear thy fancy 'd knell,
Dismal and solemn as a passing bell!

And why must harmless insects be accus'd,
When daily, hourly warnings are refus'd?
Each day, each hour, accosts my ear, or eye,
Some monitor, which bids prepare to die.

See yonder stalk! there lately grew a flow'r,
'Tis gone, its glowing colours are no more.
That bush, where roses smil'd, and breath'd perfume!
How sweet their fragrance, and how gay their bloom!
A few days since they bloom'd, now dropt and lost:
Frail mortal life, behold how vain thy boast!
Hark, near my side, the clock, with solemn sound,
Tells me how life pursues his constant round!
Life on the wings of time flies swift away;
My last will come, and this may be the day.
Each pain I feel, and every plaintive sigh,
What does it speak? this truth — "I soon must die."
Must die! Is this a melancholy sound,
When endless life begins its blissful round?
Thy poison'd arrow, Death, wounds not the heart,
Which in the Saviour's blood can claim a part.

May this blest hope (dear solace of my soul!)
With heav'nly comfort all my fears control.
While faith points upward to the blest abode
Of life immortal, and my Saviour God,
May that bright world its radiant dawn impart,
And be each hour, a Death-watch to my heart.

THE FRIEND

He is a friend, who scorns the little sphere
Of narrow self, and finds a joy sincere
To see another blest; whose gen'rous heart
To all around would happiness impart,
If happiness were his: whose bosom glows
With warmth the frozen stoick never knows.
Divine Benevolence where friendship reigns,
And piety the sacred flame maintains.
This is the tie inviolate, which binds
In mutual friendship, harmonizing minds.
A friend, thus form'd, is form'd to give delight,
To brighten joy, and gild affliction's night:
His heart exults whene'er his friends rejoice.
And ev'ry pleasing pow'r, at friendship's voice,
Awakes to life, and bids the transport rise,
In grateful adoration to the skies.
But ah, how short the bright untroubled hour!
Soon clouds arise, and storms impending low'r,
And oft they burst upon the fainting heart;
Then friendship shews her noblest, kindest art,
Sustains the drooping powers, and helps to bear

The well-divided load of mutual care.
If griefs oppress, or threat'ning woes impend,
Dear solace then, to find a real friend!
He is a real friend, whose passions know
The anguish of communicated woe;
Who feels the deep distress when sorrow mourns,
And from his inmost heart the sigh returns.
The kindred sigh conveys a strange relief:
How cordial is society in grief!
Less are the woes, and lighter are the cares,
Which gentle, sympathizing friendship shares.
When humbly at the throne of grace we bend,
And ask its kindest blessings for a friend;
When for a friend our warmest wishes rise
In holy breathings to the pitying skies;
The sacred precept warrants those desires,
And heav'n will sure approve, what heav'n inspires.

O may I make my friend's distress my own,
Nor let my heart, unhappy, grieve alone:
In sorrow, may I never want a friend,
Nor when the wretched mourn, a tear to lend.

ON CHILDREN'S PLAY

I.

Oft, when the child in wanton play-
   Exerts his little pow'rs,
And busy, trifling, toils away
   In sports the circling hours:

II.

We smile to see his infant mind
   So eager, so intent;
But growing years new follies find,
   As much on trifles bent.

III.

Youth has its toys, when pleasure's charms
   The fond pursuit invite:
But pleasure mocks th' extended arms;
   Vain shadow of delight!

IV.

What are the joys of riper age?
   By time is folly cur'd?
No, trifles still the heart engage,
   And vanity matur'd.

V.

If glitt'ring riches tempt the eyes,
   An envy'd, valu'd store;
Thus children shells and counters prize,
   And hoard and wish for more.

VI.

Or if aspiring fame employ's
   The eager, gazing train;
The paper-kite of sportive boys
   Is not more light and vain.

VII.

Unsatisfy'd, and tir'd at last.
   We must resign our breath,
Life's empty cares and follies past.
   And ev'ning close in death.

VIII.

Thus children "weary of their play,
   With fretfulness oppress'd,
Throw all their little toys away,
   And gently sink to rest.

IX.

Happy the mind, by heaven inspir'd
   To scorn earth's empty toys;
And with divine ambition fir'd,
   Pursue sublimer joys!

X.

Then, when the cares of life are o'er,
   The parting soul shall rise,
And scenes of happiness explore,
   Immortal in the skies.

THE PATH OF LIFE

What is this world with all its gay delights?
A gloomy wilderness of wide extent,
Where many winding paths perplex the choice,
And lead the unwary traveler's feet astray.
Here smiles an easy smooth-descending road,
In verdure cloth'd, and spread with blooming flow'rs
The scene how fair! — but ruin waits its end.
There rugged looks the path, thick set with thorns,
Where many toil their weary hours away
In search of happiness amid the dust.
What crowds of wretched, erring minds I see,
Still disappointed, yet persisting still,
All strangers to the way which leads to rest!
A thousand dangers, and a thousand snares
Attend their steps; before them is a scene
Of various grief; a labyrinth of woe;
A dark, damp vale of tears. Though now and then
Prosperity's gay flatt'ring sunshine smiles,
Its brightest day is short, declining fast,
If not o'ercast with sable clouds at noon.
And oft its brightest day more fatal proves
Than dark adversity's tempestuous night.
It shines with sickly ray, and spreads around
Malignant ills; malignant to the mind,
Stubborn disease, which med'cine cannot cure.
And if adversity's cold, wintry blast
Invade the shiv'ring heart, then comfort dies,
And solitary hope just lives, to warm
With some faint gleams of possible relief.

Thus pond'ring o'er the gloomy scenes of life,
The pensive muse attun'd her plaintive song.

201

Her eye dejected fix'd upon the ground,
Where thorny cares spontaneous rise, she sigh'd,
And wish'd a fairer prospect! smiling hope
Soft-whisp'ring, bids her lift her downcast eye,
And view the wild attentive. Now she sees
A beam ethereal, dawning o'er the gloom
With cheering lustre, permanent and mild.
'Tis mercy! saving mercy! she can shield
From every ill, the trembling, trusting soul.
Beneath the shelter of her guardian wing
Not gay prosperity's malignant glow
Shall scorch, nor cold adversity shall freeze.
Amid the devious labyrinth she marks
The path divine, where heav'nly wisdom leads
Her favor'd vot'ries; narrow path, but safe.
There real pleasures rise, and sacred peace
Attend their steps; if thorny cares too near
Inflict a wound, kind mercy instant pours
A sovereign balm, to ease the burning pain.
There walks humility with cautious step;
On wisdom, gracious guide, she leans secure.
A thousand lurking snares her feet escape,
And o'er her head a thousand dangers fly,
Fly harmless. Patience there, and cheerful hope
Walk hand in hand; and faith with piercing eye
Looks forward through the shades, and joyful marks
Her journey's end, the radiant seats of day.

   "Here fix your choice," immortal wisdom cries:
"To you, O sons of men, to you I call:
"O turn from erring folly. Fatal guide;
"Her way is danger, and it ends in death.
"Turn to my path, here only can you find
"Content, which wretched thousands seek in vain.

"My path is safety; and it leads to life,
"To life immo'rtal, in the realms of bliss."

  Indulgent mercy wafts the heav'nly sound,
Reviving to my heart. Yes, glorious guide,
To thy unerring conduct I resign
My steps, and bless the ever-gracious pow'r,
Which beam'd a ray of heav'n o'er this dark wild,
And led my feet to thy celestial path,
The path of peace, and life, and endless joy.

TO THE VOTARIES OF PLEASURE

Ye mirthful tribes, who careless, vain, and gay,
  In pleasure's flowery paths untiring stray;
Say, can you boast content? Ah, no; the sigh,
Involuntary, breathes your sad reply.
And conscience speaks: attend the friendly pow'r;
Indulge one serious, one reflecting hour.
Earth's soft allurements, empty, light, and vain,
Are dreams of joy; you wake to real pain.
When pleasure dawns, serenely fair and bright,
'Tis shaded soon with clouds, and lost in night:
Yet still you fondly court its flatt'ring smiles;
Again it glitters, and again beguiles.
Will you be tempted thus with painted charms,
And follow shadows with extended arms?
While nobler pleasures stand neglected by,
Nor move your heart, nor raise your languid eye?
Delights refin'd, and lasting, court your choice,

And heav'nly wisdom sues with melting voice:
"How long, deluded, wretched souls; how long
" Shall pleasure sooth you with her siren song?
"Ah fly the fatal smile, th' enchanting strain,
"And let the gay deceiver tempt in vain."
Turn at the friendly call; O yet be wise,
To real pleasures raise your cheated eyes.
May the kind admonition, deep impress'd,
Dwell on your hearts, and teach you to be blest!
Think where you tread! — the path which looks so gay.
Is ruin's sure, inevitable way.
Think — life immortal, or eternal death,
Precarious trembles on a moment's breath.
This single moment's yours — the next may bear
Your souls to endless darkness and despair.
Fly from the world's deluding, tempting wiles,
While time is yours, and heav'nly mercy smiles:
From sin, from all its soul-destroying charms,
Fly to the great Redeemer's open arms.
Now with a gentle, kind, inviting voice,
He calls, he courts you to immortal joys.
O hear those winning accents, hear and prove
The boundless blessings of his pard'ning love.
Ere long, that slighted voice, with dreadful sound,
Shall with the keenest pangs of terror wound;
Shall wound those guilty souls, who dare despise
His sov'reign grace; nor life nor glory prize.
Before his dreadful bar you must appear:
That awful, that tremendous hour, how near
To you unknown; yet ev'ry moment brings
Th' important period nearer on its wings.
How will your now unmov'd, relentless heart
Then bear the word, the dreadful word, Depart?
Depart ccndemn'd, accursed down to hell,

Where black despair, and endless torment dwell?
In time reflect, and tremble at the view,
The fatal path to death no more pursue.
Fly for your lives, to safety instant fly;
Ah, wretched ling'ring souls, why will you die?
While heav'nly patience lengthens out your day,
And God's unerring word directs the way,
O seize the fleeting hour, the precious Now,
And at the Saviour's feet for mercy bow.

ON THE PUBLIC FAST
FEBRUARY 6, 1756.

In response to the Great Lisbon Earthquake Nov. 1, 1755

I.

See, gracious God, before thy throne
Thy mourning people bend!
'Tis on thy sov'reign grace alone,
　Our humble hopes depend.

II.

Tremendous judgments from thy hand,
　Thy dreadful pow'r display;
Yet mercy spares this guilty land,
　And yet we live to pray.

III.

Great God, and why is Britain spar'd,
    Ungrateful as we are?
O be these awful warnings heard,
    While mercy cries, Forbear.

IV.

What num'rous crimes increasing rise
    O'er all this wretched isle!
What land so favor'd of the skies,
    And yet what land so vile!

V.

How chang'd, alas! are truths divine.
    For error, guilt, and shame!
What impious numbers, bold in sin,
    Disgrace the Christian name!

VI.

O bid us turn, almighty Lord,
    By thy resistless grace;
Then shall our hearts obey thy word,
    And humbly seek thy face.

VII.

Then should insulting foes invade,
    We shall not sink in fear;
Secure of never-failing aid,
    If God, our God, is near.

NATIONAL JUDGMENTS DEPRECATED
ON THE FAST. FEB. 11, 1757.

I.

While justice waves her vengeful hand
    Tremendous o'er a guilty land.
Almighty God, thy awful pow'r
With fear and trembling we adore.

II.

Where shall we fly, but to thy feet?
Our only refuge is thy seat;
Thy seat, where potent mercy pleads,
And holds thy thunder from our heads.

III.

While peace and plenty bless'd our days,
Where was the tribute of thy praise?
Ungrateful race! how have we spent
The blessings which thy goodness lent?

IV.

Pale famine now, and wasting war,
With threat'ning frown thy wrath declare;
But war and famine are thy slaves,
Nor can destroy when mercy saves.

V.

Look down, O Lord, with pitying eye;
Though loud our crimes for vengeance cry,
Let mercy's louder voice prevail,
Nor thy long-suffering patience fail.

VI.

Encourag'd by thy sacred word,
May we not plead the blest record,
That when a humbled nation mourns,
Thy rising wrath to pity turns.

VII.

O let thy sov'reign grace impart
Contrition to each rocky heart,
And bid sincere repentance flow,
A gen'ral, undissembled woe.

VIII.

Our arms, O God of armies, bless,
Thy hand alone can give success,
And make our haughty neighbors own
That heav'n protects the British throne.

IX.

Fair smiling peace again restore,
With plenty bless the pining poor,
And may a happy thankful land
Obedient own thy guardian hand.

ON THE SAME. PLEADING FOR MERCY

I.

Come, let our souls adore the Lord,
  Whose judgments yet delay,
Who yet suspends the lifted sword,
  And gives us leave to pray.

II.

In armies, fleets, or strong allies,
  No more we place our trust;
On God alone, our hope relies,
  Kind, potent, wise, and just.

III.

Great is our guilt, our fears are great:
  But let us not despair;
Still open is the mercy-seat
  To penitence and prayer.

IV.

Kind Intercessor, to thy love
  This blessed hope we owe;
O let thy merits plead above,
  While we implore below.

V.

O gracious God, for Jesus' sake,
  Attend thy Britain's cry;
Nor let the kindling vengeance break
  Destructive from thine eye.

VI.

Though justice near thy awful throne
  Attends thy dread command,
Lord, hear thy servants, hear thy Son,
  And save a guilty land.

NATIONAL JUDGMENTS AND MERCIES
A CALL TO REPENTANCE. Nov. 1757.

On the Occasion of the failed Louisbourg Expedition
Sept. 24th, 1757

I.

L ong has divine compassion strove
With this rebellious land;
O justice, long has pleading love
   Withheld thy dreadful hand.

II.

At length, ye Britons, lift your eyes,
   Your crimes no more pursue;
Behold the gath'ring tempest rise,
   And tremble at the view!

III.

See, fraught with vengeance, how it spreads!
   To mercy instant fly;
Ere yet it burst upon your heads,
   Repent, repent — or die.

IV.

Late raging storm, 'twas mercy stay'd,
   Her voice destruction heard,
Th' impetuous winds her voice obey'd,
   And awful justice spar'd.

V.

Shall every warning be in vain
   Your ruin to prevent?
Indulgent mercy calls again,
   Return, repent! repent!

VI.

The voice, ye Britons, hear with awe?
    O hear, and turn to God;
Lest mercy, long abus'd, withdraw,
    And leave you to the rod.

VII.

Almighty God, thy pow'rful grace
    Can change us, and forgive;
Can save a guilty rebel race,
    Ann say, Repent, and live,

VIII.

O let thy pow'rful grace appear,
    And justice sheath her sword;
Then shall a rescu'd nation fear,
    And love, and praise the Lord.

211

ANNE STEELE

THE INVOCATION

I.

Say, gentle Muse, who oft has deign'd
With humble solitude to dwell;
Whose cheering visits, in the lonely cell,
With tuneful numbers sooth'd my pain,
And bade the sadly pleasing strain,
   To ease my woe,
   Harmonious flow;
And pensive care sat list'ning while my song complain'd.

II.

Say, wilt thou ne'er return?
And must I ever mourn?
And must I ever tune in vain
The dull unanimated strain?
O come, the languid notes inspire,
Once more awake the sacred lyre,
And teach my song on stronger wings to rise.
   Unmindful of her heavenly birth,
My grov'ling soul sinks down to earth;
   And while she tries
   In vain to rise,
Clouds interpose, and veil the distant skies.

III.

Come, sweet Urania, come, thy cheering pow'r
   Once more impart
   To warm my heart:
To thee I would devote this solemn, silent hour.
   Retir'd from company and noise,
Amusement flies; her idle, flutt'ring train
Reflection, sighing, owns are empty, light, and vain,
And bids my heart aspire to nobler joys:

IV.

To nobler joys than earth bestows,
Were earth, in all her fairest charms,
To lure my eyes, and tempt my arms,
    And try to gain my heart.
        My heart replies
        In painful sighs
        Vain world, depart!
        Thy soft allurements all are vain;
        Thy sweetest pleasures are but gilded woes,
Thy brightest scenes are clouded soon, and dark'ning end in
pain.

V.

Come, heav'n-born faith, fair seraph, come;
How weak the muse's pow'r without thy aid!
    Thy radiant eye can pierce the gloom,
    Can guide her doubtful flight,
    Beyond the seats of night,
        And point afar
        The morning-star,
Which cheers with heav'n's sweet dawn this mortal
shade!

VI.

Here let my invocation end;
    Or rather here begin!
Bright morning-star, thy blissful ray
Can chase this mortal shade away,
        This night of death and sin.
    Before thy all-enlivening eye,
    Death, sin, and fear, and terror fly,
 And hope looks up and hails the rising day.
 Then comfort smiles, desire and faith ascend,
Kind messenger of life, on thee my hopes depend.

VII.

Bright morning-star, when wilt thou rise
   On this benighted heart?
Thou art my light, and thou my guide:
O come, and bless my longing eyes,
Dispel these gloomy clouds which hide
   Thy soul-reviving light;
   Break with immortal radiance, through the night.
And id thy healing beams, the dawn of heav'n impart

VIII.

   Thy beams alone can bring my day;
   O shine with soul-attracting ray,
     Till darkness, sin, and doubt retire,
And raise my languid heart, and bid my hope aspire
   To bliss unmingled and refin'd;
     Bright scenes unknown below,
     Without a shade of woe,
   Immortal pleasures, worthy of the mind!
Then shall the muse awake the sacred lyre;
   Then shall her sweetest notes harmonious rise,
   And bear my thoughts enraptur'd to the skies,
While love and thankful joy the votive song inspire.

TO FLORIO

I.

For blooming happiness young Florio sighs;
 And yonder, see, the lovely stranger wait!
Desire, impatient, sparkles in his eyes,
Till wealth conduct her smiling to his gate.

II.

Here, Florio, take this glass[4], and look again ;
You'll find 'tis distance makes her seem so fair.
She must be yours, — nor shall you sigh in vain-
Not blooming happiness, but wrinkled care:

III.

Companion of your life; for heaven ordains
That care with riches is a constant guest;
Yet fond, mistaking mortals court her chains,
And think her tyrant sway will make them blest

IV.

But upward point that glass of truth, and see
A fairer guest, descending from the sky,
Celestial hope! 'tis she, my friend, 'tis she
Who never pains the heart, or cheats the eye.

V.

Kind hope, she rules the mind with sweet control;
Her voice is harmony! propitious fair!
She calms, inspires, and animates the soul,
And wins a smile from gloomy frowning care.

VI.

Care plants a thorny forest on the plain,
And teasing, bids you trace that forest o'er
In search of happiness, but still in vain
Your weary steps the mazy wild explore.

---

[4] The Bible

VII.

Celestial hope relieves your anxious mind,
While through the gloom the dear supporter guides
Your doubtful way, and whispers, " You shall find
"(Though distant far) where happiness resides.

VIII.

"See, the shades open! — now direct your eye,
"A beam of glory points her bright abode,
"Beyond the reach of care, above the sky:
"This glass, this faithful glass will shew the road."

TO BELINDA

I.

Belinda to her utmost wish is blest!
But stay, my friend — that hasty thought review —
New wishes yet will rise to break your rest;
And if not lasting, can your bliss be true?

II.

True happiness is not the growth of earth,
The toil is fruitless if you seek it there;
'Tis an exotic of celestial birth,
And never blooms, but in celestial air.

III.

Sweet plant of paradise, its seeds are sown
In here and there a mind of heav'nly mould;
It rises slow, and buds, but ne'er is known
To blossom fair, the climate is too cold.

IV.

Ah no, Belinda, you have only found
Some flower that charms your fancy, gaily dress'd
In shining dyes, a native of the ground,
And think you are of happiness possess'd.

V.

But mark its date, tomorrow you may find
The colours fade, the lovely form decay:
And can that pleasure satisfy the mind,
Which blooms, and fades, the solace of a day?

VI.

O may your erring wishes learn to rise
Beyond the transient bliss which fancy knows!
Search not on earth, explore its native skies;
There happiness in full perfection grows.

ANNE STEELE

RESIGNATION

I.

Weary of these low scenes of night,
  My fainting heart grows sick of time,
Sighs for the dawn of sweet delight,
Sighs for a distant, happier clime!

II.

Ah why that sigh? — peace, coward heart,
And learn to bear thy lot of woe:
Look round — how easy is thy part
To what thy fellow-suff'rers know.

III.

Are not the sorrows of the mind
Entail'd on ev'ry mortal birth?
Convinc'd, hast thou not long resign'd
The flattering hope of bliss on earth?

IV.

'Tis just, 'tis right; thus he ordains,
Who form'd this animated clod;
That needful cares, instructive pains,
May bring the restless heart to God.

V.

In him, my soul, behold thy rest,
Nor hope for bliss below the sky:
Come, resignation, to my breast,
And silence every plaintive sigh.

VI.

Come, Faith, and Hope, celestial pair!
Calm resignation waits on you;
Beyond these gloomy scenes of care,
Point out a soul-enlivening view.

VII.

Parent of good, 'tis thine to give
These cheerful graces to the mind:
Smile on my soul, and bid me live
Desiring, hoping, yet resign'd.

VIII.

Thy smile, — -sweet dawn of endless day!
Can make my weary spirit blest;
While on my Father's hand I stay,
And in his love securely rest.

IX.

My Father, dear, delightful name!
Replete with life, and joy sincere!
O wilt thou gracious, seal my claim,
And banish every anxious fear.

X.

Then, cheerful shall my heart survey
The toils, and dangers of the road;
And patient keep the heav'nly way,
Which leads me homewards to my God.

ANNE STEELE

AN EVENING WALK

I.

F rom the philosophic grow,
  Where enlarg'd ideas rove,
   In earth, or air, collecting sweets divine:
      Or the lonely rural cell,
      Where the humble virtues dwell,
Unenvy'd dwell; and yet how fair they shine!

II.

   Meditation, pleasing guest!
   Come to this desiring breast,
And make it, like the ev'ning air, serene!
   See, what cheerful verdure spreads
   O'er the fields, and o'er the meads,
And trace the beauties of the vernal scene.

III.

   Beauties, ah how short their boast!
   Now they bloom— and now they're lost,
And all that looks so gay, shall cease to charm:
   — Melancholy thought — away—
   Not in vain is nature gay,
She bids expectant hope the bosom warm.

IV.

   Hope with ever-cheerful eye
   O'er yon verdant fields can spy
Fair plenty pour profuse the future bread:
   On the rosy-blossom 'd trees,
   Smiling — fading — now she sees
Autumnal fruits, their richer beauties spread.

V.

Meditation, come away,
  Hope attends thee, ever gay;
Come, sweet companions, tune my artless lays!
  Nature's every various grace,
  While my thoughts with wonder trace,
O may that wonder wake my heart to praise!

VI.

Can I view with languid thought,
  All the scene with blessings fraught,
Not own the bounteous hand from whence they flow?
  See, how wisdom, goodness, pow'r,
  Join to bid my heart adore,
And pay the debt of praise I hourly owe!

VII.

Praise, a tribute ah how poor!
  Language, what is all thy store,
My boundless obligations to display?
  Bid the earth-born reptile try,
  Looking upward to the sky
To count the blessings of the source of day

VIII.

Faint are all the notes I raise,
  Lord, accept my wish to praise!
To thee my heart, to thee my all belongs:
  Thy inspiring grace impart,
  Teach the breathings of my heart
To praise thee better than my feeble songs

ANNE STEELE

THE HUMBLE CLAIM

My God — important, glorious, blissful name!
Can I without a fear, assert my claim?
I fear, yet hope, I doubt, and yet desire,
Now tremble low on earth, and now aspire,
Aspire to love — ah vile, ungrateful heart!
Canst thou sincerely love, and yet depart,
So oft depart, entic'd by earthly toys,
In chase of dreams forsake substantial joys?

 His word recalls my heart, invites my trust;
That word reveals him, merciful and just:
Kind mercy, smiling power, forbids despair;
But who, O justice, who thy frown can bear?
He bore the frown, the stroke of justice, He
Who dy'd for man — O may I say, for me!
Then justice sheath'd her sword, and reconcil'd,
Own'd the full ransom paid — and mercy smii'd,
Triumphant mercy! — how divinely bright!
How angels gaz'd, and wonder'd at the sight!
Had angels cause of wonder? Man has more;
Yes, dearest Lord, I wonder, love, adore!
My Saviour, O permit my humble trust,
Permit my soul, though mourning in the dust,
To look to thee, my hope, my only stay!
And sure, thou wilt not frown my soul away,
For thou art love; thou wilt not say, "Depart,"
But, "Give me, trembling sinner, all thy heart."
To thee, my heart, dear Saviour, I resign;
Thy grace with sweet constraint can make it thine:
Vile wretched heart! thy pow'rful grace alone
Can cleanse, renew, and make it all thy own.
O let thy love, thy all-prevailing love,

Possess my heart, and every fear remove!
Then shall my soul assert her joyful claim,
Great Mediator, in thy worthy name!
Then shall I say, my God, with full delight,
While all his promises my trust invite!
My God, transporting accents! bliss divine!
Indulge the claim, O let me call thee mine!
O may my panting heart to thee aspire,
With restless wishes, with intense desire,
Till full assurance of thy love impart
The dawn of heaven to my enraptur'd heart!

Ah, what is earth, with all her flattering toys!
Ye dreams begone — I seek substantial joys!
Substantial joys those glorious words contain,
My God! — let not my heart repeat in vain,
My God! O seal my claim, and I am blest!
Here my hope terminates, my wishes rest.
Of full, unbounded happiness possest.

THE PROSPECT

To Melancholy, softly pensive power,
　　As late I gave the solitary hour;
Before my thoughts, in long succession, rose
The sadly varied train of human woes.
To contemplation's mount, serene retreat!
The muse indulgent led my willing feet;
And while I view'd th' extended prospect round,
She bade the soothing, plaintive lyre resound.

　Here, on a verdant plain bespread with flowers,
The sons of mirth indulge their sprightly pow'rs;
With roses crown'd, how blithsome, light, and gay,
They dance and sing the flying hours away!
Reflection, care, and foresight, all retreat,
For here hath pleasure only fix'd her seat:
Her wretched vot'ries court her silken chains
For present joy, nor dreams of future pains.
Death ready arm'd attends, and marks unseen,
His fated victims in the mirthful scene.
Ha! — whence that groan? — from yonder gloomy cell
So near the seats of joy can anguish dwell?
Yes, keenest anguish there and terror reign:
Oh, would the thoughtless, laughing, frolic train
Attend, nor let that warning groan be vain!

　Unlike to these, yon restless tribe behold!
Their lives, incessant toil; their idol, gold;
Close at their heels attends corroding care,
On either side, distrust and anxious fear.
To friendship strangers, and to social joys;
The wish of wealth their sordid souls employs.
Their hopes, their cares, are lost in glitt'ring dust:

The toil how fruitless! and how vain the trust!
Insidious death prepares his ruthless dart,
To rend the idol from the bleeding heart.
And now a different scene my eye surveys.
An eager throng, the candidates for praise.
To gain the envy'd height, where fame bestows
Her fairest wreath, each panting bosom glows.
The glorious prize inspires their ardent toils,
Till on their brow the dear-bought laurel smiles,
Behold the sons of valour, learning, wit;
High on an eminence sublime they sit,
With crowds of flatt'rers fawning at their feet.
But see, malignant envy stealing nigh!
She breathes — the tainted laurels droop and die.
The changeful many mark the dire disgrace,
And pluck the little pageants from their place.
Surprising change! almost ador'd before,
Now nam'd with infamy, or nam'd no more.

   Such mournful scenes, what heart unmov'd could bear?
Soft pity dropp'd the unavailing tear.
"Ah, wretched mortals! a deluded train!
"Their hopes, their joys, their busy cares, how vain;"
Are gifts like these, O earth, thy proudest boast?
Thy fav'rites prove their value to their cost.
'Tis then their real estimate we know,
When fame, wealth, pleasure, end in death or woe.
The view how doleful, did there not appear
A few of mien sedate, and cheerful air.
A happy few, whom true religion guides,
Points out their path, and o'er their steps presides!
When griefs oppress, her gentle hand sustains;
Her cheering voice can soften all their pains.
Though arrows, wing'd with danger, fly around,

She wards the stroke, or heals the smarting wound.
Her sacred dictates they with joy obey,
Nor wish to leave the heaven-directed way.
Nor fame allures, nor pleasure's silken chain,
Nor glitt'ring dust, their nobler thoughts detain:
Desire and hope sit smiling in their eyes,
With patience temper'd; while the distant skies
Attract their upward glance, and speak their care,
And speak their joy and expectation there.

Hail, heaven-taught minds! my heart your friendship claims;
Be mine your cares, and hopes, your joys and aims-.

  O for a beam of glory from above,
To bid the intervening clouds remove;
From earth's low dregs to purge the visual ray,
And clear my prospect to the realms of day.
Dim is the eye of sense; but faith supplies
(Inspir'd by heaven) what feeble sense denies.
In revelation's glass, celestial aid,
Applied by faith, what wonders are displayed!
What boundless glories open to the view!
And joys forever bright! forever new!
Unfading honors! pleasures all refin'd!
And riches lasting as th' immortal mind!
There full delight, a boundless river, flows!
There unforbid, the tree of knowledge grows!
And there the tree of life invites the taste
To fruits celestial, an immortal feast!
There an unfading verdure clothes the plains?
And constant spring in perfect beauty reigns
A paradise with every joy replete!
Nor pain, nor care invade the safe retreat:
For there the living source of bliss displays,

Without a cloud, his life-inspiring rays.
No mortal ear has known, no mortal eye,
No stretch of human thought can e'er descry,
Nor faith with heaven-imparted ardour trace
The endless glories of the blissful place.
Oh, happy fav'rites of almighty love,
Whose hopes, and cares, and hearts, are fix'd above!
Stern death to these no frown of terror wears;
Kind envoy from their Father's court, he bears
His blest commission, to dissolve the tie
Which holds their longing spirits from the sky.

Now rise my wishes high to joys divine;
O may this state, this blissful state, be mine!
Great Spring of life, to thee my heart aspires,
Forgive and animate these faint desires.
Thou ever-gracious, potent, wise, and just,
Whose promis'd aid invites my humble trust;
Instruct my feet to shun, with constant care,
The path where pleasure spreads the tempting snare:
Teach me to scorn the joys of treasur'd earth:
Ignoble aim, unworthy of my birth,
Beneath my hopes; nor let deluding fame
Allure me with the empty sound, a name!
Thy favor is my wish; for this alone
Is honor, boundless pleasure, wealth unknown,
My God, my guide, thy guardian care display,
And let thy blissful presence cheer my way,
Through life's bewilder'd maze, in every scene,
My light in darkness, my support in pain.
At death's approach, O let thy smile impart
Celestial consolation to my heart j
Thy gracious smile shall banish every fear,
And gentle death without a frown appear:

Kind messenger, to bear me to my God,
To dwell forever in thy bright abode!

DESIRING TO BID ADIEU TO THE WORLD

I.

Vexatious world, thy flattering snares
   Too long have held my easy heart;
And shalt thou still engross my cares?
     Vain world, depart.

II.

I want delights thou canst not give,
Thy joys are bitterness and woe;
My pining spirit cannot live
     On aught below.

III.

Enchanting prospects court the eye,
And gay alluring pleasures smile;
But in the fond pursuit they die:
     Ah fruitless toil!

IV.

But grief, substantial grief is here,
As gloomy as Egyptian night;
When will the smiling dawn appear
     Of true delight?

V.

How oft convinc'd shall I complain
That happiness cannot be found?
Yet sighing, mourning, still in vain,
    Cleave to the ground.

VI.

Look, Sov'reign Goodness, from the skies,
Look down with gently pitying eye;
O bid my fainting spirit rise:
    To thee I sigh.

VII.

With beams of sweet celestial light,
Dispel the dark oppressive gloom;
Display the mansions of delight,
    And bid me come.

VIIL

Those shining realms of endless day
Could I one happy moment view,
Then should my soul with transports say,
    Vain world, adieu.

OCCASIONED BY READING MR. GRAY'S HYMN TO ADVERSITY

I.

O kind Adversity, thou friend to truth!
  By thee to virtue form'd, the human mind
Disdains the vanities of heedless youth;
How roving else, and ignorant, and blind!

II.

When flatt'ring fortune shines with gaudy blaze,
In fascinating chains she holds the eye;
The mind is lost in error's fatal maze,
And dreams of lasting bliss below the sky.

III.

Thy friendly admonitions rouse the soul,
Conviction rises strong to break the snare;
Truth, (heav'nly guide!) appears with kind control,
And fortune's painted scenes are lost in air.

IV.

Though rough thy aspect, and thy frown severe,
'Tis but to bend the proud, the stubborn heart;
A soft emollient is thy briny tear,
And thy corrosives pain with healing smart.

V.

The kindest, gentlest virtues form thy train;
Reflection comes with pensive musing eye,
And humble penitence, that not in vain
Presents to heaven the supplicating eye.

VI.

Meek patience looks unmov'd on pain and care;
While cheerful hope with peace-inspiring smile,
Points forward, through the gloom, celestial fair!
The woes of life, her whisper can beguile.

VII.

Beyond the woes of life she lifts her eyes,
And often meditates a joyful flight;
By faith, her radiant sister, taught to rise,
To distant prospects of immense delight.

VIII.

O kind adversity, without thy aid,
How faintly would these virtues warm the breast!
Why should I tremble at thy darksome shade?
For who without adversity is blest?

IX.

Thy wholesome cold, like winter, kills the weeds
Which in th' uncultur'd mind luxuriant rise;
Then heav'nly wisdom sows her precious seeds,
Nor shall they want the blessings of the skies.

X.

But O may heaven thy rig'rous hand restrain,
Mayst thou correct and teach, but not destroy!
Thy needful lessons then shall not be vain,
And thy short sorrows work my lasting joy,

TO A FRIEND, ON THE DEATH OF A CHILD

I.

L ife is a span, a fleeting hour,
How soon the vapour flies!
Man is a tender, transient flower,
  That ev'n in blooming dies.

II.

Death spreads like winter's frozen arms,
  And beauty smiles no more:
Ah! where are now those rising charms
  Which pleas'd our eyes before?

III.

The once lov'd form now cold and dead,
  Each mournful thought employs;
And nature weeps her comforts fled,
  And wither'd all her joys.

IV.

But wait the interposing gloom,
  And lo, stern winter flies;
And drest in beauty's fairest bloom,
  The flow'ry tribes arise.

V.

Hope looks beyond the bounds of time;
  When what we now deplore,
Shall rise in full immortal prime,
  And bloom to fade no more.

VI.

Then cease, fond nature, cease thy tears,
  Religion points on high;
There everlasting spring appears,
  And joys that cannot die.

TO DELIA PENSIVE

I.

Say, Delia, whence these cares arise,
  These anxious cares which rack your breast?
If heaven is infinitely wise,
What heav'n ordains, is right, is best.

II.

'Tis wisdom, mercy, love divine,
Which mingles blessings with our cares;
And shall our thankless hearts repine
That we obtain not all our prayers?

III.

From diffidence our sorrows flow;
Short-sighted mortals, weak and blind,
Bend down their eyes to earth and woe,
And doubt if providence is kind.

IV.

Should heaven with every wish comply,
Say, would the grant relieve the care?
Perhaps the good for which we sigh,
Might change its name, and prove a snare.

V.

Were once our vain desires subdu'd,
The will resign'd, the heart at rest;
In ev'ry scene we should conclude,
The will of heav'n is right, is best.

SPRING AND AUTUMN

I.

When Spring displays her various sweets,
  And op'ning blossoms cheer the eyes,
And fancy ev'ry beauty meets,
Whence does the pleasing transport rise?

II.

Soon will their transient date expire,
They fly and mock the fond pursuit;
New pleasures then the thought inspire,
And bounteous Autumn yields her fruit.

III.

Where smiling beauties charm'd the sight,
Whose fragrance bless'd the vernal hours;
Nectarious fruits the taste invite,
And compensate for faded flow'rs.

IV.

Thus, when the spring of youth decays,
Though deck'd with blossoms sweet and fair,
Autumn a nobler scene displays,
If fruits of virtue flourish there.

V.

For this the vernal buds arise;
But, if no useful virtues grow,
Their worthless beauty quickly flies
And blossoms only serv'd for show

TO VARIO

I.

Go, Vario, trace creation's ample round,
   In search of happiness your cares employ;
And when the dear, important good is found,
Say is it permanent, or real joy?

II.

If real, why, when distant pleasures rise,
Does glad expectance sparkle in your eye T
Say why, when near, the satisfaction flies,
And disappointment heaves the painful sigh?

III.

Or grant your heart should all its wish possess,
How keen the fears of deprivation sting!
How can the present good have pow'r to bless,
Which hangs precarious on a moment's wing?

IV.

Be happy — what on earth! the thought how vain!
Earth cannot give a permanent delight;
As sure must fleeting pleasure yield to pain,
As day retreats before approaching night.

V.

Yet is not heav'n unkind, which shades with woe
The chequer'd scene, to bid our wishes rise;
Could real, lasting bliss be found below,
Why should we seek for mansions in the skies?

TO AMIRA ON HER RECOVERY

Once more has heav'n indulgent heard our prayers,
And spar'd your life! O be the mercy wrote,
In lasting characters of duteous love,
On every heart; and may Amira be
A living monument of grateful praise.
New mercies call for new returns of love
And glad obedience, to the bounteous hand
From whence they flow, through all our future lives,
When sorrows rise, let sweet reflection call
Past favors o'er; and while we wond'ring trace
The steps of providence, adoring, own
Pow'r, wisdom, love and truth, display 'd in all.
And these can never change; here let our souls
With humble trust, and cheerful hope recline.
May every pain be sweeten'd by content,
And calm submission to a Father's hand.
A father! O endearing, tender name!
And will the Lord of angels condescend
To call us children? Yes, almighty love
With more than tenderness paternal, deigns
To sooth our cares: how kind his gentle hand.
Who while he chastens, pities, and supports
Our fainting spirits! though an angry frown
Becloud his face, how soon the gloom withdraws t
How soon divine forgiveness smiles serene!
O may his mercies be our constant theme,
And warm our hearts, and tune our lips to praise,
And heighten joy to transport, while we view
The boundless spring of bliss from whence they flow;
Who bids our hope aspire to greater joys;
To joys beyond the reach of time or care,
Reserv'd for those who love him! may our hearts

Rise often on the wings of faith and love
To those divine abodes, where not a cloud
Of pain or sorrow spreads a moment's gloom,
To shade the blissful scene, for God unveils
His radiant face, and spreads eternal day.

TO THE SAME, ON THE DEATH OF HER CHILD

I.

So fades the lovely, blooming flower,
Frail, smiling solace of an hour!
So soon our transient comforts fly,
And pleasure only blooms to die!
To certain trouble we are born,
Hope to rejoice, but sure to mourn.
Ah wretched effort! sad relief,
To plead necessity of grief!
Is there no kind, no lenient art
To heal the anguish of the heart?
To ease the heavy load of care.
Which nature must, but cannot bear?
Can reason's dictates be obey'd?
Too weak, alas, her strongest aid!
O let religion then be nigh,
Her comforts were not made to die;
Her pow'rful aid supports the soul,
And nature owns her kind control;
While she unfolds the sacred page,
Our fiercest griefs resign their rage.
Then gentle patience smiles on pain,

237

And dying hope revives again;
Hope wipes the tear from sorrow's eye,
And faith points upward to the sky;
The promise guides her ardent flight,
And joys unknown to sense invite,
Those blissful regions to explore,
Where pleasure blooms to fade no more.

THE COMFORTS OF RELIGION

I.

O blest religion, heav'nly fair!
　　Thy kind, thy healing power,
Can sweeten pain, alleviate care,
　And gild each gloomy hour.

II.

When dismal thoughts, and boding fears
　The trembling heart invade;
And all the face of nature wears
　A universal shade:

III.

Thy sacred dictates can assuage
　The tempest of the soul,
And every fear shall lose its rage
　At thy divine control.

IV.

Through life's bewilder'd, darksome way,
   Thy hand unerring leads;
And o'er the path, thy heavenly ray
   A cheering lustre sheds.

V.

When feeble reason, tir'd and blind,
   Sinks helpless and afraid;
Thou blest supporter of the mind,
   How pow'rful is thy aid!

VI.

O let my heart confess thy power,
   And find thy sweet relief,
To brighten every gloomy hour,
   And soften every grief.

THE DESIRE OF KNOWLEDGE
A PROOF OF IMMORTALITY

What is this thinking pow'r, this active mind,
    Which nought on earth can satiate, nought can bound?
Restless it roams the wide creation o'er
In search of something more than sense can give.
Whate'er delights, the senses must decline;
'Tis short-liv'd pleasure, momentary joy.
The senses soon are tir'd, and sink to rest.
The mind, unsatisfy'd, looks onward still,
And asks delights more noble and refin'd,
More permanent and full; 'tis knowledge fires
Its ardent wish, and tempts the warm pursuit.
This is the food of minds! 'tis angels' food!
Those happy spirits feast with full delight, —
But here we only taste, and long to feed.

    Surely, the mind must be akin to heaven;
For heaven, all-wise, and infinitely good,
Implants not these sublime desires in vain.
If nought below immortal joys can fill
The mind, the mind must be immortal too.
Inquisitive and restless, now she soars
Beyond the narrow bounds of earth and time,
To reach the blissful seats, where knowledge spreads
In rich variety her boundless feast.
But soon she tires, and droops her feeble wing,
Oppress'd with heavy clay, and sinks to earth:
Yet here reluctant stays, though earth allure
With soothing arts and promises of joy.
The gay amusement for a moment smiles
In painted dreams; again the mind awakes,
And starts disdainful from the couch of ease.

Now with expanded wings, again she tempts
The airy flight; but tempts, alas, in vain;
Flutters in wild conjecture's giddy rounds,
Sinks down amid the shades of mortal night,
And mourns her fetters, and her feeble wings.

    But hope, dear comforter, relieves her care,
Celestial hope! her smiling presence cheers
The sable gloom, and beams a healing ray:
Her gentle, peace-inspiring whisper bids
Look forward to a nobler, happier state;
When minds releas'd from all the chains of flesh,
And all the toys of sense, shall rise enlarged
To perfect freedom and unbounded bliss.

ANNE STEELE

I CORINTHIANS XIII
PARAPHRASED

Were all the power of elocution mine,
      An angel's voice, and harmony divine;
The boasted gifts, with charity uncrown'd,
Were like the tinkling cymbal's empty sound.
Endow'd with knowledge — though before my eye,
Display'd the ample fields of science lie;
The pow'r of miracles could I attain,
If charity be wanting, all is vain!
To feed the hungry, and relieve the poor,
Should zeal mistaken lavish all my store;
Nay, should I give my body to the flame,
And win the glory of a martyr's name:
If charity be absent, all is lost,
My zeal is but an empty, idle boast!

   Sweet charity, Long-suff 'ring, meek and kind,
Inspires with peace and joy the humble mind.
Her heart no proud disdainful passion swells,
Nor envy in her gentle bosom dwells:
No unbecoming selfish care she knows,
But ev'ry social virtue round her flows:
Averse to take affronts her placid smile
Looks down on malice, and suspects no guile.
She finds no joy in sin's deceitful charms,
For sacred truth with nobler pleasure warms.
The num'rous ills of life she patient bears,
While faith looks upward, and forbids her fears;
Hope rises cheerful, with expectant smiles,
And all the tedious hours of pain beguiles.

Immortal charity improv'd shall shine,
When prophecies and tongues their pow'r resign;
When mortal knowledge fails its glimm'ring ray,
Lost in the blaze of full ethereal day.
Imperfect all we teach, and all we know,
In this frail state, this little world below;
But when we reach the worlds of heav'nly light,
Then shall fair knowledge shine forever bright;
Nor the least shade of imperfection rise
In all the blissful regions of the skies.

When reason dawns upon the infant mind,
How low the thoughts! the knowledge how confin'd!
But when th' increasing ray full vigour gains,
What once the child admir'd, the man disdains.
How weak the best ideas form'd below!
The fairest, brightest views which mortals know,
Like distant objects in perspective show.
But when the bright meridian shall appear,
Our eyes shall see the heav'nly glories near;
These weak, faint notions, shall forgotten die.
Amid the boundless wonders of the sky.

Faith, hope, and charity, on earth remain,
To guide our steps, and sweeten mortal pain;
But lovely charity superior shines,
Till perfect bliss the sacred flame refines.

TO A FRIEND, ON THE BIRTH OF A CHILD

I.
Come, friendship, tune the pleasing lyre,
　For harmony is thine;
Philander's joys the song inspire,
　Philander's joys are mine.

II.
Our hearts, so late oppress'd with fear,
　Forget the anxious sigh;
And dawning pleasures now appear
　In ev'ry kindred eye.

III.
Propitious heav'n that smil'd before,
　To make Philander blest,
Indulgent sends this blessing more,
　And sweetens all the rest.

IV.
The dear-lov'd blessing while we view.
　And pleasing passions rise,
Be love and praise, so justly due,
　Paid grateful to the skies.

V.
With love supreme be heav'n ador'd;
　Still may our passions own
The bounteous giver as their Lord,
　Nor idolize the boon.

TO THE MOTHER

I.

Say, while you press, with growing love,
The darling to your breast,
And all a mother's pleasures prove,
Are you entirely blest?

II.

Ah, no! a thousand tender cares
　By turns your thoughts employ,
Now rising hopes, now anxious fears.
　And grief succeeds to joy.

III.

Dear innocent, her lovely smiles
　With what delight you view!
But every pain the infant feels,
　The mother feels it too.

IV.

Then whispers busy cruel fear,
　The child, alas, may die!
And nature prompts the ready tear,
　And heaves the rising sigh.

V.

Say, does not heaven our comforts mix
　With more than equal pain;
To teach us if our hearts we fix
　On earth, we fix in vain?

VI.

Then be our earthly joys resign'd,
　Since here we cannot rest;
For earthly joys were ne'er design'd
　To make us fully blest.

THE TULIP AND THE VIOLET

I.

See yonder gaudy tulip rise,
  And to the sun her leaves display;
My fancy gives her voice and eyes,
And thus the boaster seems to say.

II.

"Queen of the gay parterre I reign;
"My glowing dyes, how bright they shine!
"The flow'rs unfold their bloom in vain;
"No flow'r has charms to rival mine.

III.

"By nature meant for regal sway,
"Tall and majestic I appear;
"Ye subject tribes, your queen obey,
"My high command, submissive hear.

IV.

"When I unfold my matchless bloom,
"And to the noon my beauties spread;
"Let no aspiring flow'r presume
"Near me, to lift her abject head."

V.

The flow'rs are silent while she speaks,
And only blush to hear her pride-
The silence now a Violet breaks,
That crept unheeded near her side,

VI.

"Thy arrogance, imperious flow'r,
"To real worth hath made thee blind;
"Thy vaunted beauties of an hour
"Are charms of an inferior kind.

VII.

"From thee no fragrant odors breathe,
"No healing gift thy leaves bestow;
"The flow'rs thou view'st with scorn beneath,
"Can more pretence to merit show.

VIII.

"The cowslip's virtues, and my own,
"Let man, let grateful man confess;
"To him our real worth is known,
"Thee he admires but for thy dress."

IX.

The friendly hint, ye list'ning fair,
Reflection bids the muse apply;
Let useful virtues be your care,
Nor boast your power to please the eye.

ANNE STEELE

CAPTIVITY

Angels, happy spirits, say,
When you trace the airy way,
Sent on messages of love,
From the radiant courts above,
Down to these abodes of night,
Far from empyrean light;
Say, can blest immortals know
Sympathy from human woe,
While you view the scenes of pain,
Captives struggling with their chain?
Hated chain, that binds to earth
Spirits of ethereal birth;
Birth at first to yours akin,
Now enslav'd, alas! by sin;
Cursed sin, the source of woe,
All the miseries below
From the hateful tyrant flow!
Yet we bear the cruel chain,
Only now and then complain;
Now and then, with mournful eye,
Raise a wish, and breathe a sigh,
Upward to our native sky.
But how soon to liberty,
Cold and negligent are we,
Sink supine, and dream of ease!
How, alas! can fetters please?
Can we hope for crowns on high,
Yet content in bondage lie,
Exiles from the blest abode,
Far from glory, far from God?
Surely if the sons of bliss
Feel a grief, it must be this.

O for one celestial ray
From the shining seats of day!
Sun of righteousness, arise,
Chase the slumbers from our eyes,
Melt the chains with heavenly fire:
Fervent love and strong desire
From thy love alone begin;
Thou canst break the power of sin;
Thou canst bid our spirits rise
Free and joyful to the skies;
Liberty and joy divine,
Sun of righteousness, are thine.

A REFLECTION, OCCASIONED
BY THE DEATH OF A NEIGHBOR

Another awful warning heaven has sent
To rouse my slumb'ring soul; — Death is abroad;
Close at my side he twangs his deadly bow.
Unerring flies the shaft, Sarissa falls:
In life's gay bloom she falls; yet I am spar'd!
But wherefore this indulgence? Gracious God,
By this new admonition, teach my heart
How precious are the swiftly flying hours
Which I supinely waste! arouse, my soul,
Why wilt thou sleep upon this sea-beat shore,
When the next wave may whelm thee in the deep,
Th' unfathom'd deep of vast eternity?

Eternity, to pure and holy souls
Joy's boundless ocean, ever calm and clear,
Where all the streams of lasting pleasure meet!
But to the sinner 'tis the dark abyss
Of black despair, where all the waves of horror,
Beyond what nature ever felt or fear'd,
Incessant beat; and not a ray of hope
Breaks through the tenfold night to cheer the gloom.
But tempest, everlasting tempest, roars.
How my soul shudders at the view!
Where am I? O for help, immediate help!
Some angel snatch me from the dreadful brink!
Some angel! no, — omnipotence descends
On mercy's wing: behold the Saviour God!
His arms are wide-extended; see, my soul,
Thy only refuge! his almighty love
Dispels my fears, while here I fix my trust.
Almighty love, thou art the fountain-head
Of all the joys, which swell th' unbounded sea
Of bliss immortal! Jesus, am I safe?
And art thou mine, my Lord, my life, my all?
O speak th' assuring word, and I am blest!
Death shall resign his terrors; let him strike,
Encircled in thy arms I'm safe forever,
For thy eternity of joy is mine.

ON THE DEATH OF MR. HERVEY

I.

O Hervey, honored name, forgive the tear,
    That mourns thy exit from a world like this;
Forgive the wish that would have kept thee here,
Fond wish! have kept thee from the seats of bliss.

II.

No more confin'd to these low scenes of night,
Pent in a feeble tenement of clay:
Should we not rather hail thy glorious flight,
And trace thy journey to the realms of day!

III.

The blissful realms, where thy lov'd master reigns,
Who taught thy pen its eloquence divine;
Whose presence now inspires to loftier strains,
While all unveil'd his boundless glories shine.

IV.

Now the celestial flame that warm'd thy breast,
And through thy heav'n-taught page resplendent shone,
Exalted joins the transports of the blest
In language ev'n to thee on earth unknown.

V.

Yes, we resign thee to thy Saviour God;
O may his love, that taught thy feet the way,
Conduct our steps to that divine abode,
Where his full glories beam eternal day!

VI.

Yet its own loss must every heart deplore,
That feels the power of Hervey's moving page,
That wish'd, (but ah, that wish avails no more!)
His life prolong'd to bless the rising age,

VII.

O lost to earth! — no, in his works he lives,
Here shall the rising age his portrait view;
Here his own pen the mind's bright image gives,
In fairer tints than painting ever knew.

VIII.

His warm benevolence, his sacred zeal,
O may some blest, surviving prophet find!
Like him who caught the mantle as it fell,
Heir to the graces of Elijah's mind.

IX.

While thus a stranger muse presents the lay
To Hervey's mem'ry due, to grace his urn
Let friendship more distinguish'd honors pay,
And teach the world departed worth to mourn.

INGRATITUDE REPROVED

I.

Ye warblers of the vernal shade,
　　Whose artless music charms my ear,
　Your lively songs my heart upbraid,
　My languid heart how insincere!
While all your little powers collected, raise
A tribute to your great Creator's praise,

II.

　Ye lovely offspring of the ground,
　Flowers of a thousand beauteous dyes,
　You spread your Maker's glory round,
　And breathe your odors to the skies:

Unsully'd you display your lively bloom,
Unmingled you present your sweet perfume

III.

Ye winds, that waft the fragrant spring,
    You whisp'ring spread his name abroad,
Or shake the air with sounding wing,
    And speak the awful power of God:
His will, with swift obedience, you perform,
Or in the gentle gale, or dreadful storm.

IV.

Ye radiant orbs, that guide the day,
    Or deck the sable veil of night;
His wond'rous glory you display,
    Whose hand imparts your useful light:
Your constant task, unweary'd, you pursue,
Nor deviate from the path your Maker drew.

V.

My God, shall ev'ry creature join
    In praises to thy glorious name,
And this ungrateful heart of mine
    Refuse the universal theme?
Well may the stars and winds, the birds and fiow'rs,
Reprove the heart that brings not all its pow'rs.

VI.

Thy grace this languid heart can raise,
    These dissipated pow'rs unite,
Can bid me pay my debt of praise
    With love sincere, and true delight;
O let thy grace inspire my heart, my tongue!
Then shall I grateful join creation's song.

ANNE STEELE

SUBMISSION TO GOD UNDER AFFLICTION,
AND DESIRING SUPPORT

Great God, I own thy justice, while beneath
 The stroke of thy chastising rod I bend;
Nor dares this wretched, guilty heart repine.
Far less I feel than merit, ev'ry stroke
How gentle! smiling mercy breaks its force,
And soft it lights, nor gives a fatal wound.
O let my soul the wond'rous pow'r confess
Of sovereign mercy, and adore the hand,
Whose just rebukes, with kind indulgence mix'd,
Are meant to teach, reclaim, and guide my feet,
Too apt to rove, forgetful of the way,
Forgetful of the end. A crown of life,
Of life immortal, is the glorious prize,
(Free gift of boundless grace!) which in the view
Of faith and humble love thy word displays;
Obtain'd by sufferings which amaz'd the world:
And shall I seek it coldly? gracious God,
Awake my languid pow'rs to active life.
Awake my faith and hope, and love and zeal,
And make me ardent run the glorious race.
Pow'r to the faint thy sacred word assures,
And strength increasing; be that gracious word
Fulfill'd to me unworthy! If thy hand,
O ever wise and good, should justly deal
Severer strokes, still let my soul behold thee,
Not as an angry judge, vindictive, frowning,
But as a tender father, who corrects
In mercy, list'ning to the humble moan
Of penitential sorrow. Were my fears
To measure suff'rings by my just desert,
Dreadful expectance! what a scene of woe!

254

The dearest comfort, ev'ry joy of life,
Would quickly take its everlasting flight,
And leave me desolate, forlorn, undone.
Hut what are earthly joys? has not my heart
Ungrateful forfeited far more than these?
Should earthly joys forsake me, should my friends.
My much-lov'd friends, by death's resistless hand
Rent from my bleeding, agonizing heart,
Leave me a miserable mourner here;
Yet, O my God, if I may call thee mine;
Amid the scene of terror, if my faith
Look up and say, My father, and my friend;
The blissful sounds will cheer my fainting soul
With peace divine, and recompense the loss
Of all that life can give, or death destroy.
And was not once this heavenly blessing mine,
Diffusing comfort through my grateful heart,
Inspiring wonder, praise, and humble love?
It was; but soon the sacred ardour sunk
To cold indiff'rence. Should heavenly love
Offended leave me to the punishment
My guilt and vile ingratitude deserves,
Despair would soon his gloomy curtains draw,
Each distant beam of cheering hope exclude,
And shade my soul in everlasting night.
But oh, th' amazing power of love divine!
Unlimited it pardons! justice pleas'd,
On mercy smiles; for lo, the Saviour's blood
Atones and cleanses every guilty stain!
'Tis this, O gracious God, dispels my fears,
Revives my hopes; in this unbounded sea
Let all my sins, and all my doubts be lost.
Lord, when this roving heart again forgets
Its duty and its bliss, let grace reclaim;

And though thy awful hand chastising strike,
Let love support me, and beneath thy frown
O may paternal tenderness appear.
Then shall I patient bear thy just rebukes,
And wait resign'd and penitent, in hope
Of bliss returning in the smile of mercy.
Then, though this mortal frame by slow degrees.
In lingering years of pain should wear away;
Or pungent griefs, too mighty, burst at once
The vital strings; or fatal accident
Wing, swift and unforewarn'd, the silent shaft
To set my spirit free; if I am thine,
To thy blest will, my God, I would submit,
Sure to be happy! Time is but a point,
And mortal pains or joys are light as air,
When vast eternity is full in view.

PLEASURE

I.

How vain a thought is bliss below!
'Tis all an airy dream!
How empty are the joys that flow
   On pleasure's smiling stream!

II.

Now gaily painted bubbles rise
   With varied colours bright!
They break, the short amusement flies-
   Can this be call'd delight?

III.

Transparent now, and all serene,
   The gentle current flows:
While fancy draws the flattering scene,
   How fair the landscape shows!

IV.

But soon its transient charms decay,
   When ruffling tempests blow;
The soft delusions fleet away,
   And pleasure ends in woe.

V.

Why do I here expect repose?
   Or seek for bliss in vain?
Since every pleasure earth bestows,
   Is but dissembled pain.

VI.

O let my nobler wishes soar
   Beyond these seats of night;
In heaven substantial bliss explore,
   And permanent delight!

257

VII.

There pleasure flows forever clear;
   And rising to the view
Such dazzling scenes of joy appear
   As fancy never drew.

VIII.

No fleeting landscape cheats the gaze.
   Nor airy form beguiles;
But everlasting bliss displays
   Her undissembled smiles.

IX.

Adieu to all below the skies,
   Celestial guardian, come!
On thy kind wing my soul would rise
   To her eternal home.

THE PILGRIM

In this dark wilderness of pain and woe
I wander mournful; oft my upward glance
Implores a cheering ray to guide my feet,
Fearful, and trembling at surrounding snares
Which lurk unseen: and oft I long for rest,
But long in vain; for ah, no safe repose
This land of danger yields! Then Jet my eyes
Look upward still to those divine abodes
Of light and joy, whence danger is excluded.
And thither let my panting heart aspire
With ardent hope! — 'Tis but to wait with patience
A few sad hours, a few more painful steps,

And life's fatiguing pilgrimage is o'er.
Soon will my weary eyelids close in death,
And these poor feeble limbs sink down to rest
In the cold bosom of the silent grave.

O could I with unshaken hope declare,
Then should my nobler pow'rs awake to life,
To life and joy immortal! happy hour!
Transporting moment! when eternal day
First breaks upon my sight! what sweet surprise!
What boundless rapture! darkness, pain and death
Banish'd at once! and everlasting light
In full meridian glory beaming round!
Joys rising bright and new, in long succession,
To set no more! and shall my weary spirit
(Which wanders now depress'd with sin and woe,)
Rise to this glory? O my gracious God,
Guide of my life, and guardian of my soul,
To thee I breathe my supplicating sigh:
Brighten my glimm'ring hope, dispel the clouds
Of gloomy fear, which hang upon my sight
Heavy and sad; let thy reviving smile,
(Fair dawn of glory!) cheer my fainting heart;
Till all the sorrows, all the pains of time,
Appear as trifles in the blissful view
Of immortality, of endless joys
Incessant flowing from the throne of God.
Then shall I wait serene, with steady faith
And glad expectance, that auspicious hour,
When death, kind angel, shall convey my soul
To light and life, to happiness and God.

259

WROTE IN AN ILL STATE OF HEALTH
IN THE SPRING

Inclement winter now resigns his pow'r,
And gentle spring begins her placid reign.
The sun, with genial warmth, awakes to life
The herbs and flowers, whose soft distilling rains
His kindly influence aid, and clothe the fields
With springing verdure; to the industrious swain
The pleasing promise of a plenteous harvest.
The trees, long stripp'd of all their leafy honors,
Shoot out anew, and with the charming season
Advancing still, unfold their annual beauties.
All nature smiles! — But I, alas, am sad!

In vain, the woods and fields resume their charms!
In vain the feather'd warblers tune their songs!
To me 'tis all a blank! untouch'd my soul
With nature's harmony! my eyes, uncharm'd
With all her beauties, cannot find a joy
In the once lovely, once delightful scene!
A gloom of sadness hangs upon my spirits.
And prompts the frequent sigh and silent tear.
Depressed by pain and sickness, all my powers
Are dull and languid, every joy is tasteless;
All nature fades, and pleasure is no more!

Ah! what is life, so lov'd, so dearly priz'd,
If health be absent? 'tis a ling'ring night
Of tedious expectation, spent in sighs,
And restless wishes for the cheerful dawn.

Thus melancholy tun'd the mourning lay:
The cheerful muse withdrawn, the gloomy pow'r,
Usurp'd her lyre, and chang'd its soothing notes
For sounds of woe; dark clouds oppressive hung
Around her seat, and spread their deep'ning shade
Till ev'ry pleasing object sunk in night.
Ah! where is faith? her heav'n-illumin'd eye
Could pierce the mental night, could raise the mind
Which sinks dejected, and beyond the gloom
Direct to fairer scenes: come, guest divine,
O come, and in thy train, let fortitude
Her useful succours bring, and meek-ey'd patience,
And smiling hope, and sweet content appear.
And let my heart with calm submission wait
Heaven's destin'd time, to hail the glad return
Of health, the best and sweetest earthly blessing.

Then shall the muse her long-neglected strain
Resume; and, by each heav'n-born guest inspired,
With grateful rapture tune the votive song
To that almighty goodness, which bestows
Its gifts unmeasur'd, undeserved, on me.
Nor let the grateful rapture be confin'd;
Since o'er the whole creation wide diffus'd,
Divine beneficence unbounded smiles,
And claims the tribute of unbounded praise

ANNE STEELE

RECOVERY FROM SICKNESS

Awake my heart, arise my joyful pow'rs,
In songs of gratitude, and love, and praise,
To God, the great deliverer's holy name!
To God, my strength, my all-sufficient refuge,
Whose pow'rful hand sustain'd my feeble frame,
Through all the tiresome scenes of pain and sickness,
And rais'd me from the borders of the grave.

Death frown'd severe, and all the prospect round
Was dark; with scarce a ray of glimm'ring light
To point my view beyond the sable veil!
Almighty goodness saw, with pitying eye,
My deep distress; my groans, and long complaints,
And sorrows reach'd the ear of heavenly mercy.
My God attended to the humble pray'r,
The mournful breathings of a helpless worm,
And sent divine supports.
The consolations of his sacred word
Bore up my fainting spirit; rays of hope
Broke through the shades of death, and bid my soul
Look up, and view her heav'nly Father's hand,
And bear his just rebukes, and patient wait
His sov'reign will! then smiling comfort dawn'd,
And hush'd my sorrows to a peaceful calm.
A lather's kind indulgent care appear'd,
And while his rod chastis'd, his arm sustain'd.

At length fair health with cheerful aspect comes:
Hail long-desir'd, delightful, welcome guest!
Gift of indulgent heaven! inspir'd by thee,
Source of a thousand joys, my full heart pants

To pour the transport in a song of praise,
A grateful tribute to th' almighty donor.

    But ah! my voice unequal to my wishes,
Forbids th' attempt, and damps the rising ardour.
Would the same pow'r which rais'd my sinking frame,
Brought back declining health, and bid me live,
Inspire the lay, and teach my song to flow
Harmonious to his wond'rous healing mercy!
Then should my tongue, with joyful rapture fir'd,
Begin the pleasing theme, and sing unwearied
Thy mercy, and thy pow'r, all-bounteous Lord,
Forever good, beneficent, and kind!

    But oh! what tongue can speak, what heart conceive
Almighty goodness? Infinitely short
The highest notes a mortal voice can raise
Must fall! As well I fondly might presume
To count the endless train of shining lamps
Which deck the azure canopy of heav'n,
My gracious God, as thy unnumber'd mercies
O may thy goodness, thy indulgent love,
Forever dwell upon my thankful heart,
And teach my future life to speak thy praise.

A RURAL MEDITATION

What soft delight the peaceful bosom warms;
When nature, drest in all her vernal charms,
Around the beauteous landscape smiles serene,
And crowns with every gift the lovely scene!
In ev'ry gift the donor shines confest,
And heav'nly bounty cheers the grateful breast.
Now lively verdure paints the laughing meads,
And o'er the fields wide-waving plenty spreads.
Here woodbines climb, dispensing odors round;
There smiles the pink, with humble beauties crown'd;
And while the flowers their various charms disclose,
Queen of the garden, shines the blushing rose.
The fragrant tribes display their sweetest bloom,
And every breezy whisper breathes perfume.

But this delightful season must decay;
The year rolls on, and steals its charms away.
How swift the gaily transient pleasure flies!
Stern winter comes, and ev'ry beauty dies.
The fleeting bliss while pensive thought deplores,
The mind in search of nobler pleasure soars;
And seeks a fairer paradise on high,
Where beauties rise and bloom, that never die.
There winter ne'er invades with hostile arms,
But everlasting spring displays her charms:
Celestial fragrance fills the blest retreats,
Unknown to earth in all her flow'ry sweets.
Enraptur'd there the mind unwearied roves
Through flow'ry paths, and ever-verdant groves:
Such blissful groves not happy Eden knew,
Nor fancy's boldest pencil ever drew.
No sun, departing, leaves the scene to mourn

264

In shades, and languish for his kind return;
Or with short visits cheers the wintry hours,
And faintly smiles on nature's drooping pow'rs.
But there the Deity himself displays
The bright effulgence of his glorious rays;
Immortal life and joy his smile bestows,
And boundless bliss forever, ever flows.

SOLITUDE

S oftly pleasing Solitude,
  Were thy blessings understood;
Soon would thoughtless mortals grow
Tir'd of noise, and pomp, and show;
And with thee retreating, gain
Pleasure crowds pursue in vain.
True, the friendly social mind
Joy in converse oft can find;
Not where empty mirth presides,
But with those whom wisdom guides.
Yet the long-continued feast
Sometimes palls upon the taste:
Kind alternate, then to be
Lost in thought awhile with thee.
Intellectual pleasures here
In their truest light appear;
Grave reflection, friendly power,
Waits the lonely silent hour:
Spread before the mental eye,
Actions past in order lie;

ANNE STEELE

By reflection's needful aid
Latent errors are display 'd:
Thus humility is taught,
Thus confirm'd the better thought.
Friends and soothing praise apart,
Solitude unveils the heart;
When the veil is thrown aside,
Can we see a cause for pride?
Empty is the heart and poor,
Stripp'd of all its fancy'd store;
Conscious want awakes desire,
Bids the restless wish aspire,
Wish for riches never found
Through the globe's capacious round.
Contemplation, sacred guest,
Now inspires the ardent breast,
Spreads her wing, and bids the mind
Rise and leave the world behind.
Now the mind enraptur'd soars;
All the wealth of India's shores
Is but dust beneath her eye;
Nobler treasures kept on high.
Treasures of eternal joy,
Now her great pursuit employ.
Mansions of immense delight!
Language cannot say how blight!
See! the op'ning gates display
Beaming for, immortal day!
See! inviting angels smile,
And applaud the glorious toil!
Hark! they tune the charming lyre;
Who can hear and not desire?
O the sweet, though distant strain!
All the joys of earth how vain!

Nearer fain the mind would rise,
Fain would gaze with eager eyes
On the glories of the skies;
But mortality denies.
Dusky vapours cloud her sight,
Down she sinks to earth and night;
Then to friendship calls again,
Gentle solace of her pain:
Friendship, with thy pleasing power.
Come and cheer the mournful hour;
Only solitude and thee
Can afford a joy for me.

TO MR. HERVEY, ON HIS THERON AND ASPASIO

I.

O sent by heaven to teach the Saviour's praise,
  And bid our hearts with pure devotion glow!
Truth shines around thee with distinguish'd rays,
And all the graces in thy language flow.

II.

Here beauteous landscapes spread their various charms,
The mind inspiring with delight serene;
With pleasing power while sacred friendship warms,
And blest religion crowns the lovely scene.

III.

Now deeply humbled, self-abas'd, we read
The abject state of Adam's wretched race;
Now smiling hope lifts up her cheerful head,
And faith adores immeasurable grace.

IV.

What glories in our great Immanuel shine!
How rich, how free, how full his merits rise!
The curse remov'd, fulfill'd the law divine;
For rebels he obeys, for traitors dies.

V.

His righteousness, immortal robe, he gives
To clothe the naked; while his flowing blood
Pours healing balm 5 the wounded sinner lives
To speak the honors of the Saviour God.

VI.

In him, what countless, endless wonders meet!
Truth, justice, mercy, reconcil'd appear:
His name, how precious! how divinely sweet!
Joy to the heart, and music to the ear.

VII.

O Hervey, be thy pleasing labours crown 'd
With bliss beyond the low rewards of fame!
Such joy be thine, as thy Aspasio found,
While many a Theron owns the Saviour's name.

THE PICTURE; TO MARINDA

Marinda's temper, open and sincere,
Despis'd the little, the dissembling arts
Which often smooth the supple fawner's brow,
While hate and stormy mischief brood within.
In friendship honest — nor profess'd esteem,
But when her heart accorded with her tongue.
She knew, by reason and reflection taught,
How vain the pleasures which the gay admire;
Her judgment bade her prize intrinsic worth
Above the low parade of outward show.
But then a warmth, impatient of control,
Would often rise and break her inward peace.
She knew, and cali'd it pride, and strove to mend
The fault acknowledg'd ; but, alas ! in vain.
Though reason said, " Content is earthly bliss;
"And patience and humility prepare
"Her peaceful lodging in the human breast."
Yet to attain these graces reason fails;
Till blest religion, heavenly form, appears!
A form no human pencil ever drew
In equal colours ! on her head a crown
Emits a lustre like the rising morn!
See in her hand the sacred book of truth!
Which she unfolding, now with heaven-taught skill
Points out the needful precept, now displays
The cheering promise of almighty aid:
Nor less than aid almighty can sustain
The fainting mind; for lo, affliction comes!
Nor comes undreaded; though Marinda oft
Had seen the frowning form, yet ne'er till now
Array'd in half its terrors; now it spreads
A more than midnight shade; ten thousand fears

269

Torment the restless scene! Marinda sinks,
O'erwhelm'd and fainting with extreme distress,
Yet struggling with her sorrow: " O for help,"
She sighs, nor sighs in vain to pitying heaven.
Two nymphs divine, of blest religion's train,
Are sent to cheer the heart-oppressing gloom;
And these can cheer when human pity mourns.
And sympathizing friendship weeps in vain.
Hope whispers comfort; and a lucid ray
Breaks through the solid night: Now Faith applies
The sacred optic, and Marinda's eye,
Through the dark clouds of mortal grief, beholds
A power omnipotent, and wise, and good,
Dispensing with parental tender care,
Her needful pains, her salutary griefs,
As kind preparatives for future joy.
Her present woes, when weigh'd with future joy,
How light! when measur'd with eternal bliss
They seem contracted to a moment's point.
Before the bright'ning prospect, proud impatience
Retreats asham'd : and now the gentle pair
Humility and Patience, pleasing guests,
Sure harbingers of sweet content, appear.
O may the gentle pair propitious tarry,
And may divine Content, by them invited,
Attend Marinda's dwelling, till this house
Of feeble texture falls; till heaven unfolds
Its shining gates to her transported eyes;
And angels, with triumphant songs, proclaim
Her blissful welcome to the realms of joy.

RETIREMENT AND MEDITATION

Kind Solitude, I love thy friendly shade;
Reflection hither bring her needful aid.
'Tis here I trace past thoughts and errors o'er,
And learn to know my weakness, and deplore.
Ah! would the serious, sad compunction last.
And teach to mend the future by the past.
'Tis here I see how empty, light, and vain,
Is gay amusement with her idle train.
And busy care, which fills the restless heart,
With real, though with unavailing smart,
Is no less vain; for sail her toils renew,
And still some farther task remains to do.
Time nor for trifling, nor for business stays;
He shakes his glass, and counts the shortening days.
And see the ebbing sands, how fast they run!
How soon the little remnant will be done!
Shall vanity employ my precious hours?
Or earth's low cares engross my active powers?
For nobler ends my time and powers are given,
Nor cares nor pleasures fit the soul for heaven.
And can I hope to reach that blissful place?
Yet sleep supine, or linger in the race.
Alas, my heedless heart, how apt to stray,
When earthly trifles tempt my thoughts away!

All my celestial hopes on God depend;
His smile my life, his favor is my end.
How little do I know, or love his name!
And yet to spirits of immortal frame,
Knowledge is food, and love the vital flame.

What is the business and the joy above,
But this, to know, to worship, and to love?
For this, my pow'rs were giv'n ; this great employ
Should be my ardent wish my constant joy.
How shall I know him? all his works declare
Their Maker's name; heav'n, earth, and sea, and air,
Confess the great, the wise, the pow'ful God;
And nature joins to spread his praise abroad.
But yet at awful distance I adore,
For he is holy: his tremendous pow'r,
His dreadful justice — oh, how fierce thy blaze!
And prostrate sinners tremble, while they praise.
How shall I know and love him? In his word
Appears the gracious, kind, forgiving Lord!
let me trace the heavenly transcript o'er,
And learn to know and serve, and love him more.
'Tis here, his brightest, sweetest glories shine,
In Jesus' face, how lovely! how divine!
Here mercy smiles, and with resistless charms
Invites the sinner to the Saviour's arms.
Here wonders rise, and all my thoughts transcend,
Justice appeas'd, almighty power my friend;
Forgiveness, peace, and free access to God,
And life, and glory through a Saviour's blood!

Lord, when these blissful wonders I explore,
I long to know, and love, and praise thee more.
In these blest moments fain my thoughts would rise,
Lose this dull earth, nor rest below the skies;
Those happy seats of knowledge, love, and joy,
Where every pleasing power finds sweet employ;
Where praise and love, in everlasting songs,
Rise ardent from ten thousand thousand tongues.
For Jesus and salvation, charming theme,

Inspires the strain, and feeds th' immortal flame.
O how my panting spirit longs to join
The sacred choir in ecstasies divine!
But ah! this load of clay retards my flight:
When shall I reach those mansions of delight?
Short is the transport, soon my fears arise,
And snatch the lovely prospect from my eyes.
Should I be banish'd from that blest abode,
And never, never see my Saviour God,
(My saviour God! for O my trembling heart
From those reviving accents cannot part)
Banish'd from thee, my hope, my life, my light,
To death, despair, and everlasting night —
The thought is horror! — No, my heart shall stay
Here at thy feet, and wait thy healing ray,
To chase the dismal gloom; one smile of thine.
One sweet forgiving smile, is bliss divine.

O let me hear thy soul-reviving voice,
To heal my sorrows, and renew my joys:
Reveal, confirm my int'rest in thy love,
And guilt, and fear, and darkness shall remove,
So fly the mournful shades of gloomy night,
When radiant morn displays her cheering light.

Jesus, let thy almighty love inspire
My heart, my voice, and tune the sacred lyre,
Let thy unbounded grace be all my theme,
And songs of joy resound thy lovely name;
Till I forsake this dark abode of clay,
And death unfolds the gates of endless day.
Then shall I learn the blissful strains above,
And all my soul be harmony and love.

NO TRUE HAPPINESS BELOW

By daily observation are we taught
(Experience too confirms the mournful truth)
That perfect bliss on earth is never found.
When roses, gay and blooming, strew the path,
Sharp thorns intrude among them, scattered thick.
Nor can we scape unwounded; sense of pain
Forbids delight; and all we ask is ease.
We taste a moment's ease; our wishes rise
In vain for happiness, the restless sigh
Still heaves, the painful vacancy remains.
If pleasure laughs a moment, is the joy,
Or is the sigh which follows, most sincere?
When sweet content serenely smiles around,
Like a fair summer evening, ah, how soon
The charming scene is lost! the deep'ning shades
Prevail, and night approaches dark and sad,
Till the last beam faint-glimm'ring dies away.

Father of spirits, who hast form'd my soul
Capacious of immortal happiness,
O send a beam of heav'n, dispel the gloom,
Direct my upward view, and point my path
To thee, in whom alone my soul can find
That perfect bliss I seek in vain below.

TRUE PLEASURE IN DIVINE MEDITATION

Come, sacred contemplation, heavenly guest,
And bring the muse to bless the lonely hour.
Unbind my fetter'd thoughts, and bid them rise
Above these low, dull, tiresome, empty scenes,
To nobler objects; spread the mental feast,
A rich variety. The heaven -born mind
Should never meanly stoop to feed on trash,
Nor mingle with the appetites of sense.
The heaven-born mind requires immortal food,
Such food as earth, with all her fancied sweets.
Can never furnish; all her fancied sweets
Are bitterness; her most substantial food
Is airy chaff, and only starves the mind.
Ye happy spirits, blest inhabitants
Of paradise, Oh! could you aid my flight
To your abodes, or bring a blissful taste
Of your divine enjoyments down to earth;
How would my soul disdain the joys of sense,
And look on all the good below the skies
Unworthy of her care! — alas, in vain
My thoughts extend their feeble flutt'ring wings;
A misty gloom hangs heavy all around;
I sink to earth — which yet my soul disclaims,
Unworthy of her birth!— .see while I gaze
Intent, its scenes in quick succession pass;
Each gay delusive form, which seem'd to please,
Is gone ; and nought remains but sad reflection.

And is there nothing permanent but grief?
No real good in all the varied scenes,
Which tire and pain the disappointed heart?
Yes, sad reflection, though in sable robe

Array'd, with mournful aspect, is my friend,
And brings me real good ; else my fond heart
Might still pursue in vain these empty shews,
Nor stay to ask for pleasures more sincere.

   Then let me listen to her friendly lore,
And learn the just, the real estimate
Of all below the skies. — But O let faith,
And hope, celestial visitants, be here;
And cheer my soul with some delightful views
Of true, substantial, undecaying good
In fair perspective; distant scenes of bliss
Immortal, far beyond the reach of sense.
Let faith ascend with heaven-directed flight,
And smiling hope sit fast upon her wings,
And bear my thoughts, and bear my heart on high.

   O thou supreme, eternal source of good!
Of good, which knows no shadow of decay!
Wilt thou, all-gracious, beam one heavenly smile,
Break through the gloom, and raise my grov'ling soul;
And with resistless, sweet attraction, draw
To thee, the centre of immortal joys!
O bid my faith, and bid my hope ascend;
For on thy vital smile alone, they live,
Thy favor is the food, the life of souls;
This only can afford sincere delight,
And give a relish to inferior sweets:
Without it, all creation is a blank!
A dreary void! — O could my spirit dwell
Beneath thy cheering smiles, feast on thy love,
And in full view adore thy bright perfections;
This would be life indeed, a heaven below!
This only can refine the joys of earth,

And sweeten all its cares; thus nature's charms
Would wear a pleasing aspect, while my soul
Should trace the radiant footsteps of her Lord
In every lovely scene which nature yields;
And all that charms the eye, the ear, or taste.
Be fairer, sweeter, as it flows from thee.

THE FAITHFULNESS OF GOD

Isaiah 54:10.

I.

Almighty Sovereign, gracious Lord,
How full, how firm, thy royal word!
Thy love, how condescending and how kind!
Nor can the power of language more,
With all its force, with all its store,
Confirm the sacred deed, or more securely bind.

II.

Sooner the mountains shall depart,
And from their firm foundations start,
Than thy eternal kindness shall remove!
Or I be shaken from thy heart,
If ever there I had a part,
If ever I possest an int'rest in thy love.

III.

Yes, Lord, thy promises are clear,
    Thy power and faithfulness appear;
Nor can I doubt omnipotence and grace:
    But ah! myself, my sins I fear,
    These springs of doubt are ever near,
These gloomy clouds which rise and hide thy lovely face.

IV.

O let thy mercy's healing ray
    Arise, and chase these clouds away;
Thy spirit's witness, evidence divine,
    Beam o'er my soul with sacred light;
    Then shall my joys all pure and bright,
Unclouded and serene, with pleasing lustre shine.

LOVE TO CHRIST

John 21:17

Omniscient Lord, before whose awful eye,
    All undisguis'd, thy creatures' actions lie;
Thou seest my heart through every winding maze,
Each secret thought thy piercing glance surveys.
My saviour God — and can I call thee mine?
Can I each idol-vanity resign?
Can I to thee appeal without a fear,
Thou know'st I love thee with a flame sincere?
Alas! I doubt my vile deceitful heart;
Back from my lips the half-form'd accents start:
A thousand meaner objects share my love,
From thee, from thee my foolish passions rove;

My conscious soul shrinks at the solemn test,
And yet I fain would hope, I love thee best!
I fain would hope! unworthy, base return!
Can it be love, and yet so faintly burn?
Didst thou forsake thy radiant courts on high?
And freely lay thy dazzling glories by?
Assume the human form, and wear the chains
Of guilty rebels doom'd to endless pains?
Bear all our sins, remove the ponderous load
Of vengeance due from an incensed God?
And bleeding, dying on the cross, atone
For mortal crimes in agonies unknown?
Touch'd with the melting pow'r of love divine,
Can I refuse this worthless heart of mine?
See, dearest Lord, obedient to thy call,
Asham'd, repentant, at thy feet I fall,
And would resign myself, my soul, my all!
O let this stubborn heart, this flinty rock,
Soften'd by heav'nly love, with sorrow broke,
Bath'd in the fountain of thy bleeding veins,
Be fully cleans'd from all its guilty stains;
Till I can say, without a rising fear,
Thou, who know'st all things, know'st my love sincere.

ANNE STEELE

DEVOTION

Happy the mind where true devotion glows!
Immortal flame, enkindled from above,
It upward rises, and to God alone,
Its sacred source, its everlasting centre,
Aspiring, trembling, points; attraction sweet,
And powerful, though unseen, directs its aim.
But ah! too oft its force abated sinks,
Damp'd with the gloomy fogs of sin and fear:
The last faint spark scarce glimm'ring to the sight,
And near expiring seems, till wak'd to life
By that all-powerful word which gave it birth.
But thus inspir'd, devotion flames anew,
And bears the soul above those heavy clouds,
Which frequent rise and clog its feeble wings.
Unfetter'd thus, when thought expatiates free,
What sweet enticements nature's charms afford
To her Creator's praise, whose hand bestows
Unnumber'd gifts, in fair variety
Dispens'd, where'er the gazing eye can reach,
Or pleasing meditation lead the thought.
Life and its joys depend upon his smile;
Blest with his smile, the soul can see his hand
In every varying scene, and taste his love
In every good his bounteous hand bestows.
Inspir'd by him, the mind enraptur'd views
His bright perfections in his wond'rous works,
The wise, the powerful, and the gracious God!
Wide o'er the fruitful fields and verdant meads
His bounty smiles! amid the blooming flowers
Almighty skill appears, the breezy gale
Wafts on its wing, his goodness in their sweets!
On the clear winding rill his goodness flows!

Descends in kindly showers to bless the earth,
Or silent falls in soft refreshing dews!
In yon bright orb, the source of light and heat,
His glory shines with dazzling fervid ray!
And mildly beams in every twinkling star!
In all the God appears! the father smiles!
Omnipotent and wise, and good, and kind!
His works all beauteous! all harmonious join!
And charm the eye, and entertain the soul;
Bid silent wonder mingle with delight,
And flow in adoration, love, and praise.

ENCOURAGEMENT TO TRUST IN GOD

1 Peter 5:7

I.

Engaging argument! here, let me rest
With humble confidence and faith entire:
What less than this can calm my troubled breast?
What more can my distrustful heart desire?

II.

Encouraged by so full, so sweet a word,
Fain would my soul forbid intruding fears:
To thee, almighty Father, gracious Lord!
Fain would I bring my load of anxious cares.

III.

But can a vile, a guilty creature, dare
Aspire to hope for favors so divine?
Aspire to claim an interest in thy care,
Or boldly call the glorious blessing mine?

ANNE STEELE

IV.

O let my spirit's sacred influence seal
The kind assurance to my doubling soul,
Thy pard'ning love, thy tender care reveal;
The blissful view shall all my fears control.

THE WISH

S hould lavish wealth display her shining stores,
Or smiling fame her noblest wreaths present;
Should pleasure, drest in all her soothing charms,
Approach, their proffer'd joys were all in vain
To tempt my better hopes. There's nothing here
To feed th' immortal mind; no earthly good
Can fill my large desires, sublime they soar
Beyond this narrow scene of transient joy,
To God, the spring of life, the source of bliss,
Of perfect bliss, and everlasting life!

    Low at thy glorious feet, eternal God,
I prostrate fall, and humbly breathe my wish.
I ask not riches, 'tis but gilded care,
Nor fame, nor pleasure, fleeting shadows all,
And vain delusive dreams of happiness!
No, 'tis thy gracious presence, Lord, I ask,
The cheering beams of thy almighty love:
To these, earth's brightest charms appear no more
Than glow-worms lost amid the blaze of noon.
An int'rest in thy favor, O my God,
Is all my wish — for this alone contains

282

Full happiness. — One ray of solid hope
That thou art mine, is worth a thousand worlds.
Thy presence, Lord, can gild the shades of death,
And turn the darkness to celestial day.
At thy approach, black doubt and gloomy fear
Retreat like mists before the rising sun.
While joys immortal dawning o'er the soul,
Diffuse new life, and give a taste of heaven.
O could I see, on thy dear hand imprest
In lasting characters my worthless name;
Could I without a wav'ring doubt behold
Thy blissful face, and say, thou art my God!
Not earth with all the charms it has in store
Should bribe my love, or draw my heart from thee

DIVINE CONTEMPLATION

I.

How blest the minds which daily rise
To worlds unseen beyond the skies,
  And lose this vale of tears!
 On heaven-taught pinions while they soar,
 And joys unknown to sense explore,
How low the cares of mortal life! how mean its bliss appears!

II.

 O for the wings of faith and love,
 To bear my thoughts and hopes above
   These little scenes of care!
 Above these gloomy mists which rise,
 And pain my heart, and cloud my eyes,

To see the dawn of heavenly day, and breathe celestial air.

III.

Yet higher would I stretch my flight.
And reach the sacred courts of light,
   Where my Redeemer reigns:
Far-beaming from his radiant throne
Immortal splendors, joys unknown,
With never-fading lustre shine o'er all the blissful plains.

IV.

Ten thousand times ten thousand tongues
There join in rapture-breathing songs,
   And tune the golden lyre
To Jesus their exalted Lord;
Dear name, how lov'd! and how ador'd!
His charms awake the heavenly strain, and every note inspire.

V.

No short-liv'd pleasure there beguiles,
But perfect bliss forever smiles,
   With undeclining ray:
Thither rny thoughts would fain ascend,
But ah! to dust and earth they bend,
l'etter'd with empty vanities, and chain'd to lifeless clay.

VI.

Dear Lord, and shall I ever be
So far from bliss, so far from thee,
   An exile from the sky?
O break these chains, my wishes fire,
And upward bid my heart aspire;
Without thy aid I cannot rise, O give me wings to fly.

REFUGE IN DISTRESS

In a frail, shattered bark, I trembling ride;
Beneath me sin a boundless ocean spreads.
Amid the dreadful waves, or swell'd with tempest,
Loud threat'ning ruin, and immediate death;
Or smiling with a smooth deceitful calm,
But hiding rocks and sands and sure destruction,
A helpless voyager! nor skill nor strength,
To 'scape the danger, or outlive the storm.
Tempestuous winds with direful fury rise,
And waves, with terror fraught, incessant rage,
To plunge me in the fathomless abyss.
Thick clouds and darkness hide the face of heav'n;
No friendly star appears to point my course
To the wish'd haven of rest, the seats of bliss,
Ah! must I sink, forever lost? ---

See! through the dreadful gloom a cheering ray
With heavenly radiance break! a glimpse of hope,
A smile of pity from the Saviour's face!
To him I lift my suppliant hands and eyes,
To him my voice with trembling accent raise,
Lord, save me or I perish!
O thou, my refuge, and my only hope,
Draw near to my assistance; let thy arm,
Thy potent arm of mercy, oft extended
To sinking dying wretches, be my stay.

Thy sovereign voice can still the raging sea,
Can hush the warring winds and waves to peace.
And bid the clouded sky be all serene
O speak, and smiling comfort shall attend
The charming sound, and drive my fears away.

285

Thou art my star: O let thy beams impart
Light to my eyes, and comfort to my soul.
Direct my course, and let thy gracious arm
Be ever near, my all-sufficient guard.
Then shall I never sink, though storms should rise,
And winds and waves in all their fury rage;
But o'er the swelling surge securely ride,
Thy cross my anchor, and thy word my guide:
Till death shall land me on the blissful shore,
Where sins, and fears, and dangers are no more.

HOPE REVIVING IN THE CONTEMPLATION
OF DIVINE MERCY

Ye restless, dark, distracting fears, be gone!
For mercy, kind, inviting mercy, smiles;
No more, my trembling soul, indulge no more,
These gloomy doubts; shall diffidence prescribe
Limits to sovereign, free, unbounded mercy?
With transport let me hear, with joy obey
The blissful word, which bids my soul approach
The throne of grace, and ask, nor ask in vain,
For pardon, life, and peace j a full supply
For all my wants: divine beneficence!
The object, how unworthy! Gracious God,
Increase my rising hope to thankful joy,
And bid my heart with pleasing rapture trace
The wonders of thy love: amazing theme!
The song of angels, and the bliss of heaven!

How shall my heart receive the vast idea,
Or feeble words express it? Scanty power
Of human thought — the force of language fails,
And soaring wishes flag their strongest wing!
The starry heav'ns, immeasurably high
Are raised above the globe; but higher far
Thy thoughts, thy ways, above my utmost reach
What finite pow'r can ever comprehend
The infinite extent of love divine?
Launch'd on the boundless ocean, every thought
Is lost in pleasing wonder! love divine!
Created wisdom's most exalted pitch
Angelic force can never sound the depth,
Th' unfathomable depth! can never reach
Th' immeasurable height!

   Yet may I meditate, adoring low
Its countless glories, in the sacred word
Display'd, and shining all serene and mild.
And while I meditate, O may I feel
Its quick'ning, healing, life-diffusing ray,
And all my soul subdu'd by love and mercy;
Mercy, which in th' eternal purpose dwelt
For man, (lost, guilty, miserable man!)
Long ere the worlds arose, or man was form'd.
Mercy, which mov'd the Son of God to leave
Th' immortal splendors of his glorious throne,
For this low world, array'd in mortal flesh,
To suffer all the sorrows, pains, and woes
Of human nature in its lowest form;
A servant! Oh, what miracles can mercy,
What wonders can almighty love perform!
Almighty love, which bore the cruel scoffs,
The restless spite, and persecuting rage

Of impious, harden'd wretches! — patient bore!
When with a single frown he might have sunk them
Quick to the caverns of eternal death.

   But, Oh! yet farther let my soul pursue
The wond'rous labyrinth of love divine,
And follow my Redeemer to the cross;
Nail'd to the cross, his hands and feet all torn
With agonizing torture! — Can my heart
Behold those wounds, and not weep tears of blood?
His blood was shed for sin, his sacred side
Deep pierc'd, pour'd forth the vital crimson flood,
Ordain'd to cleanse and expiate mortal crimes.
For mortal crime what loads of wrath unknown
Were due! Almighty justice, arm'd with terrors,
Pour'd the full vial on his guiltless head,
Of vengeance for the infinite offence
Of guilty man against its sacred laws.
He bore it all! he in the sinner's stead
Sustain'd the dreadful storm, and by his death
Th' immortal work was finish'd I full atonement,
Full satisfaction made; amazing scene!
Stupendous sacrifice! mysterious love!
He died! — the Lord of life, the Saviour died!
All nature sympathizing felt the shock!
Earth groan'd, and trembled to her inmost centre!
The sun withdrew his beams, and wrapt his face
In sable clouds, and midnight's deepest shade,
To mourn the absence of a brighter sun,
The sun of righteousness eclips'd in death!
A short eclipse! for soon he rose again
All-glorious, and resum'd his native skies!
There, with full brightness and unclouded ray,
Forever shines, dispensing light and bliss

Through the bright worlds of uncreated day.

His rays far-beaming, visit this dark world;
And through the clouds of guilt, the shades of death.
Break the fair glimmerings of ethereal morn:
O may they reach this dark, cold, lifeless heart,
And kindle light divine, and vital warmth
Through all my powers! Arise, O blissful Sun,
Dispel the clouds of sin, and doubt, and sorrow:
Shine with all-potent and resistless beams,
And, in the sweet assurance of thy love,
Spread the bright dawn of heaven around my soul.
And when this mortal part, this feeble frame,
Sinks down, and mingles with its native dust;
Let my free, joyful soul, exulting rise
On angel-wings, to those divine abodes,
Where thy bright presence in full glory shines;
Transform'd to thy fair image, cloth'd in light,
Mix with the tuneful choir, thy love redeem'd,
In endless praise : — O bliss beyond conception !
In silent rapture all my soul adores.

EUSEBIA AND URANIA,
OR
DEVOTION AND THE MUSE

EUSEBIA.

Say, dear Urania, silent why so long '?
I languish for thy sweet-reviving song.
Wilt thou unkind, neglect a sister's moan,
And leave me wretched to complain alone r
Oft has thy lyre my ardent joys express'd,
And breath'd the ardent wishes of my breast.
Oft have thy sympathizing strings complain'd.
And gently sooth'd my heart with anguish pain'd.
Once more, Urania, try thy pleasing power,
And animate this dull, this languid hour.

URANIA.

Thy active life must wake the silent strings;
For when Eusebia breathes, Urania sings.
But fainting efforts, and unmeaning sighs
Can never teach the feeble notes to rise.
'Tis gratitude and love, 'tis warm desire,
Or grief sincere attunes the heaven-taught lyre.
When thy heart labours with the sense of pain,
In sympathizing accents I complain:
And when from earth thy soaring thoughts arise,
My kindred notes attend them to the skies.
Ah! where is now the heart-oppressing sigh:
Or where the ardent wish that pierc'd the sky?
Does not Eusebia sleep supine on earth,
Almost forgetful of her heavenly birth?

EUSEBIA.

No more, my friend – at length, alas! I see
The change, the mournful change, is all in me.
My heavenly birth! — the thought awakes my pain;
And shall I sleep regardless of the chain,
The hateful chain, which holds me from the skies?
Nor once look upward with desiring eyes?
Ah, wretched state! yet, dear Urania, say,
Extinguished is the joy-inspiring ray?
Lost is that heavenly flame in mortal night,
Which once attractive led our upward flight:
Its vital warmth these fetters could unbind,
And earth no more detain the heaven-born mind.

URANIA.

Extinguish'd! No — immortal is the flame
Which animates my dear Eusebia's frame.
Though late with such a sickly beam it shone,
When fainting accents breath'd thy languid moan:
Celestial love can never, never die,
It will revive, and seek its native sky;
To its divine Original it tends,
And on almighty power its life depends.
Though earth-born vapours gloomy intervene,
And cloud, with night's dark shade, the mournful scene,
If love's unchanging source his beams display,
The intercepting gloom shall fleet away,
And grateful transport hail the rising day.

EUSEBIA.

Thou friendly power, how kind thy cheering strain!
This blissful hope will mitigate my pain.
Arise, O Sun of righteousness, arise,
With sweet attraction draw me to the skies.
Thy healing beams my every grief can chase,
Great Spring of life, unveil thy radiant face.

Awake desire, and hope, and love, and joy,
Till heaven alone my raptur'd soul employ!

URANIA.

And heaven alone deserves Eusebia's care;
The loveliest scenes on earth no more are fair
When Jesus is withdrawn; his smiles bestow
A glimpse of heaven, a paradise below.
Then Oh, what splendor fills those happy plains,
Where in full glory our Immanuel reigns!
Diffusing life, and love, and joys unknown,
Through all the blissful myriads round his throne.
Ten thousand thousand tuneful voices raise
Their sweetest, loftiest notes to sing his praise;
While all the golden harps of heaven resound
Triumphant love with endless glory crown'd.

EUSEBIA.

Transporting view! O for a seraphs wing–
To bear me to thy courts, my Lord, my King!
O happy state! how sweet, divinely sweet,
To bend adoring at thy glorious feet!
How should I wonder that my pow'rs could be
So languid here, so cold to heav'n and thee!
Blest hour of liberty, when we shall rise,
Urania, to those ever-smiling skies!
Where not a cloud shall spread its transient gloom,
But undeclining joys immortal bloom.
There shall thy soothing lyre no more complain,
But tun'd to rapture breathe a nobler strain.
Ecstatic praise and boundless joy inspire '
The meanest voice in that immortal choir.
Come, my Urania, aid my rising thought;
In the bright hope be every care forgot.

URANIA.

Hail, glorious hope; how sweet the distant view!
Ye little cares of earth and time adieu.
Fain would I stretch my willing, joyful flight,
With my Eusebia, to those worlds of light;
Where praise and harmony, unknown below,
Forever with unwearied ardour flow.
But, ere we reach the blissful seats of day,
Eusebia's earthly mansion must decay;
Then death, (kind friend,) shall bid the pris'ner rise,
And join the raptur'd concert of the skies.
Meanwhile Urania joins her sister's cares,
Partakes her joy, and in her sorrow shares.
And if thy smile inspire the humble song,
Thy name, dear Saviour, shall employ her tongue;
And Jesus, and Salvation, shall resound
In echoes of delight the groves around.
Divine employ! to sing thy lovely name,
While list'ning angels join the glorious theme!

AMBITION

I.

L et Fame the shining annals spread-
Where she records her mighty dead,
And boasting, promise an immortal name!
    Vain is her boast, her proud parade
    Sinks in oblivion's dreary shade;
Time, all-destroying time, forbids the claim.

II.

    Let her employ her utmost power,
    With radiance gild the present hour,
('Tis all she can) her fairest wreaths display;
    What is the envy'd prize, decreed
    The living Conqu'ror's glorious meed?
At best, the fading triumph of a day.

III.

    The Christian seeks a nobler prize,
    A fairer wreath attracts his eyes,
Divine ambition in his bosom glows;
    His hopes a crown immortal fires;
    Jesus, the Lord of his desires,
On faith, and humble love, the crown bestows.

IV.

    Honors unconscious of decay,
    While ages rise and roll away,
Secur'd by perfect truth's unchanging word;
    The victor's palm> the robe of state,
    Laid up in heaven, the Christian wait,
Triumphant through his dying, rising Lord

V.

His name, enroll'd among the just.
When sculptur'd monuments are dust,
And mortal glory sinks in endless night;
Shall with immortal lustre shine,
Wrote by the hand of love divine
In life's fair book, in characters of light.

VI.

Such is the Christian's glorious prize;
Thus high his hopes, his wishes rise,
Inspir'd by blest ambition, heaven-born flame!
O thou, the source of bliss divine,
My heart renew, exalt, refine!
Nor let me bear, in vain, the Christian's name.

CHRIST THE CHRISTIAN'S LIFE

I.

O for the animating fire
  That tun'd harmonious Watts's lyre
    To sweet seraphic strains!
Celestial fire, that bore his mind
(Earth's vain amusements left behind)
    To yonder blissful plains.

II.

There Jesus lives, (transporting name!)
Jesus inspir'd the sacred flame,
    And gave devotion wings?
With heaven-attracted flight she soar'd,
The realms of happiness explor'd,
    And smil'd, and pitied kings.

III.

Come, sacred flame, and warm my heart,
Thy animating power impart,
    Sweet dawn of life divine!
Jesus, thy love alone can give
The power to rise, the power to live;
    Eternal life is thine.

IV.

If in my heart thy heavenly day
Has e'er diffus'd its vital ray,
I bless the smiling dawn;
But oh, when gloomy clouds arise,
And veil thy glory from mine eyes,
I mourn my joys withdrawn.

V.

Then faith, and hope, and love decay;
Without thy life-inspiring ray,
      Each cheerful grace declines;
Yet I must live on thee, my Lord,
For still in thy unchanging word
      A beam of comfort shines.

VI.

The vital principle within,
Though oft depress'd with fear and sin,
      Can never cease to be;
Though doubt prevails, and grief complains,
Thy hand omnipotent sustains
      The life deriv'd from thee.

VII.

O come, thou life of every grace,
Reveal, reveal thy lovely face,
      These gloomy clouds remove;
And bid my fainting hope arise
To thy fair mansions in the skies,
      On wings of faith and love.

VIII.

There life divine no languor knows,
But with immortal vigour glows,
      By joys immortal fed:
No cloud can spread a moment's night,
For there thy smiles immense delight
      And boundless glory shed.

THE COMPLAINT AND RELIEF

When pensive thought recalls the scenes of life,
    And full in view the varied landscape rises;
While mem'ry draws the line, and fancy paints
The mingled light and shade in due proportion;
Intruding melancholy often blends
Her sable dye, and deepens every shade,
Till all appears a mourning piece of woe;
And my impatient heart at length exclaims,
Ah, what is life? what glimpse of real joy
Has ever smil'd to bless the gloomy scene?
Anxieties, and fears, and pains, and sorrows,
Thick interwoven, rise in every part,
Through all the dreary wild: If e'er delights
Seem'd buckling here and there amid the thorns,
Touch'd by the wasting canker, soon they fell;
Or nipp'd by chilling wintry blasts, declin'd:
Nor one fair blossom ever cheer'd my sight.

   So withers all my bloom of life away!
So pain and sickness waste this sinking frame!
The ling'ring hours roll heavily along,
All dark and sad; save where some transient gleam
Lights a short blaze, and vanishes away,
Birth of a moment! — Such is mortal bliss!—
Is mortal bliss no more? Is this the all
Of happiness that earth can e'er bestow?
A momentary ray! a short-liv'd meteor!
Let me reflect again — were blooming health,
That best, that dearest earthly blessing mine,
Were pleasure mine, and all its tempting charms
Still brighten'd with unsullied innocence;
Should fortune smile auspicious on my life,

And lavish pour her gifts beneath my feet;
Could all the gifts of fortune, health, or pleasure,
Give permanent delight, or solid bliss?
Ah no! they all are empty, vain, and fleeting!
Earth's fairest gifts united, can't bestow
One happy hour of real satisfaction.
Can air suffice the craving appetite,
Or empty shadows yield substantial good?

Man has desires, capacious as his soul,
Desires, which earthly joys can never fill.
Can mortal food sustain the immortal mind,
Or her unbounded wishes fix on ought
Below the skies, as equal happiness?

No, were the brightest scenes of mortal bliss
Display'd before me, crown'd with young delights;
Should smiling pleasures rise in fair succession,
The earth all blooming, all serene the sky;
The thoughts of death would cloud the gay meridian
With midnight shades! — And see, the tyrant comes!
His arrow flies! — Down sinks the golden scene
In everlasting darkness! --

But Oh! the soul, that never-dying part,
Survives the ruin! then her vast concerns
Appear in all their infinite importance.
On worlds unknown, amaz'd the stranger enters,
Heir to eternity of bliss, or woe.
Eternity — delightful, dreadful name!
What mind can grasp the infinite idea?

Eternity of woe! tremendous sound,
Fraught with despair! unutterable horror!
What heart can bear the distant apprehension
Of the ten thousandth part of half its terrors?
Eternity of bliss! transporting thought!
But thought can never reach the faintest shadow
Of joys forever bright, forever full!

What awful, infinite concerns depend
On this poor, slender, trembling thread of life!
Time — how inestimable is the treasure!
How precious every day, and every hour!
And could my foolish, my repining heart
Complain, they move too heavy? Gracious God,
Forgive the rash complaint, the guilty folly!
By thee instructed, O may I employ
The fleeting remnant of my precious time
In that important work for which 'tis giv'n,
In preparation for eternity.
Confiding still in thy almighty arm,
My God, my strength, (all impotence myself)
On thee I lean: O make me persevere,
And ardent striving grasp the blessed hope
Thy sacred word displays — the blessed hope
Of life eternal through a Saviour's death!
Be this my refuge, my unfailing comfort,
In every painful hour! O may thy spirit
Apply that healing balm for every wound,
A dying Saviour's blood! that full atonement
For all my guilt! that source of purity
To sinful souls! that antidote for death!
That fountain of immortal happiness!
And nought below immortal happiness
Can satiate the desires, the vast desires,

Which animate the soul, which bid it rise
Above this dying globe, this nest of worms.

   And may a worm, a little particle
Of breathing dust, (for such the frame that holds
This soul, this vital spark of heavenly flame,)
Aspire to mix with angels? Yes, for man,
For sinful man renew'd, hath heaven decreed
A place amongst those spotless sons of light.
The rebel-angels from their glory fell,
Whelm'd in the depth of everlasting woe,
Without one ray of mercy; while for man-
Here let me pause and wonder — while for man,
For guilty, rebel man, the Saviour bled!
For traitors, doom'd to never-ending torture,
He bled to purchase life, and happiness!
Redeeming loye and mercy is the source,
The boundless ocean of immense delight,
Where all our thoughts are lost in vast amazement.
Redeeming love is the delightful theme
Which tunes the golden harps of paradise
To notes of ecstasy! to endless rapture!
This can irradiate all the gloomy scenes
Of mortal life, and tune the jarring strings
Of nature! — This can change the deepest groans
Of pain and sorrow, all to harmony,
And joy, and praise! — O may its sacred power
Reach this poor languid heart, enkindle life
Through all my fainting frame, and raise my soul
To join with angels in the strains of heaven!

   My Saviour God, O loveliest, dearest name,
That e'er my ear receiv'd, or tongue pronounc'd!
While hoping, yet almost afraid to hope,

That thou art mine, I breathe the charming sounds
In faltering accents; wilt thou, gracious, seal
My humble claim, exalt my trembling hope
To full assurance? Let thy Holy Spirit
With pow'rful and convincing attestation
Confirm my wav'ring faith, reveal my name,
My worthless name, in thy fair book of life,
In everlasting characters engraved.
Disperse my fears, and fill my inmost soul
With joy unspeakable and full of glory.

   O blissful state! on earth my wish supreme!
Sweet prelibation of immortal joys!
Possess'd of this, I could resign the world,
Nor heave a sigh, nor shed one parting tear.
Then death were welcome, and the frowning aspect
Of nature's foe would change to heav'nly smiles.
Then would I spurn the globe, and rise attended
By guards celestial to the realms of bliss:
To thy bright presence, O my Saviour God;
To dwell forever in the vast delights
Thy smiles bestow! there in transporting strains
To join the heavenly chorus; all my powers
Uniting in immortal praise, and honors,
To thy ador'd, to thy exalted name.
There Jesus and salvation, boundless theme,
Shall swell the boundless song; and tune the notes
To ecstasy! the rapture-breathing strain
Unmeasur'd, but by vast eternity.

A THOUGHT IN SICKNESS

I.

How weak, how languid is th' immortal mind!
Prison'd in clay! ah, how unlike her birth!
These noble powers for active life design'd,
Depress'd with pain and grief, sink down to earth.

II.

Unworthy dwelling of a heaven-born guest!
Ah, no! — for sin, the cause of grief and pain,
Taints her first purity, forbids her rest;
And justly is she doom'd to wear the chain.

III.

To wear the chain — how long? till grace divine
By griefs and pains shall wean from earthly toys;
Till grace convince, invigorate, refine,
And thus prepare the mind for heavenly joys.

IV.

Then, O my God, let this reviving thought
To all thy dispensations reconcile;
Be present pains with future blessings fraught,
And let my cheerful hope look up and smile.

V.

Look up and smile, to hail the glorious day,
Jesus, to thee this blissful hope I owe,
When I shall leave this tenement of clay,
With all its frailties, all its pains below.

VI.

Jesus, in thee, in thee I trust, to raise
Renew'd, refin'd, and fair, this frail abode;
Then my whole frame shall speak thy wond'rous praise,
Forever consecrated to my God.

A REFLECTION ON A WINTER EVENING

I.

Now faintly smile day's hasty hours,
　　The fields and gardens mourn,
Nor ruddy fruits, nor blooming flowers
　　Stern winter's brow adorn.

II.

Stern winter throws his icy chains,
　　Encircling nature round:
How bleak, how comfortless the plains!
　　Late with gay verdure crown'd.

III.

The sun withdraws his vital beams,
　　And light and warmth depart,
And drooping, lifeless, nature seems
　　An emblem of my heart.

IV.

My heart, where mental winter reigns.
　　In night's dark mantle clad,
Confin'd in cold inactive chains,
　　How desolate and sad!

V.

Ere long the sun with genial ray
　　Shall cheer the mourning earth,
And blooming flowers and verdure gay
　　Renew their annual birth.

VI.

So, if my soul's bright sun impart
　　His all-enlivening smile,
The vital ray shall cheer my heart;
　　Till then, a frozen soil.

VII.

Then faith, and hope, and love shall rise
   Renew'd to lively bloom,
And breathe accepted to the skies,
   Their humble, sweet perfume.

VIII.

Return, O blissful sun, and bring
   Thy soul-reviving ray;
This mental winter shall be spring,
   This darkness cheerful day.

IX.

But while to this low world confin'd
   Where changeful seasons roll,
My blooming pleasures will decline,
   And winter pain my soul.

X.

O happy state, divine abode,
   Where spring eternal reigns;
And perfect day, the smile of God,
   Fills all the heavenly plains.

XI.

Great source of light, thy beams display,
   My drooping joys restore,
And guide me to the seats of day,
   Where winter frowns no more.

THE ELEVATION

I.

While I survey the azure sky
   With wonder and delight,
   A thousand beauties meet my eye,
A thousand lambent glories deck the night.
   I do not ask to know their names,
   Nor their magnitude inquire;
   What avails it me to prove
   Which are fix'd, and which remove?
   Let the sons of science rove
   Through the boundless fields of space,
   And amazing wonders trace;
   Bright worlds beyond those starry flames,
My nobler curiosity inspire.

II.

   When o'er the shining plain,
   Thought ranges unconfin'd,
   Night with her sparkling train
   Awhile may entertain,
   But cannot fix the mind.
The restless mind, insatiate still,
(Which all creation cannot fill,)
      Fain would rise
      Beyond the skies,
And leave their glitt'ring wonders far behind.
   Beyond them brighter wonders dwell,
      By mortal eyes unseen;
   Not angel eloquence can tell
The endless glories of the blissful scene.
   Wonders, all to sense unknown!
   Glories, seen by faith alone!
Come, faith, with heaven-illumin'd ray,

Arise, and lead the shining way,
     And teach my longing mind
     The path of life to find;
  A path proud science never found
  In all her wide, unwearied round;
A path by bold philosophy untry'd:
Nor will I ask the twinkling eyes of night;
The sacred Word alone directs my flight,
Nor can I miss my way with this unerring guide.

III.

From awful Calvary the flight begins;
     For there the burthen'd mind
     Divine relief can find;
  'Tis there she drops her load of sins;
Accursed load, which held her from the skies!
     'Tis love, almighty love,
     Which bids the load remove,
And shews the heavenly way, and bids my soul arise
  Jesus, the true, the living way
  To the blissful realms of day!
  Come, dearest Lord, my heart inspire
  With faith, and love, and warm desire;
And bear me, raptured, to the blest abode,
Thy glorious dwelling, O my Saviour God.

IV.

  In those happy worlds are given
  To the favorites of heaven,
     Mansions brighter far
     Than the brightest star
  Which gilds the fair ethereal plains.
Stars must resign their temporary ray,
These shine resplendent with immortal day,
Nor cloud, nor shade, their spotless glory stains.
     Radiant mansions, all divine!

They shall forever, ever shine
  With undecayiug light;
When stars no more shall set and rise,
  And all these fair expanded skies
Are roll'd away, and lost in everlasting night.
V.
  Adieu, ye shining fields of air,
  Ye spangled heavens, that look so fair,
    And smiling court the eye;
  Your fading beauties charm no more,
While contemplation lost in sweet amaze,
Dwells on the splendors of a brighter sky:
But, O my soul, at humble distance gaze,
    With trembling joy adore.
  There reigns th' eternal source of light,
  Full-beaming from his awful throne
Dazzling glories,— oh, how bright !
    To thought unknown.
  Too strong th' unsufferable day
  For the strongest angel's eye!
  Seraphs veil'd and prostrate lie
    Adoring at his feet;
  But love attempers every ray,
And mingles holy awe with bliss divinely sweet
VI.
  Ecstatic joy! immense delight!
  Here fainting contemplation dies,
  The glory overwhelms her sight;
  Nor faith can look with steadfast eyes.
  No more, my soul, attempt no more
  Those awful glories to explore,
  From frail mortality conceal'd.
    Yet in the sacred word
    I may behold my Lord;

In those celestial lines
A ray of glory shines,
Pointing upward to the skies;
Scenes of joy, though distant, rise,
To faith, and hope, and humble love reveal'd

VII.

Jesus, whom my soul adores,
O let thy reviving ray,
(Sweet dawn of everlasting day,)
With heavenly radiance cheer my fainting powers;
And when I drop this mortal load,
Free and joyful to the sky
Let my raptur'd spirit fly,
With unknown swiftness wing the aerial road,
And find a mansion in thy bright abode.
Transporting thought — and shall I see
The heavenly friend who died for me?
While seraphs tune the golden lyre,
Jesus, to thy charming name,
Let me join the blissful choir,
Thy love the everlasting theme!
But not the joy-resounding lay,
Harmonious o'er the worlds above,
Through endless ages can display,
Dear Saviour, half the glories of thy love,

WRITTEN IN MAY,
AFTER A SEASONABLE SHOWER OF RAIN

I.

How chang'd the face of nature shows,
How gay the rural scene!
A fairer bloom the flowers disclose,
  The meads a livelier green.

II.

While bounty clothes the fertile vale,
  And blossoms on the spray,
And fragrance breathes in every gale,
  How sweet the vernal day!

III.

And hark! the feather'd warblers sing!
  'Tis nature's cheerful voice;
  Soft music hails the lovely spring,
  And woods and fields rejoice.

IV.

How kind the influence of the skies!
  These showers, with blessings fraught,
Bid verdure, beauty, fragrance rise,
  And fix the roving thought.

V.

O let my wondering heart confess,
  With gratitude and love,
The bounteous hand that deigns to bless
  The garden, field, and grove.

VI.

That bounteous hand my thoughts adore,
  Beyond expression kind,
Hath sweeter, nobler gifts in store,
  To bless the craving mind.

VII.

That hand, in this hard heart of mine
    Can make each virtue live
And kindly showers of grace divine
    Life, beauty, fragrance give.

VIII.

O God of nature, God of grace,
    Thy heavenly gifts impart!
And bid sweet meditation trace
    Spring blooming in my heart!

IX.

Inspir'd to praise I then shall join
    Glad nature's cheerful song:
And love and gratitude divine
    Attune my joyful tongue.

TO AMIRA ON THE DEATH OF HER SON

I.

Enough to nature and to grief is paid,
    Indulge no more these unavailing tears;
Not all your comforts in the grave are laid,
    Through grief's dark shade a lucid ray appears.

II.

A ray of heaven fair beaming through the gloom!
    Bids fainting hope lift up her languid eyes;
While faith directs her view beyond the tomb,
    To those bright scenes where joys immortal rise.

III.

Cleans'd, in the Saviour's blood, from every stain,
  Think with what transport you will meet above,
(Forever free from sin and grief and pain)
  The dear, departed object of your love!

IV.

Then, though your bleeding heart its loss deplore,
  O yet be each repining thought supprest,
That sovereign hand, which cannot err, adore,
  Here, may your heart with full affiance rest.

V.

Indulgent mercy blends, with lenient skill,
  Sweet cordials with the bitter cup of woe:
And many a friend, and many a comfort still,
  Are kindly spar'd to cheer your stay below.

VI.

Your stay, perhaps for high important ends,
  May be prolong'd through many circling years,
A blessing to your partner, children, friends,
  And future comfort pay your present tears.

VII.

May humble resignation calm your breast,
  And faith enjoy, with heaven illumin'd eye,
A prospect of the regions of the blest,
  Where pleasures bloom, that never, never die!

DESIRING TO LOVE CHRIST AND OBEY HIM

John 14:15

I.

J esus my Lord, in thy dear name unite,
    All that my heart calls great, or good, or sweet;
Whate'er inspires with wonder or delight,
    In thee, thou fairest of ten thousand, meet.

II.

Do I not love thee? Ah, my conscious heart
    Nor boldly dares affirm, nor can deny;
O bid these clouds of gloomy fear depart,
    With one bright ray from thy propitious eye!

III.

Do I not love thee? can I then allow,
    Within my breast pretenders to thy throne?
O take my homage, at thy feet I bow!
    No other Lord my heart desires to own.

IV.

Take, take my passions in thy sovereign hand,
    Refine and mould them with almighty skill;
Then shall I love the voice of thy command,
    And all my powers rejoice to do thy will.

V.

Thy love inspires the active sons of light,
    With swift-wing'd zeal, they wait upon thy word;
O let that love, in these abodes of night,
    Bid my heart glow to serve my dearest Lord!

VI.

Come love divine, my languid wishes raise!
   With heavenly zeal this faint cold heart inflame,
To join with angels in my Saviour's praise,
   Like them, obey his will, adore his name!

VII.

But can the mind, with heavy clay opprest,
   To emulate seraphic ardour rise?
While sin pollutes her joys, forbids her rest,
   How can she join the worship of the skies?

VIII.

Yet he commands to love and to obey,
   Whose hand sustains those happy spirits there;
In him, my soul, who is thy guide, thy stay,
   In him confide, to him commit thy care.

IX.

Jesus my Lord, O give me strength divine!
   Then shall my powers in glad obedience move;
Receive the heart that wishes to be thine,
   And teach, O teach me to obey and love!

TRUE HAPPINESS

I.

Celestial content, inexhaustible treasure!
  The man that enjoys thee requires no addition;
In thee he possesses wealth, honor, and pleasure;
  O happy condition!

II.

With pity he looks on the many, pursuing
  The trifles of earth with such eager attention,
And straining, in chase of their utter undoing,
  (Tho' distant) unfolding.

III.

On inviolate truth while his hopes are depending,
  Nor terrors affright, nor afflictions depress him;
Assur'd, tho' to death's gloomy mansions fast tending
  His God will still bless him.

IV.

Releas'd from the sorrows of time his glad spirit
  Shall leave its weak partner, and joyfully soaring,
The promis'd possession begin to inherit;
  With angels adoring.

V.

He knows that his body, the grave now detaining,
  In Jesus' bright image hereafter arising,
Shall surely rejoin him, no sorrow remaining,
  Corruption despising.

VI.

Then with heaven's fair armies in triumph ascending
  Partake of delights ever new and abounding;
Enraptur'd before the bright throne lowly bending
  Salvation resounding.

WAITING FOR MORNING

Psalm 30:5

L ong and mournful is the night,
  Mental night of gloomy fear:
    Source of comfort, source of light
    When, O when wilt thou appear!
Thy beams alone can bid the gloom depart,
And spread celestial morning o'er my heart.
    Morning of that glorious day
    Which the blest enjoy above,
    Where with full unclouded ray
    Shines thy everlasting love:
Where joy triumphant fills the bright abode,
O happy world! fair paradise of God!

    Thither if the heart aspire,
    Shall it, Lord, aspire in vain?
    Shall the breathings of desire
    Rise with unavailing pain?
O thou my guide, my solace, and my rest,
In this sad desert shall I rove unblest?

    Sure the Lord of life is near
    Though a cloud his face conceal:
    Jesus, when wilt thou appear,
    When thy cheering beams reveal?
When shall thy beams of soul-reviving light
Dispel this gloomy cloud, this mental night?

Not in vain aspires the heart
That depends on thee alone;
Light and joy thou wilt impart,
Radiant dawn of bliss unknown.
Here let me wait beneath thy guardian wing
Till from thy smile celestial morning spring.

THE HAPPY MAN

From the 23rd Psalm

Happy the man of heavenly birth,
Beyond the proudest boast of earth
Whom mercy thus sustains:
To scenes of living verdure led,
Plenty and peace their blessings spread,
And not a thought complains.

Conducted by his gracious guide
Where streams of sweet refreshment glide,
And fed with food divine;
God is the guardian of his rest,
Beneath his smile, serenely blest,
He bids his soul recline.

Yet, should his feet forgetful stray,
His guide restores, and points the way
   To safety, life, and peace;
Still mindful of his glorious name,
A faithful God is still the same,
   His paths are righteousness.

Should gloomy shades the path o'erspread,
Dark as the mansions of the dead,
   His heart no terrors wound:
His heavenly guardian ever near,
Sustains his hope, forbids his fear,
   And comfort smiles around.

The constant bounty of his Lord,
With rich provision spreads his board,
   Amid repining foes:
While peace and gladness on his head
Their sweetest odors hourly shed,
   His cup with bliss o'erflows:

O happy portion! lot divine!
Thus shall indulgent goodness shine
   On all his future days;
Forever near his guardian God
Shall mercy fix his blest abode
   And tune his soul to praise.

SUPPORT IN TROUBLE

Though terrors late alarm'd my breast,
    And rais'd a threatening tempest there,
    Yet, Lord, my passions own thy hand,
    The storm subsides at thy command,
    And now my calmer thoughts attest
Thy well-try'd love, thy long experienc'd care.

    Faith, scarce discern'd a glimpse of light,
    Hope languish'd with dejected eye,
    Reason, (weak empress of the mind)
    To passion had the helm consign'd,
    Loud was the storm and dark the night,
But thy supporting, guardin hand was nigh.

    Almighty Saviour, gracious Lord,
    Thou only refuge of my soul,
    Thy sovereign voice when I can hear,
    I gain new strength to combat fear,
    Hope rests on thy unchanging word,
Thy word can every rising fear control.

    Hence, guilty diffidence be gone,
    With all thy train of boding fears;
    Let faith and calm expectance wait,
    And cheerful hope, with eye sedate,
    Look up and watch the smiling dawn
That through the sable veil of night appears.

That smiling dawn derives its ray
From the full source of light divine;
O sun of righteousness, impart
Thy healing radiance to my heart!
Increasing till celestial day
Dispel the gloom, and joy unclouded shine.

THE COMPLAINT OF THE MIND

Why is the heaven-descended mind
(For nobler purposes design'd)
So close attach'd to frail unthinking clay?
    Fain would she taste the joys of light
    And meditate her upward flight;
But her weak partner cannot bear the day.

    If now and then a ray divine
    With sweet attractive lustre shine,
And upward tempt her half expanded wings:
    The pains or appetites of sense
    Retard her flight with fair pretense,
And chain her joyless down to trifling things.

How blest the unbodied minds above,
   Who still desire, delight, and love,
And nought impedes the work, or clouds the joy!
   No listless inattention there,
   Nor tempting toy, nor gloomy care;
Celestial pleasure smiles without alloy!

   O happy period! blissful day!
   (Hope, cheerful hails its distant ray,
Though rising tears stand trembling in her eyes)
   When this gross heavy clay refin'd,
   A fit companion for the mind,
To active, joyful, endless life shall rise!

   Jesus, to thee alone I owe
   Each cheering glimpse of heaven below,
And thou canst bid the longing mind ascend:
   Though dull mortality impede,
   She spurns the weight if thou but lead;
On thee alone her strength and hope depend.

   O speak the word! her joyful wings
   Shall leave this scene of little things
For the fair regions of immense delight!
   One kind assuring word of thine
   Confirms the bright reversion mine,
And faith shall bid adieu to earth and night.

WRITTEN IN PAINFUL ILLNESS

Indulgent father, ever gracious God,
Low at thy feet submissive I adore
Thy chastening hand, nor murmur at the rod:
Yet thy supporting arm, I must implore.

Thou holy, wise, and kind, O bid my heart
In patient silence wait thy sovereign will!
Sweet consolation let thy voice impart,
And say to every anxious thought "be still."

Say to my heart, that often hath prefer'd
To thy kind ear, the supplicating sigh;
"Be comforted, be strong, thy suit is heard;
Behold my all-sufficient grace is nigh!"

Oft have I wish'd to have my heart refin'd
By cleansing grace; desir'd, and long'd to wear
The bright resemblance of my Saviour's mind,
His gentle, humble virtues copied there.

O may the rod the happy end promote
To humble, cleanse, renew this heart of mine!
And may thy grace assist me to devote
Its powers to thee alone for they are thine!

If the short remnant of my fleeting time
Be near its period; teach, O teach my soul
On faith's fair wing, to reach that blissful clime
Where time's quick-circling wheels no more shall roll!

Oppress'd with pain my feeble powers decay,
The springs of life wear out, the vital flame
Seems quivering near its exit. Is the day
At hand which shall dissolve this mortal frame?

If this frail tottering mansion soon should fall,
Art thou, my soul, prepar'd to take thy flight?
Prepar'd, at thy almighty Father's call,
To quit, with joy, the scenes of mortal night?

Or canst thou patient see death's threatening dart,
And oe'r the expecting grave long-lingering bend,
To drop thy dying partner, loth to part,
While yet thy hopes and wishes upward tend?

What mean these questions?—all depends on thee
My Saviour God: speak to my trembling heart:
Say "thou art mine," that word is life to me,
And I can smile at death's tremendous dart!

Whether he threaten long, or sudden rend
This mortal frame, and set my spirit free;
That moment let thy angel guards attend,
And bear me safe to life, to heaven and thee.

ANNE STEELE

DESIRING A THANKFUL DEVOTION TO GOD

My great preserver, to thy gracious hand
My life, my safety, and my all I owe;
New gratitude thy favors still demand,
And still my numerous obligations grow.

Oft has thou listen'd to my humble prayer,
Oft, at my cry, unwearied mercy came:
O be thy goodness, thy indulgent care,
My constant refuge, my delightful theme!

When warm'd with grateful love to thee my Lord
My thoughts begin to count thy favors o'er,
The boundless sum, what numbers can record?
How vain the attempt! astonish'd I adore!

Yet I may love thee, this is thy command,
Thy kind command, O make me all thy own!
My powers, my passions, Lord, are in thy hand,
And thou canst mould them for thy use alone.

This worthless heart, to thee I would resign,
Poor as it is, thy sovereign hand can raise
A monument to thee, enrich, refine,
And there inscribe thy mercies and thy praise.

Thy wondrous praise, not all creation's tongues
In one harmonious concert, can display;
Not the celestial choir's enraptur'd songs,
Through vast eternity's unbounded day.

And shall a reptile of the dust, aspire
To join with angels in their high employ?
Lord, at thy feet, I lay my trembling lyre
In silent awe, yet mix'd with humble joy.

Yet, if thou bid me try the heavenly theme,
And bless me with thy smile, my lyre again
On every string shall sound thy glorious name,
Thy sile shall animate the feeble strain!

If thou accept, and aid my wish to praise,
Then shall my heart with glad devotion bring
(But ah, how mean thy gift!) her sweetest lays
To thee, my gracious God, my glorious King.
All I enjoy, and all I hope is thine,
Unworthiness, alone, belongs to me;
Inspire me, O my God, with love divine,
And make my life a hymn of praise to thee.

ANNE STEELE

THE HAPPINESS OF THE CHILDREN OF GOD

2 Corintians 6:18

Extensive promise! O what hopes divine,
What rich delight, the gracious words impart!
My father! when my faith can call thee mine,
A ray of heaven illuminates my heart.

Lord, if thy word confirm my heavenly birth,
And bid me say "my father," then I live;
Not all the tenderest, dearest names on earth,
Can half the pleasure, half the transport give.

The Lord Almighty deigns (amazing thought!)
To call us children, (once the heirs of woe,)
Sweet words of consolation, richly fraught
With all the blessings mercy can bestow.

His eye, attentive marks his childrens way,
He guides them safe though dangers lurk unseen:
Though sorrow's gloomy clouds o'ershade the day,
Secure, on his Almighty arm they lean.

His ear, indulgent to their feeble prayer,
Receives each rising wish, each plaintive sigh;
His kind, compassionate, paternal care
Knows all their wants, and will those wants supply.

When foes unnumber'd rise, and fear alarms,
His constant love immediate succour lends,
Encircled in their father's guardian arms,
Foes rise in vain, omnipotence defends.

All needful, present good, his hand provides,
But what their future portion? Angels tell,
(For mortal language fails,) where he resides,
What blooming joys, what boundless raptures dwell.

But not the natives of that glorious place,
Not all the bliss resounding songs above,
Can e'er display the riches of his grace;
Or count the endless wonders of his love.

O could those distant seats of joy impart
A moment of their bliss! how would it raise,
How would it animate this languid heart,
In these dark regions, to begin his praise!

Yet from his word, a bright enlivening ray
Shines on my heart, while all my powers adore;
Jesus, whose wondrous love mark'd out the way,
Jesus, the heavenly friend, is gone before.

Fair mansions in his father's blest abode
That heavenly friend prepares, and joys unknown
By him presented to their Father God,
His children bow before the eternal throne.

In his prevailing, his accepted name,
Father, my soul adores beneath thy feet;
Let his full merits plead my humble claim,
And raise my hope to joy divinely sweet.

DESIRING THE GRACIOUS PRESENCE OF GOD

Alas! my heart where is thy absent God,
Arise and search, nor languish hopeless here,
See o'er creation's frame diffus'd abroad,
His power, his wisdom and his love appear!

But chiefly of his sacred word enquire,
There faith and hope diviner glories trace,
Seek with the ardor of sincere desire,
For nature's father is the God of grace.

His sacred word invites me to his feet,
Reveals forgiveness rich and full and free,
The voice of mercy, how divinely sweet!
O be the heavenly accents spoke to me!

God of my life, thy radiant face reveal!
For thou art near though clouds obstruct my sighs
Thy voice divine can every cloud dispel,
O speak and give me comfort, give me light!

Thy word permits, commands to seek thy face,
Nor shall the humble mourner seek in vain:
Thou wilt reward the search, thy word of grace
Inviolate forever must remain.

Thy word of grace—rich treasure of delight!
(O let my soul recall her comforts past)
Not morn's fair dawn is dearer to the sight!
Nor honey sweeter to the longing taste.

And shall those heavenly sweets no more be mine?
Return ye, blissful moments to my heart!
Dispel the cloud, O God of mercy, shine,
And life and peace and happiness impart!

THE PRESENCE OF GOD, THE ONLY COMFORT
IN AFFLICTION

In vain, while dark affliction spreads
Her melancholy gloom,
Kind providence its blessings sheds
And nature's beauties bloom.

For all that charms the taste or sight
My heart no wish respires;
O for a beam of heavenly light
When earthly hope expires.

Thou only center of my rest,
Look down with pitying eye,
While with protracted pain opprest
I breathe the plaintive sigh.

Thy gracious presence, O my God,
My every wish contains,
With this, beneath affliction's load
My heart no more complains.

This can my every care control,
    Gild each dark scene with light;
This is the sunshine of the soul,
    Without it all is night.

My Lord, my life, O cheer my heart
    With thy reviving ray,
And bid these mournful shades depart
    And bring the dawn of day!

O happy scenes of pure delight!
    Where thy full beams impart
Unclouded beauty to the sight
    And rapture to the heart.

Her part in those fair realms of bliss
    My spirit longs to know:
My wishes terminate in this,
    Nor can they rest below.

Lord, shall the breathings of my heart
    Aspire in vain to thee?
Confirm my hope, that where thou art
    I shall forever be.

Then shall my cheerful spirit sing
    The darksome hours away,
And rise on Faith's expanded wing
    To everlasting day.

330

FAITH AND HOPE IN DIVINE GOODNESS, ENCOURAGED BY PAST EXPERIENCE

Psalm 23:6

L ord while my thoughts with wonder trace
Thy favors past through all my days;
My thankful heart adores thy grace,
I trust that goodness which I praise.

Still from the same eternal spring
Thy various, constant bounties flow;
Beneath the shelter of thy wing
I view serene the shades of woe.

Ev'n death's tremendous vale appears
No more in gloomy terrors drest;
Thy smile, my God, forbids my fears
While on thy gracious hand I rest.

Through the dark scenes of mortal care,
To humble faith's enraptur'd eye
The distant prospect opens fair,
Of radiant mansions in the sky.

Yes, Lord, in thy divine abode
My soul desires, and hopes a place,
To dwell forever near my God,
And view unveil'd thy lovely face.
With all my powers renew'd, refin'd,
To join the blissful choir above;
In strains immortal, unconfin'd
To celebrate my Saviour's love.

A THOUGHT OF LIFE AND DEATH

The cares of mortal life, how vain!
　　How empty every joy!
While grief, and weariness, and pain
　　The fainting mind employ.

But O, that nobler life on high,
　　To which my hopes aspire!
Does not prompt the frequent sigh,
　　And wake the warm desire?

When now and then a heavenly ray
　　Attracts my upward view,
Almost I hail the approach of day,
　　And bid the world adieu.

Those happy realms of joy and peace
　　Fain would my heart explore,
Where grief and pain forever cease,
　　And I shall sin no more.

No darkness there shall cloud the eyes,
　　No languor seize the frame;
But ever active vigor rise
　　To feed the vital flame.
But ah!—a dreary vale between
　　Extends its awful gloom;
Fear spreads, to hide the distant scene,
　　The horrors of the tomb.

The thoughts of death's envenom'd dart,
   The parting pangs I fear,
Alarm this timorous, fainting heart,
   And still it lingers here.

O for the eye of faith divine,
   To pierce beyond the grave!
To see that friend, and call him mine,
   Whose arm is strong to save!

That friend who left his throne above,
   Who met the tyrant's dart,
And (O, amazing power of love!)
   Receiv'd it in his heart.

Here fix my soul, for life is here,
   Light breaks amid the gloom;
Trust in the Saviour's love, nor fear
   The horrors of the tomb.

Jesus, in thee alone I trust,
   O tell me I am thine!
I yield this mortal frame to dust,
   Eternal life is mine.

DESIRING A FIRMER AFFIANCE[5]
IN GOD UNDER AFFLICTIONS

Why is my heart with grief opprest?
 Can all the pains I feel or fear,
Make thee, my soul, forget thy rest,
 Forget that God, thy God is near?

Hast thou not often call'd the Lord
 Thy refuge, thy almighty friend?
And canst thou fear to trust that word
 On which thy hopes of heaven depend?

Mortality's unnumber'd ills
 Are all beneath his sovereign hand;
Each pain which this frail body feels
 Attends, obedient, his command.

Lord, form my temper to thy will!
 If thou my faith and patience prove,
May every painful stroke fulfill
 Thy purposes of faithful love.

O may this weak, this fainting mind,
 A father's hand adoring see;
Confess thee just, and wise, and kind,
 And trust thy word and cleave to thee.

---

[5] A pledging of faith, as a marriage contract. A trust or confidence.

TRUSTING IN HIS MERCY
WITH HUMBLE SUBMISSION AND HOPE

Indulgent still to my request,
How free thy tender mercies are!
With full consent my thoughts arrest,
My gracious God, thy faithful care.

The hand that holds the rod I see;
That gentle hand I must adore;
That goodness, how divinely free,
Which my expectant hopes implore!

Thy hand sustains me lest I faint,
Or at the needful stroke repine;
Thy ear attends to my complaint;
The tenderest pity, Lord, is thine.

And can my heart desire in vain,
When he who chastens bids me sue,
That every sorrow, every pain
Be blest to teach, reclaim, renew?

O yet support thy feeble child,
Till thy correcting hand remove!
Be all thy purposes fulfill'd,
And bid me sing thy sparing love.

INTREATING THE PRESENCE OF GOD
IN AFFLICTION

L ow at thy gracious feet I bend,
My God, my everlasting friend,
Permit the claim, O let thy ear
My humble suit indulgent hear!

No earthly good my wish inspires;
Great is the boon my soul desires,
But thou hast bid me seek thy face,
Hast bid me ask thy promis'd grace.

O may thy favor (bliss divine!)
With fuller, clearer radiance shine!
Brighten my hopes, dispel my fears,
Till not a cloud of grief appears!

But O my heart, reflect with shame,
Canst thou prefer so bold a claim?
Conscious how often thou hast stray'd,
By empty vanities betray'd.

How oft, ungrateful to thy God,
Have trifles call'd thy thought abroad;
Till heavenly pity saw thee roam,
And bade affliction bring thee home.

And when the snares of earth were broke
By kind affliction's needful stroke,
Hast thou not own'd, with humble praise,
That just and right are all his ways?

Yes, gracious God, before thy throne
My vileness, and thy love I own;
O let that love with beams divine,
Forgiving, healing, round me shine!

Whene'er, ungrateful to my God,
This heedless heart requires the rod,
Thy arm, supporting, I implore,
The hand that chastens can restore.

O may the kind correction prove
A fruit of thy paternal love!
Wean me from earth, from sin refine,
And make my heart entirely thine!

Then shall my thankful powers rejoice,
And wake to praise this feeble voice:
While mercy, power, and truth employ
My love, my wonder, and my joy.

ANNE STEELE

ACKNOWLEDGING HIS GOODNESS
IN SUPPORTING AND RESTORING

Now to thy heavenly Father's praise,
   My heart thy tribute bring:
That goodness which prolongs my days
   With grateful pleasure sing.

Ye humble souls, who love the Lord,
   Come join the pleasing theme;
His mercy, power, and truth record
   And bless his glorious name.

Whene'er he sends afflicting pains,
   His mercy holds the rod;
His powerful word the heart sustains,
   And speaks a faithful God.

A faithful God is ever nigh
   When humble grief implores;
His ear attends each plaintive sigh,
   He pities and restores.

No more let diffidence prevail
   Our comforts to destroy:
His tender mercies never fail,
   Be these our sweet employ.

Ah! how unequal to the theme
   Our feeble efforts prove!
Ye heavens resound his glorious name,
   While we adore and love.

Yet fain my grateful soul would bring
    Her tribute to thy throne;
Accept the wish, my God, my King,
    To make thy goodness known!

O be the life thy hand restores
    Devoted to thy praise!
To thee, be sacred all my powers,
    To thee, my future days!

Thy soul-enlivening grace impart,
    A warmer love inspire;
And teach the breathings of my heart
    Dependence and desire.

DESIRING TO PRAISE GOD
FOR THE EXPERIENCE OF HIS GOODNESS

Psalm 36:7

The loving kindness of the Lord,
    (Delightful theme!) demands my lays:
Thou, worthy to be lov'd, ador'd,
O teach my heart to sing thy praise!

In vain my heart with pleasure tries,
My God, to count thy mercies o'er;
So numerous and so bright they rise,
I gaze, I wonder, I adore!

Yet, all the powers I have are thine,
For thee, those powers I would employ;
And dedicate to love divine,
With humble gratitude and joy.

The sweet experience of thy grace
Which animates my voice to sing;
Incites my soul to seek thy face,
And trust the shelter of thy wing.

Thy guardian wing alone can bless;
I find repose and safety there;
The kindest refuge of distress
A sure relief in every care.

O let the wretched sons of woe
To thee apply, on thee depend:
And bid the drooping mourners know
In thee a never-failing friend.

Could e'er one soul in deep distress
That fled to thee for refuge say,
"Indulgent mercy would not bless,
and justice frown'd my hopes away?"

Ah no, a thousand thousand tongues
Thy love and truth, adoring own,
And offer their united songs
With grateful joy before thy throne.

Not e'en those happy minds can trace,
With all their powers renew'd, refin'd,
The boundless glories of thy grace,
O thou omnipotently kind!

Ah how shall these poor languid powers
With frail mortality opprest,
Display the grace my soul adored?
How speak the transports of the blest?

Dear Lord, accept my heart's desire,
Till death shall close these mortal days!
Then bid me join the heavenly choir,
And sing thy everlasting praise!

ANNE STEELE

PENITENCE AND HOPE

Dear Saviour, when my thoughts recall
   The wonders of thy grace;
Low at thy feet asham'd I fall,
   And hide this wretched face.

Shall love like thine be thus repaid?
   Ah vile, ungrateful heart!
By earth's low cares detain'd, betray'd,
   From Jesus to depart.

From Jesus, who alone can give
   True pleasure, peace, and rest:
When absent from my Lord, I live
   Unsatisfy'd, unblest.

Be he, for his own mercy's sake,
   My wandering soul restores:
He bids the mourning heart partake
   The pardon it implores.

O, while I breathe to thee, my Lord,
   The penitential sigh,
Confirm the kind, forgiving word
   With pity in thine eye!

Then shall the mourner at thy feet,
   Rejoice to seek thy face;
And grateful own how kind! how sweet!
   Thy condescending grace.

DEVOTING THE HEART TO JESUS

Jesus, what shall I do to show
  How much I love thy glorious name?
Let my whole heart with rapture glow
Thy boundless goodness to proclaim.

Yes, dearest Lord, my heart is thine,
Sacred to thee be all its powers!
O bid me give to love divine
The little remnant of my hours!

Thou narrow heart, ye fleeting hours,
How mean the tribute you can raise!
The grace my thankful soul adores,
Claims an eternity of praise!

Lord, if a distant glimpse of thee
Can give such sweet, such rich delight;
What must their joy, their transport be
Who dwell forever in thy sight?

To that bright world my heart aspires,
Where all the glories of thy face
Unveil'd, shall fill the soul's desires,
And tune the song to boundless grace!

O teach my heart, my life, my voice
To celebrate thy wondrous love!
Fulfill my hopes, complete my joys,
And bid me join the songs above.

ANNE STEELE

THE LOVE OF CHRIST EXCITING
THANKFUL DEVOTION

O dearer to my thankful heart
  Than all the circling sun surveys!
Thy presence only can impart
Light, peace, and gladness to my days.

Beneath thy soul-reviving ray,
Ev'n cold affliction wintery gloom
Shall brighten into vernal day,
And hopes and joys immortal bloom.

Vain world, be gone with all thy toys;
I have no room for trifles here:
My heart aspires to nobler joys;
Thy fairest glories disappear.

Bright realms of bliss, where Jesus reigns,
My wish, my care, my hope invite:
Where raptur'd seraphs tune their strains
To themes of infinite delight

See, Lord, thy willing subject bows
Adoring low before thy throne:
To thee, I gladly pay my vows;
Thou art my sovereign, thou alone.

Smile on my soul, and bid me sing,
In concert with the choir above,
The glories of my Saviour King,
The condescensions of his love.

Amazing love! that stoop'd so low,
To view with pity's melting eye
A wretch deserving endless woe!
Amazing love!—did Jesus die?—

He died, to raise to life and joy
The vile, the guilty, the undone,
O let his praise my hours employ,
Till hours no more their circles run!

He died!—ye seraphs tune your songs,
Resound, resound the Saviour's name:
For nought below immortal tongues
Can ever reach the wondrous theme.

ON RECOVERY FROM SICKNESS

Lord of my life, to thee my powers belong,
Thy mercies are my chief, my darling theme;
To thee be first inscrib'd the votive song
With warmest gratitude, with love supreme;
On thee my life and all its powers depend,
My gracious guardian, my unchanging friend.

O be that life, which thy indulgent hand
Sustain'd when sinking to the shades of death,
Devoted to thy praise, whose kind command
Restores my wasting strength and shortening breath.

Be my remaining hours entirely thine,
My strength and breath employ'd in work divine.
Yet next to heaven to friendship's honor'd name
The lay which grateful love inspires is due;
With lenient hand she nurs'd the vital flame,
When faintly glimmering it almost withdrew:
Heaven smil'd indulgent on her tender care,
Blest were her efforts, answer'd was her prayer.

The lay which friendship claims heaven will approve,
Since first to heaven the grateful strains aspire:
Sacred to filial and fraternal love,
Be the next labours of the tuneful lyre.
O may the love that animates my lay
Procure acceptance for the thanks I pay.

But never can these languid notes express
My heart's warm wishes ardent as they rise;
Yet he, who knows their meaning, he can bless;
Unmeasur'd bounty every good supplies.
O be the friends who claim my grateful love,
A blessing here, completely blest above.

OCCASIONED BY HEARING A FRIEND
COMMEND MY VERSES

Could all the powers of eloquence divine
But half the glories of my Lord display,
How I should wish those unknown powers were mine
To animate and raise the votive lay.

O could I rise, one happy minute rise!
And hear the music of the blissful choir,
Would not my heaven-enraptur'd mind despise
The sweetest notes that tune this feeble lyre.

Yet is the subject of their song the same,
Not angels know a nobler theme than mine;
Thy grace Emmanuel, bliss-inspiring name!
Awakes the strain to ecstasy divine.

That grace, which smiles approving on their lays,
Bends lower still and kindly deigns to own
A mortal's wishes to attempt thy praise,
When humble love presents them at thy throne.

My Lord, my life, does not thy love inspire
The warmest highest wish this bosom knows?
O let that love employ this feeble lyre
Till with diviner force the passion glows!

Till (every mortal weakness left in dust)
Immortal life commences, then my tongue
To thee, dear object of my hope and trust,
With heaven's full choir shall tune a nobler song.

347

WISHING FOR REAL PLEASURE

How long, forgetful of thy heavenly birth,
Wilt thou my soul so fondly cleave to earth?
How long low-hovering o'er these seats of pain,
Wilt thou expect felicity in vain?
The joys of time could never be design'd
A portion worthy of the immortal mind.
What is it thus detains these wretched eyes,
Detains my heart whene'er it seeks to rise,
And holds back half my wishes from the skies?

When soothing fancy paints, with mimic art,
Her pictur'd joys to catch my cheated heart,
So fair, so bright the varied colours glow,
Almost they can disguise the blended woe.
But soon the momentary forms decay,
Steal from my gaze, and vanish quite away.
Convinc'd the flattering scenes are empty air,
Beneath my thought unworthy of my care,
Can I pronounce the gay delusions fair?

Earth's fairest pleasures which allure my sight,
Are but the fleeting shadows of delight!
Shall airy phantoms thus my powers employ,
Powers that were form'd to grasp substantial joy?
Shall vanity enslave this freeborn mind,
And chains of sense my nobler passions bind/
Alas in vain I strive, in vain I sigh,
In vain my fetter'd thoughts attempt to fly
And weakly fluttering mean the distant sky!

O thou whose eye surveys my inmost heart,
Thy grace, thy all prevailing grace impart,
Dissolve these chains which keep my soul from thee,
And bid this wretched struggling heart be free.
O come thou bright, thou everlasting fair,
Thou only worthy object of my care!
Thy dazzling beauties to my view display,
And earth shall vanish at the blissful ray,
Like night's dark shades before the rising day.

Immortal charms shall all my powers control,
And fix each wandering passion of my soul,
Thy love the sacred source of endless joy
Shall all my heart and all my thoughts employ.
Earth would be heaven in such a state as this,
And time a foretaste of eternal bliss.
But ah! how soon the charming vision flies!
Stay blest ideas, teach my soul to rise,
Nor let me wish in vain for heaven below the skies!

ANNE STEELE

A REFLECTION ON THE CLOSE OF THE YEAR

Occasioned by hearing the bells at midnight

Is this a theme of mirth? who can rejoice
That time, important time so swiftly flies;
And scorn reflection's monitory voice,
The friendly power that woos us to be wise?

Forever ye departed months, adieu!
What heart that knows your value can be gay?
What heart that asks reflection's conscious view,
How many hours fled unimprov'd away?

Yet oft her warning voice, e'er yet they past,
Cry'd, "Seize the precious minutes make them thine:
Ah how wilt thou account for so much waste
Or treasure lent for purposes divine?

O let my heart her needful dictates hear,
To her the solemn midnight hour I give,
And ask, while musing on the finish'd year,
How I have spent the time, and why I live?

How have I spent the time? reflection say?
She answers "wasted many a precious hour,
In careless indolence lost many a day,
When heaven demanded every active power.

Why do I live? "Past errors to deplore,
Low at the feet of sovereign grace to bow,
For strength divine intreat (while I adore,)
To dedicate to heaven the fleeting now."

Jesus, to thee, to thy atoning blood,
To thy unsully'd righteousness I fly:
O thou, my judge, my Saviour, and my God,
Instruct me how to live and how to die.

DESIRING A CHEERFUL RESIGNATION
TO THE DIVINE WILL

Why breathes my anxious heart the frequent sigh?
Why from my weak eye drops the ready tear?
Is it to mark how present blessings fly?
Is it that griefs to come awake my fear?

O may I still with thankful heart enjoy
The various gifts indulgent heaven bestows!
Nor let the ungrateful diffidence destroy
The present good with fears of future woes.

Nor let me curious ask if dark or fair
My future hours, but in the hand divine
With full affiance leave my every care,
Be hope, and humble resignation mine.

Celestial guests! your smile can cheer the heart
When melancholy spreads her deepening gloom:
O come, your animating power impart,
And bid sweet flowers amid the desert bloom.

Yes, here and there, amid the dreary wild,
A spot of verdure cheers the languid eye:
And now and then, a sun-beam warm and mild,
Sheds its kind influence from a clement sky.

My God, my guide, be thou forever near,
Support my steps, point out my devious way,
Preserve my heart from every anxious fear,
Gild each dark scene with thy enlivening ray.

Be earth's quick changing scenes or dark, or fair,
On thy kind arm, O bid my soul recline:
Be heaven-born hope (kind antidote of care)
And humble cheerful resignation mine.

THE BLIND MAN'S PETITION

Luke 18:38

G reat Saviour, born of David's race,
O look, with pity look this way!
A helpless wretch implores thy grace,
Implores thy mercy's healing ray!

Jesus, thou Lord of life divine,
To whom the sons of woe complain:
Is not unbounded mercy thine?
And can I ask, and ask in vain?

Did ever supplicating sigh
In vain to thee its grief impart?
Or mournful object meet thine eye,
That did not move thy melting heart?

Around thee crowd a plaintive throng,
I hear their importuning cries;
And now from every thankful tongue
I hear the glad Hosannah rise.

O look, with pity look on me,
Wrapt in the mournful shades of night!
My hope depends alone on thee,
Speak Lord, thy word shall give me light!

'Tis mercy, mercy I implore!
Speak, Lord, thy humble suppliant raise!
Then shall my heart thy grace adore;
Then shall my tongue resound thy praise.

REST AND COMFORT IN CHRIST ALONE

Where shall I fly but to thy feet,
  My Saviour, my almighty friend?
Dear names, beyond expression sweet!
On these my hopes of bliss depend.

Where shall I rest but on thy grace,
Thy boundless grace divinely free?
On earth I find no resting place;
Dear Saviour, bid me come to thee!

Though sin detains me from my Lord,
I long, I languish to be blest:
O speak one soul reviving word,
And bid me come to thee, my rest.

When I this wretched heart explore,
Here no kind source of hope appears;
But O my soul, that grace adore,
Free grace, which triumphs o'er my fears.

Jesus, from thy atoning blood,
My only consolation flows;
Hope beams from thee my Saviour God,
My soul no other refuge knows.

TO — ON THE DEATH OF HER FATHER

Though nature's voice you must obey,
  Think, while your swelling griefs o'erflow,
That hand, which takes your joys away,
That sovereign hand can heal your woe.

And while your mournful thoughts deplore
The parent gone, remov'd the friend!
With hearts resign'd, his grace adore,
On whom your nobler hopes depend.

Does he not bid his children rise
Through death's dark shades, to realms of light?
Yet, when he calls them to the skies,
Shall fond survivors mourn their flight?

His word (here let your soul rely)
Immortal consolation gives:
Your heavenly Father cannot die,
Jesus the friend, forever lives.

O be that dearest friend your trust,
On his almighty arm recline;
He, when your comforts sink in dust,
Can give you comforts more divine.

355

ANNE STEELE

TO AN INFANT THREE WEEKS OLD

Can I bid thee, lovely stranger,
Welcome to a world of care?
Where attends thee many a danger,
Where awaits thee many a snare?

Hence, away, ye dark surmises,
Hope presents a fairer scene;
Many a blooming pleasure rises,
Many a sunbeam shines serene.

O may providence defend thee!
Circled in its guardian arms,
Dangers may in vain attend thee,
Safe amid surrounding harms.

Shall I wish the world caressing?
Wish thee pleasure, grandeur, wealth?
No—but many a nobler blessing;
Wisdom, virtue, friendship, health.

May'st thou know the gracious donor,
Early know, and love and praise!
Then shall real wealth and honor,
Peace and pleasure crown thy days.

356

BREATHING AFTER GOD

Where is my God? does he retire
   Beyond the reach of humble sighs?
Are these weak breathings of desire
Too languid to ascend the skies?

Where is my God? can he be mine
And yet so long conceal his face?
And must I every joy resign
Nor hope for his returning grace?

Hence guilty diffidence depart,
His goodness never can decline;
He sees this weak, this trembling heart
That yet aspires to call him mine.

He hears the breathings of desire,
The weak petition if sincere,
Is not forbidden to aspire,
And hope to reach his gracious ear.

Look up my soul with cheerful eye,
See where the great redeemer stands,
The glorious advocate on high,
With precious incense in his hands.

He sweetens every humble groan,
He recommends each broken prayer;
Recline thy hope on him alone,
Whose power and love forbid despair.

Teach my weak heart, O gracious Lord,
With stronger faith to call thee mine,
Bid me pronounce the blissful word,
My father God with joy divine.

FILIAL SUBMISSION

Hebrews 12:7

And can my heart aspire so high,
 To say, "my Father God!"
Lord, at thy feet I fain would lie,
 And learn to kiss the rod.

I would submit to all thy will,
 For thou art good and wise;
Let every anxious thought be still,
 Nor one faint murmur rise.

Thy love can cheer the darksome gloom,
 And bid me wait serene;
Till hopes and joys immortal bloom,
 And brighten all the scene.

My father—O permit my heart,
 To plead her humble claim,
And ask the bliss those words impart
 In my Redeemer's name.

HUMBLE TRUST

Why should my pining spirit be
So long a stranger to my Lord,
When promises divinely free,
Invite me in his sacred word?

Does he not bid the weary come,
And call the wretched sons of grief,
To him their refuge and their home,
Their heavenly friend, their sure relief?

Yes by the kindest, tenderest names,
My Lord invites my humble trust;
My diffidence he gently blames,
How soft the censure and how just.

This trembling frame worn out with pains
On thee my guardian God depends;
And while my fainting heart complains,
To thee the plaintive groan ascends.

Though all the powers of nature fail,
And life's pale trembling lamp decline;
Thy grace can bid my faith prevail,
Can give me fortitude divine.

That grace which bids my hope aspire
Can every anxious fear remove,
Can give me all my soul's desire,
The full assurance of thy love.

HYMN TO JESUS

Shall loyal nations hail the day,[6]
That crowns their king with loud acclaim?
And shall not saints their homage pay,
To their beloved Saviour's name?
Ye saints, resound in joyful strains,
Jesus, the King of glory reigns!

Jesus who vanquish'd all your foes,
Who came to save, who reigns to bless,
From him your every comfort flows,
Life, liberty, and joy, and peace.
Resound, resound in joyful strains,
Jesus, the King of glory reigns!

Yes, thou art worthy, dearest Lord,
Of universal endless praise;
With every power to be ador'd,
That men or angels e'er can raise.
Let heaven and earth unite their strains,
Jesus, the King of glory reigns!

_____

[6] The coronation of King George III

But earth, nor heaven can e'er proclaim,
The boundless glories of their king;
Yet must our hearts adore his name,
Dear name, whence all our blessings spring!
Resound, resound in joyful strains,
Jesus, the King of glory reigns!

How mean the tribute mortals pay,
How cold the heart, how faint the tongue;
But Lord thy coronation day,
Shall tune a more exalted song;
Resounding in immortal strains,
Jesus, the King of glory reigns!

He comes, he comes, with triumph crown'd,
In dazzling robes of light array'd,
Faith views the splendor dawning round,
Earth's fairest lustre sinks in shade.
Resound, resound in joyful strains,
Jesus, the King of glory reigns!

THE KING OF SAINTS

Come, ye that love the Savior's name,
   And joy to make it known:
The sovereign of your hearts proclaim,
   And bow before his throne.

Behold your King, your Savior crown'd
   With glories all divine;
And tell the wondering nations round
   How bright those glories shine.

While majesty's effulgent blaze
   Surrounds his awful brow;
E'en angels tremble as they gaze,
   And veil'd adoring bow.

But love attempers every ray,
   Love, how divinely sweet!
That stoops to view the sons of clay,
   And calls them to his feet!

Infinite power and boundless grace,
   In him unite their rays:
You that have e'er beheld his face,
   Can you forbear his praise?

When in his earthly courts we view
   The glories of our King;
We long to love as angels do,
   And wish like them to sing.

And shall we long to wish in vain?
  Lord, teach our songs to rise!
Thy love can animate the strain,
  And bid it reach the skies.

O happy period! glorious day!
  When heaven and earth shall raise,
With all their powers the raptur'd lay,
  To celebrate thy praise.

HYMN FOR THE LORD'S DAY MORNING

Great God, this sacred day of thine
  Demands the souls' collected powers;
May we employ in work divine,
These solemn, these devoted hours!
O may our souls adoring own
The grace which calls us to thy throne!

Hence, ye vain cares and trifles fly,
Where God resides appear no more,
Omniscient God, thy piercing eye,
Can every secret thought explore.
O may thy grace our hearts refine,
And fix our thoughts on things divine.

The word of life dispens'd to day,
Invites us to a heavenly feast;
May every ear the call obey,
Be every heart a humble guest!
O bid the wretched sons of need,
On soul-reviving dainties feed!

Thy Spirit's powerful aid impart,
O may thy word with life divine,
Engage the ear, and warm the heart;
Then shall the day indeed be thine:
Then shall our souls adoring own
The grace which calls us to thy throne.

HAPPY POVERTY, OR THE POOR IN SPIRIT BLESSED

Matthew 5:3

Ye humble souls, complain no more,
Let faith survey your future store,
How happy, how divinely blest,
The sacred words of truth attest.

When conscious grief laments sincere,
And pours the penitential tear;
Hope points to your dejected eyes,
A bright reversion in the skies.

In vain the sons of wealth and pride,
Despise your lot, your hopes deride;
In vain they boast their little stores,
Trifles are theirs, a kingdom yours:

A kingdom of immense delight,
Where health, and peace, and joy unite;
Where undeclining pleasures rise,
And every wish hath full supplies:

A kingdom which can ne'er decay,
While time sweeps earthly thrones away;
The state which power and truth sustain,
Unmov'd forever must remain.

There shall your eyes with rapture view,
The glorious friend that dy'd for you;
That dy'd to ransom, dy'd to raise
To crowns of joy, and songs of praise.

Jesus, to thee I breathe my prayer,
Reveal, confirm my interest there!
Whate'er my humble lot below,
This, this my soul desires to know!

O let me hear that voice divine,
Pronounce the glorious blessing mine!
Enroll'd among thy happy poor,
My largest wishes ask no more.

THE NECESSITY OF RENEWING GRACE

How helpless, guilty nature lies,
Unconscious of its load!
The heart unchang'd can never rise,
   To happiness and God.

The will perverse, the passions blind,
   In paths of ruin stray:
Reason debas'd can never find,
   The safe, the narrow way.

Can ought beneath a power divine
   The stubborn will subdue?
'Tis thine, almighty Savior, thine
   To form the heart anew.

'Tis thine the passions to recall,
   And upwards bid them rise;
And make the scales of error fall
   From reason's darken'd eyes.

To chase the shades of death away,
   And bid the sinner live!
A beam of heaven, a vital ray
   'Tis thine alone to give.

O change these wretched hearts of ours,
   And give them life divine!
Then shall our passions and our powers
   Almighty Lord, be thine.

THE PEARL OF GREAT PRICE

Matthew 13:46

Ye glittering toys of earth adieu,
   A nobler choice be mine;
A real prize attracts my view,
   A treasure all divine.

Be gone, unworthy of my cares,
   Ye specious baits of sense;
Inestimable worth appears,
   The pearl of price immense.

Jesus, to multitudes unknown,
   O name divinely sweet!
Jesus, in thee, in thee alone,
    Wealth, honor, pleasure meet.

Should both the Indies at my call,
   Their boasted stores resign,
With joy I would renounce them all,
    For leave to call thee mine.

Should earth's vain treasures all depart,
   Of this dear gift possess'd;
I'd clasp it to my joyful heart,
    And be forever bless'd.

Dear sovereign of my soul's desires,
   Thy love is bliss divine;
Accept the wish that love inspires,
    And bid me call thee mine.

PSALMS,
ATTEMPTED IN VERSE

PSALM I

Happy the man, whose heaven-directed feet
Avoid the crowded path where sinners meet;
Who shuns the lofty seat of impious pride;
Of men, who dare Jehovah's law to deride.
He in that sacred, venerable law,
(Inspiring Holy Thoughts and pious awe,)
Continual meditates with new delight;
Guide of his day, and Solace of his night!
Beneath heavens kindest influence he shall grow,
Like a fair tree where cheering waters flow:
whose grateful boughs confess the happy foil,
And crown'd with autumn's richest bounty smile.
Fading and secure his hope shall stand,
And prosperous be the labours of his hand.

Not so the sinners hope; he soon shall find,
It flies like chaff before the driving wind.
How will the guilty tribes their sentence bear,
When God in awful judgment shall appear?
Then shall no sinner stand before his face,
Or in the blest assembly find a place.
The Lord looks down, and guides his children's way,
Safe to the regions of eternal day.
But oh, the flowery paths which sinners tread,
To darkness and to sure perdition lead.

ANNE STEELE

PSALM II.

I.

W hy do the heathen nations rise
　With unavailing rage?
Why thus to dare the avenging skies,
　In impious plots engage?

II.

Proud monarchs meet, and breathing war,
　Raise their vain threatenings high
Against the Lord, and boldly dare
　His chosen king defy.

III.

"Shall we submit to his commands,
　"And bend the suppliant knee?
"No, let us break the servile bands,
　"We are, and will be free."

IV.

Heavens awful sovereign, thron'd on high,
　Surveys their airy dreams,
He smiles contempt; in ruin lie
　Their vainly labor'd schemes.

V.

His dreadful anger now awakes;
Their hearts what terrors wound!
　Almighty power affronted speaks,
　And wrath attends the found!

VI.

My chosen king exalted see,
　"On Zion's sacred Hill!
"Attend the solemn fixed decree,
　"And learn Jehovah's will!

VII.

"Thou art my son, thee I proclaim
　"Earth's universal Lord;
"Of powers, and potentates supreme,
　"Thy name shall be ador'd.

VIII.

"Ask, and I give to thee alone,
　"The heathens wide domain;
"And earth's remotest ends shall own
　"Thy uncontested reign.

IX.

"Who will not to thy scepter bow,
　"Shall feel thy iron rod;
"And crush'd in helpless ruin, show
　"The vengeance of a God."

X.

Be wise, ye monarchs, learn to fear
　The power, of powers supreme;
With awful, trembling joy revere
　The Lord's exalted name.

XI.

While mercy, with inviting rays,
　Shines radiant in his eyes,
Approach; for should his anger blaze,
　The unpardoned rebel dies

XII.

When fury kindling it in his eye,
　Each guilty breast alarms;
Happy the fools who gladly fly
　For refuge to his arms.

ANNE STEELE

PSALM III

I.

Lord, how my numerous foes increase!
How fast my troubles rise!
To thee, the sacred spring of peace,
    My wearied spirit flies.

II.

My numerous foes awake my fears,
    While they exulting boast,
"No heavenly aid for him appears,
    "And all his hopes are lost."

III.

Be thou, my glory, and my shield,
    Wilt all my fears control;
A strong defense thy arm shall yield,
    And raise my drooping soul.

IV.

To God I breath'd my ardent cry,
    He, gracious, heard my prayer;
It reached his sacred throne on high,
    And he remov'd my care.

V.

I laid me down and slept secure,
    I wak'd, for God was nigh;
Sustain'd by his Almighty power,
    My guard his watchful eye.

VI.

What though ten thousand foes in arms
    Against me should appear;
And war resound its dire alarms,
    I will not yield to fear.

VII.

Arise, O Lord, with saving power
  In my defense engage;
As oft thy potent arm before
  Has crush'd their impious rage.

VIII.

Salvation, Lord, is thine alone,
  And all thy saints shall find
The bliss my thankful heart has known,
  A God forever kind.

PSALM IV

I.

O LORD, my strength, my righteousness,
  Attend my humble prayer;
Oft thou hast heard me in distress,
  Renew thy ancient care.

II

How long shall scoffers turn with lies
  My glory into shame?
Ah, cease these envious vanities,
  Nor wound my injur'd name.

III.

For know, the man of upright heart,
  As his peculiar care,
The Lord himself has set apart
  And when I call will hear.

IV.

With trembling awe my heart survey,
　And every sin repent;
Let true contrition close the day,
　And future guilt prevent.

V.

The sacrifice the Lord will own,
　If thus you seek his face,
Thus humbly bow before his throne,
　And trust his pardoning grace.

VI.

Vain is the toilsome search of good
　In all things here below;
By smile alone, my gracious God,
　Can real bliss bestow.

VII.

Thy smile, whence all my comfort springs,
　With gladness fills my heart;
No joy increasing affluence brings,
　Such pleasure can impart.

VIII.

My days by the kind of preference blest,
　From thee my safety flows;
Thy favor guards my nightly rest,
　It gives me sweet repose.

PSALM VIII

I.

O LORD, how glorious is the name
Through the wide earth's extended frame,
Majestic glories form thy seat,
And heaven adores beneath thy feet.

II.

Thy power from tender babes can raise
A monument of wondrous praise:
At thy command, the infant song
Shall still the proud blasphemers tongue.

III.

When all by shining works on high
I meditate with raptured eye,
The silver moon, the starry train
Which guild the fair ethereal plain

IV.

Lord, what is man, that he should share
Thy notice, thy indulgent care?
That man, frail child of earth, should be
The favorite of the Deity?

V.

His place by forming hand assign'd
But just below the angelic kind;
With noblest favors circled round,
And with distinguish'd honors crown'd:

VI.

Invested him with power and sway,
In bid the subject brutes obey;
Sovereign of all thy works below,
To him the meaner creatures bow:

VII.

The bleating flocks, the lowing herds,
The gliding fish, the flying birds;
All that the earth's wide circuit yields,
Natives of air, of seas, or fields

VIII.

But still the man adoring own,
That thou, O Lord, art King alone;
And through the earth's extended frame.
Declare the glories of by name.

PSALM XIII

I.

How long wilt thou, O God of grace,
Forget my wonted to love?
How long conceal thy shining face,
   Nor bid the cloud remove?

II.

How long shall my dejected soul,
   (Thus pondering o'er her woes,)
In vain endeavor to control
   The power of inward foes?

III.

Lord, hear my prayer, and heal my woes,
   Arise with cheering light;
Or soon these wretched eyes will close
   In everlasting night.

IV.

The powers of darkness will rejoice
   To see my life decay,
In triumph with insulting voice
   Around her trembling prey

V.

But, Lord, thy mercy hitherto
   Has been my only trust;
Let mercy now by joys renew,
   And raise me from the dust.

VI.

Then shall my heart and tongue proclaim
   The bounties of my God,
My songs with grateful rapture flame,
   And spread thy praise abroad.

PSALM XVI

Preserve me, oh my God; on thee alone
   With humble confidence my soul relies,
By thee encouraged oft with holy pleasure,
Yet mix'd with trembling, I have made my claim
To thy regard, and said, thou art my God.
But oh, to thee my best, and noblest service
Is poor and worthless! Yet their good who love thee
I would consult; where'er the image dwells
My soul delights, and I would show thy saints,
How much my heart reveres that excellence
Which bears that blessed resemblance of my God.
  Unnumbered woes shall be their fatal lot,

Who follow Idol Gods; their impious rites
I will not join, nor shall my faithful lips
But with abhorrence e'er pronounce their names.

   The Lord is mine, the portion of my choice,
My sure support, my blessed inheritance.
Thy favor, (O my God, my happy lot
continue still,) is all my wish, my joy.
Thy gracious hand has, with indulgent care,
Marked out my lines; my prospects are serene;
A pleasant heritage, and ample share
Of every good! O let me bless the Lord,
Whose heavenly counsel guides my doubting soul,
While in the silent watches of the night
Constructive meditation warms my heart.
The Lord is ever near, my guard, my guide:
Blessed with his presence, what can e'er remove
The lasting basis of my sacred joys?
Exulting gladness fills my grateful heart,
And bids my tongue and all my powers rejoice.
This flesh, this dying frame shall rest in hope
To rise, and join anew the parting soul;
For thou wilt never leave me in the grave,
Nor can a pure refined ethereal spirit
E'er mingle with the dust and foul corruption.
Thy hand shall guide me in the path of life:
The path of life to thy bright presence leads,
The boundless ocean of immortal joy;
To thy right hand, where pleasures all divine
Triumphant smile in everlasting bloom.

PSALM XIX

The heavens declare their Maker's glorious name;
  The spacious firmament's extended frame,
And all the shining wonders it displays,
Proclaim the God, and teach the world his praise.
Each rising day repeats instructive songs,
And closing night the wondrous theme prolongs:
Nor speech nor language wants the sacred strain;
'Tis nature's harmony, nor tun'd in vain.
Delightful music I hear the heaven-taught mind
Sweetness beyond the reach of sounds can find.
Through all the world the sacred lines are spread,
And earth's remotest ends may wondering read.
From hence the rising sun his light displays,
And glads all nature with his cheerful rays.
So the young bridegroom on his nuptial day
Exulting smiles, and all the scene is gay.
Like supportive youth contending in the race,
When joyful ardour paints the glowing face,
With rapid speed, now from the radiant east
His race begins, now gains the distant west;
Each deep recess his piercing beams explore,
And nature owns his all enlivening power.

  But with diviner beams, the sacred word
Shines o'er the soul, and guides it to the Lord.
Unerring guide, which heavenly light supplies,
Transforms the heart, and makes the simple wise!
In God's commands see truth and goodness join!
Immortal rectitude in every line.
'Tis his celestial light and knowledge flows,
And nobler joy that all creation knows.
That pure devotion which his fear inspires,

To him its sacred source directs its fires.
His precepts with eternal splendor shine,
All spotless truth, and righteousness divine.
Immortal treasure! All the glittering store
Of golden mines, compar'd to these, how poor!
Here heavenly food abounds, divine repast!
More sweet than honey to the longing taste:
Here gentle admonitions warn my heart,
When my frail steps would from thy way depart.
Obedience to thy laws, my sovereign Lord,
Brings peace and joy, an ample rich reward.
The errors of my heart, ah, who can trace?
Lord, I implore thy purifying grace;
Preserve thy servant from each willful stain,
From sin's destructive power and hateful reign:
Then shall my life be right, my heart sincere,
And free from deadly guilt, adore thy care.

   Let these petitions of my lips arise,
Warm from my heart accepted in thine eyes;
propitious hear the humble suit I bring,
oh Lord, my strength, my Saviour and my King.

PSALM XXIII

I.

The Lord, my shepherd and my guide,
  Will all my wants supply;
In safety I shall still abide
  Beneath his watchful eye.

II.

Amid the verdant flowery meads,
  He makes my sweet repose;
When pain'd with thirst he gently leads
  Where living waters flow

III.

If from his fold I thoughtless stray.
  He leads the wanderer home;
And shews my erring feet the way
  Where dangers cannot come.

IV.

Though hastening to the silent tomb,
  And death's dark shades appear:
Thy presence, Lord, shall cheer the gloom,
  And banish every fear.

V.

No evil can my soul dismay,
  While I am near my God;
My comfort, my support and stay,
  Thy staff and guiding rod.

VI.

Thy constant bounties me surround,
  Amid my envious foes;
My favor'd head with gladness crown'd
  My cup with blessings flows.

VII.

Thus shall thy goodness, love and care
   Attend my future days;
And I shall dwell forever near
   My God and sing his praise.

PSALM XXIV

The earth through all her wide dominion owns
  Her Maker; his are all her ample stores;
Her numerous tribes, dependent on his hand,
Partake his bounty and confess his care.
His potent hand has founded on the seas
The wondrous fabric, rising firm and fair
In just proportion, 'midst the swelling floods.

  But who, of all his creatures, may aspire
To lift their eyes to his divine abode?
Who of the guilty race of man can hope
To stand before his holy seat undaunted?
Or bear the glance of that all-piercing eye,
Which beams immortal purity and truth?
He, whom almighty grace has cleans'd from guilt,
Whose heart and life confess'd the sacred change;
Who dares not in the purpose of his soul
Consent to sin, or harbour secret guile.
He shall be crown'd with blessings from the Lord,
Shall stand with joy before his Saviour God,
In his eternal righteousness array'd.

These are the happy souls that seek the Lord,
That humbly seek thy face, O God of Jacob.

   Lift up your heads, O ye celestial gates!
Unfold your leaves, ye everlasting doors!
With conquest crown'd, the king of glory comes!
Who is this king of glory? 'tis the Lord
Strong in the field, victorious in the fight.

Lift up your heads, O ye celestial gates,
Ye everlasting doors, with joyful speed
Unfold your shining leaves! Behold he comes!
The king of glory comes! The Lord of hosts!
The conquering God! He is the king of glory.

PSALM XXVII

I.

The Lord, my Saviour, is my light;
   What terrors can my soul affright?
While God my strength, my life is near,
What potent arm shall make me fear?

II.

When cruel foes, the sons of strife,
Came furious to devour my life;
Their vile designs at once o'erthrown,
Confess'd the power that cast them down.

385

III.

Should numerous hosts besiege me round,
My steadfast heart no fear shall wound:
Though war should rise in dread array,
God is my strength, my hope, my stay.

IV.

This only boon my heart desires,
For this my ardent wish aspires,
This will I seek with restless care,
Till God attend my humble prayer:

V.

In his own house to spend my days,
My life devoted to his praise;
There would my soul his beauties trace,
And learn the wonders of his grace.

VI.

When troubles rise, my guardian God
Will hide me safe in his abode!
Firm as a rock my hope shall stand,
Sustain'd by his almighty hand

VII.

Now shall my head exalted rise
Above surrounding enemies;
While my glad offerings to the Lord,
With grateful songs, his praise record.

VIII.

Thou sacred spring of all my joys,
Whene'er I raise my plaintive voice,
O let thy sovereign mercy hear,
And answer all my humble prayer.

IX.

When thou with condescending grace
Hast bid me seek thy smiling face,
My heart replied to thy kind word,
Thee will I seek, all gracious Lord.

X.

Hide not from me thy blissful ray,
Nor angry frown my hopes away;
Thy saving help has still been near,
God of my life, renew thy care.

XI.

Should every earthly friend depart,
And nature leave a parent's heart;
My God, on whom my hope depend,
Will be my father and my friend.

XII.

O teach me, Lord, thy sacred way,
Uphold my steps, nor let me stray;
While enemies and fears alarm,
Extend thy kind, thy guardian arm.

XIII.

Leave not my life to impious foes,
Whose rage no sense of justice knows;
Against my innocence they rise,
And breathe out cruelty and lies.

XIV.

My hope was ready to depart,
But faith sustain'd my fainting heart;
I trusted in a gracious God,
And live to spread his praise abroad.

XV.

Ye humble souls, in every strait
On God with sacred courage wait;
His hand shall life and strength afford,
O wait continual on the Lord.

PSALM XXIX

G ive to the Lord, ye potentates of earth,
Sons of renown, who glory in your might,
Give to the Lord immortal power and praise!
Confess the awful glories of his name,
To whom alone immortal praise is due,
Amid his sacred courts, where holiness
Resplendent shines, your adorations pay.
Hark! How his voice tremendous breaks the clouds:
The God of glory thunders; Dreadful sound!
O'er the wide ocean storm and terror spread---
'Tis God amid the storm and terror speaks!
Resistless power dwells in that awful voice;
In every accent majesty divine.
See Lebanon with all his honors bend!
And towering cedars broken spread the ground,
A stately ruin! 'tis the breath of God
Which shakes the solid hills, unmov'd before;
And Lebanon and Sirion start alarmed.
So bounds the wanton heifer o'er the mead;
So starts the unicorn arous'd to flight.
Ethereal flames attendant wait his voice;
Dividing, blaze along the vaulted skies,

And flash bright horrors o'er a guilty world.
The wilderness through all her wide extent,
Astonish'd hears her mighty Maker's voice;
And Kadesh trembles through her deepest glooms.
The frighted hinds in pangs confess his power;
The forest haunts disclos'd, each deep recess
Appears, and wonders at the sudden day.
While in his temple, every praiseful tongue
Resounds with loud acclaim his glorious deeds,
On the wild tempest, and rolling flood,
The God of nature sits, he reigns supreme,
Forever reigns, when nature is no more.
The Lord, the fountain of immortal power,
With strength divine his people will sustain;
On these, while storms and tempests shake the world,
He smiles serene, and calms their rising fears,
With the sweet earnest of eternal peace.

PSALM XXX

I.

Thee, Lord, my thankful soul would bless,
  Thee all my powers adore!
Thy hand has rais'd me from distress,
  My foes rejoice no more.

II.

O Lord, my God, oppress'd with grief,
  To thee I breath'd my cry!
Thy mercy brought divine relief,
  And wip'd my tearful eye.

III.

Thy mercy chas'd the shades of death,
  And snatch'd me from the grave;
O may thy praise employ that breath
  Which mercy deigns to save.

IV.

Come, O ye saints, your voices raise
  To God in grateful songs:
And let the memory of his grace,
  Inspire your hearts and tongues.

V.

His frown, what mortal can sustain?
  But soon his anger dies;
His life-restoring smile again
  Returns; and sorrow flies.

VI.

Her deepest gloom when sorrow spreads,
  And light and hope depart,
His smile celestial morning sheds,
  And joy revives the heart.

VII.

Beneath thy protecting arm
    How did my soul rejoice!
And fondly hop'd no future harm
    Should ever shock my joys.

VIII.

Lord, 'twas thy favor fix'd my rest;
    Thy shining face withdrew,
And troubles fill'd my anxious breast,
    And pain'd my soul anew.

IX.

Again to thee, O gracious God,
    I rais'd my mournful eyes;
To thee I spread my woes abroad,
    With supplicating cries.

X.

What glory can my death afford?
    In the dark grave confin'd,
Shall senseless dust adore the Lord,
    Or call thy truth to mind?

XI.

Hear, O my God, in mercy hear,
    Attend my plaintive cry;
Be thou, my gracious helper, near,
    And bid my sorrows fly.

XII.

Again I hear thy voice divine
    New joys exulting bound;
My robes of mourning I resign,
    And gladness girds me round.

XIII.

Then let my utmost glory be
  To raise thy honors high;
Nor let my gratitude to thee
  In guilty silence die.

PSALM XXXI

I.

Lord, in thy great, thy glorious name,
I place my hope, my only trust;
Save me from sorrow, guilt and shame,
Thou ever-gracious, ever-just.

II.

Attentive bow thy pitying ear,
Let mercy fly to my relief,
Be thou my refuge, ever near,
A sure defense from all my grief.

III.

Thou art my rock, thy name alone
The fortress where my hopes retreat;
O make thy power and mercy known,
To safety guide my trembling feet.

IV.

Preserve me from the fatal snare
Of secret foes, who plot my fall;
And make my life thy tender care,
My God, my strength, my hope, my all.

V.

To thy kind hand, O gracious Lord,
My soul I cheerfully resign;
My Saviour God, I trust thy word,
For truth, immortal truth, is thine.

VI.

I hate their works, I hate their ways,
Who follow vanity and lies;
But to the Lord my hopes I raise,
And trust his power who built the skies.

VII.

In thee, my God, I will rejoice,
While mercy makes my soul her care;
For thou hast heard my mournful voice,
In all my sorrows God was near.

VIII.

Thou hast not left my life to groan,
Where chains and tyrant foes oppress;
Enlarg'd by thee, my feet have known
The sweets of liberty and peace.

IX.

Thy wonted mercy, Lord, renew,
See how my inward troubles rise;
My melting soul with pity view,
And these dejected weeping eyes.

X.

My life is spent in grief and tears,
In sighs my hours roll slow away,
My strength decays, while sins and fears
Sink all my frame in deep decay.

XI.

While black reproaches blot my fame
And neighbors join the cruel foes,
My friends who now forget the name,
With horror fly, and shun my woes:

XII.

Till from their memory I slide,
And sink in dark oblivion's shade,
A broken vessel thrown aside,
And mix unheeded with the dead.

XIII.

I heard the cruel slander rise,
While foes and fears beset me round;
I heard the murderous bands devise
To crush me helpless to the ground.

XIV.

But I haved trusted in thy name,
O Lord, my hope, my fix'd abode;
And still avow'd my humble claim,
(O sweet support!) thou art my God.

XV.

My life, my all, is in thy hand;
Let thy almighty power control
The rage of this remorseless band,
And save my persecuted soul.

XVI.

O let thy favor, bliss divine!
Thy smile with heavenly radiance break,
And round thy fainting servant shine;
O save me for thy mercy's sake.

XVII.

Leave not my hope to sink in shame,
God of my prayer, in whom I trust;
Let wicked men, who hate thy name,
Lose all their glory in the dust.

XVIII.

Deep in the grave be lying tongues
In everlasting silence laid,
Whose proud disdain, and slanderous wrongs,
The injur'd innocent invade.

XIX.

What endless bliss, O bounteous Lord,
(Immensely great, divinely free!)
Hast thou reserv'd for their reward,
Who fear thy name, and trust in thee?

XX.

Thy gracious hand shall near thee hide
These happy favorites of thy care;
Safe at thy feet they shall abide,
Nor pride, nor slander reach them there.

XXI.

Blest be the Lord, forever blest,
Whose mercy bids my fears remove;
The sacred walls which guard my rest,
Are his almighty power and love.

XXII.

I rashly said, I Sink, I die,
Cut off, abandon'd to despair;
Yet thou, my God, hast heard my cry,
And gracious answer'd all my prayer.

XXIII.

Ye saints, to whom his mercy flows,
O love, forever love the Lord;
While on the proud his hand bestows,
A dreadful, and a just reward.

XXIV.

Ye humble souls, who seek his face,
Let sacred courage fill your heart;
Hope in the Lord, and trust his grace,
And he shall heavenly strength impart.

PSALM XXXII

Blest is the man, whose crimes are all remov'd
By grace divine, whose trembling guilty soul
Kind mercy covers with spotless robe.
How blest, when awful justice frowns no more!
Acquitted at the throne supreme, and cleans'd
His inmost heart from every guileful thought.

When deep suppress'd my inward lay,
Nor found the solace of complaining speech;
Heart-breaking groans were all my griefs could know,
And this weak frame sunk down in swift decay.
Thy awful hand vindictive press'd my soul,
And day and night my unremitting pains
Dry'd up the springs of life with parching thirst.
At length, low prostrate at thy throne of grace,
(My heart dissolv'd in penitential woe.)
I mourn'd my sins, and told my sorrows there.

'Twas then, my God, thy kind forgiving smile
Remov'd my griefs, and cancel'd all my guilt.
For this, shall every pious mourning soul
Before thy throne present his humble prayers,
And find a God of sovereign mercy there.
When floods of sorrow roll their swelling waves,
Sure they can never reach him near his God.
Thou art my refuge, thou, my safe defense;
Here will I hide, whene'er my troubles rise,
And trust thy power, thy faithfulness and love;
Til thy preserving, thy delivering hand,
To grateful transport tunes my raptur'd song

  Come, while I teach, ye uninstructed, hear
The voice of one by long experience wise;
My watchful care shall guide your dubious way.
Bend unresisting to the hand of heaven;
Nor like the brute, whom reason never taught,
Impatient of restraint, with heedless rage,
Pursue the path ungovern'd passion leads.
Unnumber'd sorrows wait the sons of guilt,
Their just reward: but he whose humble trust,
Fix'd on the Lord, inspires obedient love,
Shall be secure; for heavenly mercy spreads
Her everlasting arms, his sure defense.
Rejoice, ye pious souls, for God is yours,
Guard of your lives, and center of your joys.
Let shouts of praise the heart felt rapture speak,
Sincere and boundless as the bliss you share.

PSALM XXXIII

Rejoice, ye righteous, in the Lord rejoice;
For praise is lovely when heart sincere
Inspires the lips, and tunes the grateful strain.

   Awake the harp! The exalted theme demands
New strains of Joy! Let every charming sound
That art or nature knows awake to praise!

   The word of God is sacred, just and right,
Inviolably firm, and all his works
With glorious evidence attest his truth.
In holiness and justice he delights,
And perfect recititude is his alone.
Earth, fill'd with blessings from his bounteous hand,
Declares the boundless good ness of the Lord.

   His potent word spread the wide arch of heaven;
The starry host obey'd the voice divine,
And instant kindled through the fair expanse.
He leads the waters through their sandy beds;
The waters own his hand, and to the sea
Obedient bring their congregated stores.
Let universal nature fear the Lord,
Let all the inhabitants of earth adore,
With awful reverence their Creator's name.
He spake! The sovereign mandate was obey'd;
Fix'd on his firm decree all nature stands.

The heathen nations, strangers to the Lord,
In vain their impious counsels would pursue;
In vain their deep contrivances are laid:
He sees and disappoints their idle schemes
Which ere thy take effect, are lost in air.
The counsel of the Lord shall stand forever,
His sacred purposes be all fulfill'd,
And future ages witness to the truth.

How blest the nation who can call the Lord
Their God, their guardian friend! His chosen people,
His inheritance; distinguish'd lot!

From heaven, where in eternal majesty
He sits enthron'd, his awful eye beholds
The sons of men; from his supreme abode
He views the inhabitants of this low world;
He made their hearts, he sees their every thought,
And weighs the various actions of their lives.
No powerful monarch by his numerous host
Surrounded, is preserv'd, if God withdraw
His kind protection; mortal strength is weak
In all its pride, and impotent to save.
In vain the warlike horse his aid supplies,
To speed his helpless, trembling master's flight;
Nor strength nor speed eludes the pursuing fate.

But oh, with watchful eye, and tender care,
The Lord regards the souls that fear his name,
And on his sovereign mercy fix their hope:
He guards their lives from every deathful stroke.
Nor war shall hurt them, nor shall famine waste.
On him we wait, our God, our help, our shield;
On him with humble confidence depend:

In him our souls forever shall rejoice;
For we have trusted in his holy name.
O be thy mercy, O Lord, our constant trust,
Our blissful portion, mercy large and full,
Unbounded and immortal as our hopes!

PSALM XXXIX

I.

When I resolv'd to watch my thoughts,
To watch my words and all my ways,
Left I should with unwary faults
Offend the God my life should praise;

II.

In mournful silence long restrain'd,
My thoughts were press'd with secret grief;
My heart with sad reflection pain'd,
In silence found no kind relief.

III.

While thus inward anguish burn'd,
My straightn'd speech at length found way;
My tongue in broken accents mourn'd
Before my God, and try'd to pray.

IV.

Almighty Maker of my frame,
Teach me the measure of my days,
Teach me to know how frail I am,
And spend the remnant to thy praise.

V.

My days are shorter than a span,
A little point my life appears;
How frail at best is dying man!
How vain are all his hopes and fears!

VI.

Vain ambition, noise and show!
Vain are the cares which rack his mind!
He heaps up treasures mix'd with woe;
And dies, and leaves them all behind.

VII.

O be a nobler portion mine;
My God, I bow before thy throne,
Earth's fleeting treasures I resign,
And fix my hope on thee alone.

VIII.

Save me, by thy almighty arm,
From all my sins, and cleanse my faults;
Then guilt nor folly shall alarm
My soul, nor vex my peaceful thoughts.

IX.

Beneath the chastening of thy hand,
Let not my heart or tongue repine;
But filent and submissive bend,
And bear the stroke because 'tis thine.

X.

But O let mercy soon prevail,
Thy awful anger to remove;
The stroke is just, but I am frail,
Thy sparing goodness let me prove.

XI.

Frail man, how soon his beauty flies!
He sins, and God afflicts with pain;
Crush'd like the feeble moth he dies;
His strength, how impotent and vain!

XII.

Lord, wilt thou gracious hear my cry,
Pity my tears and heal my woe?
As were my fathers, so am I,
A wretched stranger here below.

XIII.

O spare me, and my strength restore,
Ere my few hasty inutes flee;
And when my days on earth are o'er,
Let me forever dwell with thee.

PSALM XLII

I.

As the poor hart tir'd in the chase,
Pants for the cool refreshing flood,
So pants my soul for streams of grace,
Thy cheering visits, O my God.

II.

For God my thirsty spirit longs,
The sacred spring of living joy;
When shall I come with thankful songs,
Before my God? Divine employ!

III.

Through the sad night and mournful day
My flowing tears have been my food,
While taunting foes continual say,
"And where is now thy Saviour God?

IV.

My melting soul in grief is spent,
When I resolve my happier days;
When with the joyful throng I went
To thy abode with songs of praise.

V.

Why, O my soul, thus sunk in woe?
Why thus with restless sorrows torn?
Hope thou in God; my song shall flow,
For his bright presence will return.

VI.

My heart sinks down oppress'd with grief;
Yet, O my God, I'll call to mind
Those seasons past, for my relief,
When I was blest and thou wast kind.

VII.

Thy terrors overwhelm my soul,
Wave after wave, with dreadful roar;
So stormy seas like mountains roll
And swelling billows drown the shore.

VIII.

Yet will the Lord command his care,
His love (sweet morn!) shall cheer mine eyes;
And mix'd with praise my nightly prayer,
God of my life, to thee shall rise.

IX.

To thee, I'll cry, my God, my rock:
Ah, why hast thou forgot thy care?
Why mourn I thus beneath the stroke
Of foes, who drive me near despair?

X.

Their sharp reproaches pierce my heart
With daily anguish, while they say
(The thought is like a pointed dart,)
Where is thy God, thy boasted stay?

XI.

Why sinks my fainting spirit down?
Why do restless passions mourn?
What, though my God a moment frown,
His blissful smile will yet return.

XII.

Then shall I spread his power abroad,
His smile my drooping hope shall raise;
My light, my health, my Saviour God,
Shall tune my sighs to songs of praise.

PSALM XLVI

God is our strength, omnipotence our stay
Our refuge, present still when troubles rise.
Safe in his care, no fear hall reach our souls,
Though earth be from her firm foundations mov'd,
And mountains with tremendous shock are torn,
Deep from their ancient habits torn, and hurl'd
With dreadful dash, amidst the roaring waves;
Though the waves roar and boil with restless rage,
And threat with hideous swell the trembling world.

   There is a river of immortal peace,
Clear springing from the high eternal throne,
Which flows in blissful streams through all the groves
Of paradise, --- from eternal spring
Some rivulets descend, to cheer
The city of our God, the sacred place
Of his abode on earth; though all around
Be discord and commotion, she shall dwell
Unmov'd, serene, and safe, for God is there:
His arm omnipotent is ever near
Her present help, her all-sufficient guard.

   The heathen rag'd with war, the empires shook,
And all was uproar, noise and wild confusion!
His awful voice was heard, and all was hush'd,
And earth dissolv'd in silence!
The Lord of hosts is with us; Israel's God
Is our defence, our everlasting refuge.
The Lord! Behold the wonders of his hand!
The mourning nations, desolate and waste,
Confess the power of his tremendous frown.
Through the wide earth he bids stern war to cease,

The earth obeys, and war is heard no more.
With one light touch he breaks the useless bow,
Shivers the spear, and burns the warlike chariot.
He speaks! --- the world in deep attention held,
Awaits sacred sounds! "Be still and know
"That I am God, among the heathen tribes
"I will be honor'd; through the spacious earth
"My name shall be exalted and ador'd!"
   The Lord of hosts is with us; Israel's God
Is our defense, our everlasting refuge.

PSALM XLVII

Ye happy tribes, proclaim your sacred joys;
   Let shouts of triumph to the heavens ascend!
The Lord most high with awful power presides,
And rules the earth with universal sway!
Subdu'd by him, her haughty foes shall sink,
And conquered nations bend beneath our feet.
He shall select our blest inheritance;
The favor'd sons of Jacob shall enjoy
The same Almighty love their father shar'd.

   Hark the glad shout! Our God to conquest leads,
And warlike sounds proclaim his glorious name!
Join every voice and hymns of joyful praise;
Our God, our King demands the sacred song;
Repeat his praises in immortal strains.
For God is King supreme, o'er all the earth
With uncontested power his scepter rules
And while his praise employs the tuneful voice,
That all your hearts adore the name you sing.

Sole monarch of the world, Jehovah reigns!
The heathen empires trembling own his power,
And holiness around his awful throne.
Assembling princes lead the praiseful throng,
To Abraham's God with grateful homage pay,
And leave their votive shields beneath his feet.
Great is the Lord! His high exalted name
Forever with unrivaled glory shines!

PSALM LI

I.

Lord, let thy mercy, full and free,
Vile as I am, extend to me;
And bid my numerous crimes remove,
All Cancell'd by thy sovereign love.

II.

O wash this guilty heart of mine,
For cleansing grace is only thine;
I own my sins, and still they rise
With recent horror to my eyes.

III.

Against the God I love and fear,
My aggravated crimes appear;
"Tis this alone awakes my smart,
And fills with grief my fainting heart.

IV.

While humbly prostrate in the dust,
I own thy awful sentence just;
My soul adores thy sacred word,
Forever righteous is the Lord.

V.

Soon as my infant life began.
And nature fram'd the future man,
So soon did sin its taint impart,
The dire contagion seiz'd my heart.

VI.

Since inward truth thy laws require,
That inward truth, O Lord, inspire;
Through all my soul let wisdom shine,
And give me purity divine.

VII.

O let the sacred hyssop prove,
Blest emblem of thy cleansing love;
Thy sovereign mercy can bestow,
A heart more pure than falling snow.

VIII.

Let thy reviving word impart
Peace, joy and pardon, to my heart;
Then shall this broken frame rejoice,
And bless thy kind, thy healing voice.

IX.

Let all my sins, (though deep their dye,)
Forever in oblivion lie;
Forever blot the dreadful score,
And view the long account no more.

X.

Create my inmost powers anew,
Make all my heart sincere and true;
O cast me not in wrath away,
Nor hide thy soul-enlivening ray.

XI.

Restore thy favor, bliss divine!
Those heavenly joys that once were mine;
Let thy own spirit kind and free,
Uphold and guide my steps to thee.

XII.

Then will I teach thy sacred ways,
With Holy zeal proclaim thy praise;
Till sinners leave the dangerous road,
Forsake their sins and turn to God.

XIII.

O cleanse my guilt, and heal my pain,
Remove the blood polluted stain;
Then shall my heart adoring trace,
My Saviour God, thy boundless grace.

XIV.

Then shall my joyful tongue proclaim
In grateful strains, thy glorious name;
Inspir'd by thee, my song shall flow,
And all thy wondrous mercy show.

XV.

If sacrifice would please my God,
My offerings should thy altars load;
But vain were all my offr'd store
For blazing altars please no more.

XVI.

This is the gift I would impart,
A humble, broken, contrite heart;
A broken heart, repentant sighs,
O God, thou never wilt despise.

XVII.

O let thy goodness, Lord, appear,
To Zion, once thy chosen care;
Sustain'd and built by power divine,
Let Salem's walls distinguish'd shine.

XVIII.

To thee, the pious sacrifice
Accepted then shall daily rise;
Again the grateful offerings flame,
And glad devotion bless thy name.

PSALM LXV

I.

Before thy throne, O God of grace,
Thy soul would her vows perform;
Her ardent vows in deep distress –
O be her grateful praise as warm

II.

O thou hear'st our humble cry,
Our God, our refuge and our stay;
To thee, shall mourning sinners fly,
To thee, shall every nation pray.

III.

Though sin prevails with dreadful swy,
And hope almost expiring lies,
Thy grace shall purge our sins away,
And bid our dying hopes arise.

IV.

Happy the man approv'd by thee,
Near to his God, thy chosen care;
Thy constant goodness he shall see,
The bounties of thy table share.

V.

Whene'er thy injur'd people's cries
Ascend before thy awful throne,
All dreadful bright thy terrors rise,
And make thy grace and justice known.

VI.

Thou art the confidence and stay
Of the wide earth's remotest ends;
And those who try the dangerous sea,
On thee their hope, their all depends.

VII.

Thy awful word with potent sound
Firm bade the solid mountains stand;
Thy power encircles nature round;
All nature rests upon thy hand.

VIII.

That word which stills the raging seas,
When loud waves tempestuous roar
Commands the warring world to peace;
And noise and tumult are no more.

IX.

Thy dreadful signs display'd abroad,
Fill trembling nations with surprise;
The trembling nations own the God,
And lift their supplicating eyes.

X.

The rising morn, the closing day,
Repeat thy praise with grateful voice;
Each in their turns thy power display,
And laden with thy gifts rejoice.

XI.

Earth's wide-extended varying scenes,
All smiling round thy bounty show;
From seas or clouds, full magazines,
Thy rich dissuasive blessings flow.

XII.

Now earth receives the precious feed,
Which thy indulgent hand prepares!
And nourishes the future bread,
And answers all the sower's cares.

XIII.

Thy sweet refreshing showers attend,
And through the ridges gently flow,
Soft on the springing corn descend;
And thy kind blessing makes it grow.

XIV.

Thy good ness crowns the circling year,
Thy paths drop fatness all around;
Ev'n barren wilds thy praise declare,
And echoing hills return the sound.

XV.

Here spreading flocks adorn the plain,
There plenty every charm displays;
Thy bounty cloaths each lovely scene,
And joyful nature shouts thy praise.

PSALM LXXVII

I.

To God, I rais'd my earnest cries,
  To God, who rules the earth and skies;
His sovereign mercy deign'd to hear
My loud complaints with pitying ear.

II.

The tedious day was spent in grief,
In humble prayer I sought relief;
But day and night the restless smart
Deny'd sweet comfort to my heart.

ANNE STEELE

III.

I thought on God with terrors arm'd;
New troubles then my soul alarm'd!
Then over whelming sorrows rose,
Nor could complaining ease my woes.

IV.

Thy terrors, Lord, forbid my rest,
And silent anguish fills my breast;
And now in sad reflection rise
Past days and years before my eyes.

V.

My nightly songs I call to mind,
And try some gleam of joy to find;
But search this wretched heart in vain,
For all is darkness, grief and pain.

VI.

Will God forever leave his care?
Must I no more his favor share?
Shall long lost mercy ne'er prevail?
And can his word forever fail?

VII.

Array'd in frowns his angry face,
Has God forgot his wonted grace?
And clos'd the full, the boundless store
Of mercy, ne'er to open more?

VIII.

But I rebuke my drooping heart,
Far hence ye guilty fears depart:
Still will I call past comforts o'er,
And trust almighty love and power.

IX

This drooping heart again hall trace
The ancient wonders of thy grace;
The mighty works my God has wrought,
Shall employ my voice, my thought.

X.

Thy way, O God, thy wondrous way,
While in thy temple I survey,
Struck with astonishment, I cry,
Where is a power so great, so high?

XI.

Whoe'er surveys thy works must own
That thou art God, and thou alone;
Thy favors to thy chosen care
The wonders of thy power declare.

XII.

Thy potent arm, forever near,
Control'd their foes, control'd their fear;
And Jacob's sons, (distinnguish'd race!)
Confess'd thy kind delivering grace.

XIII.

The full clouds pour'd their watery store;
Amid the storms impetuous roar,
Thy dreadful arrows flew abroad,
And sounding skies proclaim'd the God!

XV.

Thy awful voice in thunder broke,
Heacen listen'd while the Almighty spoke;
While o'er the world keen lightenings spread,
Earth trembled with unusual dread!

415

XVI.

Thy path, O Lord, thy tractless way
Lies in the deep unfathom'd sea;
No mortal thought can ever trace
Thy steps of wisdom, power and grace.

XVII.

Thy people found thy guardian care;
Where'er thy wander'd, God was there;
Till guided by thy prophet's hand,
They reach'd secure the promis'd land.

PSALM LXXXIV

I.

How lovely, how divinely sweet,
O Lord, thy sacred courts appear!
Fain would my longing passions meet
The glories of thy presence there.

II.

With strong desire my spirit faints,
I languish for thy blest abode;
This throbbing heart, oh, how it pants!
And all my powers cry out for God.

III.

The sparrows near thy altar live,
And swallows there a nest obtain;
My God, my King, and wilt thou give
To birds, what I desire in vain?

IV.

Oh, blest the men, blest their employ,
Whom thy indulgent favors raise
To dwell in these abodes of joy,
And sing thy never-ceasing praise.

V.

Happy the men, whom strength divine
With ardent love and zeal inspires!
Whose steps to thy blest way incline,
With willing hearts and warm desires.

VI.

Through Baca's thirsty vale they go;
But God commands, and springs arise,
And flowers descend with copious flow,
To yield the pilgrim full supplies.

VII.

Still thy pursue the painful road,
Increasing strength surmounts their fear;
Till all at length before their God,
In Zion's glorious courts appear.

VIII.

O Lord of hosts, attend my prayer,
Our father's God thy ear incline;
Shield of our livs, reveal thy care,
And on thy own anointed shine.

IX.

One day within thy sacred gate,
Affords more real joy to me,
Than thousands in the tents of state;
The meanest place is bliss with thee.

X.

God is a sun; our brightest day
From his reviving presence flows;
God is a shield, through all the way,
To guard us from surrounding foes.

XI.

He pours his kindest blessings down,
Profusely down on souls sincere:
And grace shall guide, and glory crown
The happy favorites of his care.

XII.

O Lord of hosts, thou God of grace,
How blest, divinely blest is he,
Who trusts thy love and seeks thy face,
And fixes all his hopes on thee!

PSALM LXXXVIII

I.

O Lord, my life, My Saviour God,
  Hear, while I spread my woes abroad;
While day and night my mournful cries
Before thy throne incessant rise

II.

Let thy indulgent pitying ear
Incline to my distressful prayer;
With sorrow my full heart o'erflows,
And o'er me soon the grave will close.

III.

My strength is lost, my life resign'd,
Among the dead my place assign'd;
Cut from life, from hope and thee,
Scarce are the slain more lost than me.

IV.

Low in the grave my hopes are laid,
And darkness spreads its deepest shade;
Thy dreadful wrath afflicts my soul,
Like whelming waves thy terrors roll.

V.

Far from these wretched eyes remov'd,
Are all the friends whom once I lov'd;
They fly my sorrows, while I moan,
Confin'd, unpity'd, and alone.

VI.

In vain to ease my hopeless woe,
The streaming tears incessant flow;
To thee, O Lord, I breathe my cries,
And stretch my hands and lift my eyes.

VII.

Wilt thou from dust thy wonders raise?
And shall the dead awake to praise?
Thy kindness shall the grave record?
Or life destroy'd adore thy word?

VIII.

Where ne'er one cheering ray of light
Breaks through the deep, the solid night,
Shall thy almighty power be known?
Thy truth, shall dark oblivion own?

IX.

Yet still to thee my cries ascend;
My earnest cries, O Lord, attend;
My nightly groans, my morning prayer,
Shall seek the still with restless care.

X.

Why, Lord, wilt thou reject my soul?
Thy smile can all my cares control;
Why wilt thou hide thy blissful face,
While I in vain implore thy grace?

XI.

Afflict'd long have I complain'd,
And long a dying life sustain'd;
Expressless pain thy frowns impart,
Distracting horrors wound my heart.

XII.

Thy fierce displeasure who can bear?
'Tis death array'd in black despair;
Like swelling floods thy terrors rise,
O'erwhelm my heart, and comfort dies.

420

XIII.

My dearest friends who shar'd my heart,
Far from those mournful scenes depart;
While o'er my solitary head
Dark shades and dismal silence spread.

PSALM XC

I.

Lord, thou hast been thy children's God,
All-powerful, wise, and good, and just,
In every age their safe abode,
Their hope, their refuge, and their trust.

II.

Before thy word gave nature birth,
Or spread the starry heavens abroad,
Or form'd the varied face of earth,
From everlasting thou art God.

III.

Destruction waits thy awful word,
While mortal hope expiring mourns;
Obedient nature owns her Lord,
And dying man to dust returns.

IV.

Great Father of eternity,
How short are the ages in thy sight!
A thousand years, how swift they fly,
Like one short, silent watch of night!

V.

Thy anger, like a swelling flood.
Comes o'er the world with dreadful sway;
The tempest speaks the offended God,
And sweeps the guilty race away.

VI.

Uncertain life, how soon it flies!
Dream of an hour, how short our bloom
Like spring's gay verdure now we rise,
Cut down ere night to fill the tomb.

VII.

Consum'd by thy vindictive frown,
Our blessings and our lives decay;
Our spirits sink despairing down,
And every comfort dies away.

VIII.

Full in thy view our crimes appear,
Thy eye beholds each secret fault,
And marks, in holiness severe,
The sins of every inmost thought.

IX.

Our days, alas, how short their bound!
Though slow and sad they seem to run,
Revolving years roll swiftly round,
A mournful tale, but quickly done.

X.

Perhaps to threescore years and ten
Protracted; or if longer still,
Ah, what can more, but lengthened pain,
The last sad tedious period fill?

XI.

What mortal thought can comprehend
The awful glories of thy throne?
Not all the terrors fear can lend,
Can make thy dreadful vengeance known.

XII.

Teach us to count our shortening days,
And with true diligence apply
Our hearts to wisdom's sacred ways,
That we may learn to live and die.

XIII.

O may thy favor, Lord, return,
Nor thy bright presence long delay;
Nor let thy servants vainly mourn,
And weep their wretched lives away.

XIV.

Soon let thy mercy cheer our hearts,
And tune our grateful songs of praise;
And let the joy thy smile imparts,
Enliven all our future days.

XV.

O make our sacred pleasures rise,
In sweet proportion to our pains,
Till ev'n the sad remembrance dies,
Nor one uneasy thought complains.

XVI.

Let thy almighty work appear.
With power and evidence divine;
And may the bliss thy servants share,
Continued to their children shine.

XVII.

Thy glorious image fair imprest,
Let all our hearts and lives declare;
Beneath thy kind protection blest,
May all our labours own thy care.

PSALM XCIII

I.

The Lord, the God of glory, reigns,
In robes of majesty array'd;
His rule omnipotence sustains,
And guides the worlds his hands have made.

II.

Ere rolling worlds began to move,
Or ere the heavens were stretch'd abroard,
Thy awful throne was fix'd above;
From everlasting thou art God.

III.

The swelling floods tumultuous rise,
Aloud the angry tempest roar,
Lift their proud billows to the skies,
And foam and lash the trembling shore.

IV.

The Lord, the mighty God, on high,
Controls the fiercely raging seas;
He speaks! And noise and tempest fly,
The waves sink down in gentle peace.

V.

Thy sovereign laws are ever sure,
Eternal holiness is thine;
And, Lord, thy people should be pure,
And in thy blest resemblance shine.

PSALM XCVII

The Lord, the mighty God exalted reigns;
Rejoice, O earth, ye numerous isles adore!
Around his seat are clouds and darkness spread,
Too strong its splendors for created eyes.
His throne, on holiness and justice fix'd,
Eternal stands! Before his awful face
Bright, yet devouring flames, tremendous blaze,
And with resistless fury blast his foes!
His lightenings flash'd bright horrors o'er the world;
Earth saw and trembled to her inmost center!
While conscious of their Maker's awful presence,
The solid hills like wax dissolv'd away,
And all creation own'd the present God!
The heavens in shining characters display
The wonders of his power, and bid the world
Behold them and adore their mighty former.
Confusion waits on those who blindly serve
The gods their hands have made; deluded mortals!
How weak their idols, and how vain their boast!
Let all the highest names, in earth and heaven,

With reverence bow before the Lord alone.
Zion with rapture all the wonders heard,
And Judah's daughters triumph'd in his name
His righteous judgments are his people's joy.
Thou, Lord, art high exalted o'er the earth.
Far above all the shining thrones of heaven.
      Ye favorites of the Lord, who love his name,
O fly, abhorrent fly, from every sin:
So shall your souls by his almighty care
Be still preserv'd, and sav'd from all your foes.
Bright scenes of happiness await the righteous;
And springing joys in future prospect rise,
To crown the upright soul with endless bliss.
Rejoice in God, ye saints, and grateful raise
Your hearts, your tongues, in praises to his name,
His holy name, your everlasting joy.

PSALM CII

I.

Lord, hear thy servant's humble prayer,
  And let my mournful cry
Ascend, and reach thy gracious ear,
  And move thy pitying eye.

II.

O do not hide thy blissful face,
  When fears and sorrows rise;
But hear, and let thy sovereign grace
  Return with quick supplies.

III.

My days like smoke consume away,
  And this poor dying frame
Sinks down to ruin and decay,
  Scorch'd with affliction's flame.

IV.

My spirit fails, my hopes decline,
  Like withering grass thy fade;
And while beneath thy stroke I pine,
  How tasteless is my bread!

V.

My strength, with oft-repeated groans,
  Is wasting fast away,
And leaves this skin, these feeble bones,
  To wrinkles and decay.

VI.

Like a poor solitary fowl
  Which in the desert roves,
Or like the melancholy owl
  That nightly haunts the groves;

VII.

I spend the watchful night alone,
Slow moves the tiresome shade,
While like the plaintive bird, I moan,
All desolate and sad.

VIII.

While all the day my cruel foes
   In sharp reproaches join,
And more to aggravate my woes,
   Against my life combine.

IX.

My taste no food with comfort cheers,
   'Tis ashes mix'd with woe;
And mingling with my drink, my tears
   In briny torrents flow.

X.

What comfort e'er can cheer my taste,
   Beneath thy angry frown?
Rais'd by thy smile, I once was blest,
   But thou hast cast me down.

XI.

I sink with hope's departing ray,
   And life expiring fails;
So faint shadow dies away,
   When gloomy night prevails.

XII.

But thou, O Lord, shalt still endure,
   Thy truth shall ne'er decay;
Thy love unalterably sure,
   While ages roll away.

XIII.

In Zion's cause thou wilt arise,
Thy mercy dawns around;
The time is come, her sorrow flies,
And all her hopes are crown'd.

XIV.

That Zion, which thy servants love;
  Each heart her memory wears;
Their passions o'er her ruins move,
  In sadly pleasing tears.

XV.

So shall the heathen nations fear
  The Lord's exalted name:
Earth's haughty monarchs low revere
  Thy majesty supreme.

XVI.

When Zion's God, with power array'd,
  Shall build her frame anew,
Then shall his glory be display'd
  To our admiring view.

XVII.

O let the humble destitute
  Ne'er sink in sad despair;
The Lord will hear their mournful suit,
  And answer all their prayer.

XVIII.

His truth, his mercy, and his power
  Shall fill the blest record;
And future ages shall adore
  And love and praise the Lord.

XIX.

From heaven, his high eternal throne,
   (O condescending grace!)
The almighty looks with pity down
   On earth's low worthless race.

XX.

He sees the groaning prisoner's pain;
   And brings a kind reprieve;
His hand shall loose the fatal chain,
   And bid the victim live:

XXI.

Live to declare his glorious name,
   And spread his praise abroad,
And in his sacred courts proclaim
   The mercy of his God.

XXII.

Assembled there his saints attend,
   And songs of praise repeat;
And there united nations bend,
   And worship at his feet.

XXIII.

In life's mid-way my strength declin'd,
   But 'twas my Father's hand;
My shortening days flew swift as wind,
   At his supreme command.

XXIV.

I said, to thee my God I pray,
   Whose years forever last;
O take me not so soon away,
   Ere half my days are past,

XXV.

Earth's foundations thou hast laid;
    The heavens, (a glorious frame!)
By thy almighty hand were spread,
    And speak their Maker's name.

XXVI.

Their shining wonders all shall fade;
    By thy controling power,
Chang'd like a vesture quite decay'd;
    But thou shalt still endure.

XXVII.

Thy bright perfections, all divine,
    Eternal as thy days,
Through everlasting ages shine,
    With undiminish'd rays.

XXVIII.

Thy servant's children still thy care,
    Shall own their father's God;
To latest times thy favor share,
    And spread thy praise abroad.

PSALM CIII

I.

Awake my soul, awake my tongue,
My God demands the grateful song,
Let all my inmost powers record
The wondrous mercy of the Lord.

II.

Divinely free, his mercy flows,
Forgives my crimes, allays my woes,
And bids approaching death remove,
And crowns me with indulgent love.

III.

He fills my longing soul with good,
Substantial bliss! Immortal food!
Youth smiles renew'd in active prime,
And triumphs o'er the power of time.

IV.

In him the poor opprest shall find
A friend almighty, just and kind;
His glorious acts, his wondrous ways,
By Moses taught, proclaim his praise.

V.

How free his plenteous mercies flow!
But his reluctant wrath how slow!
He chides, but soon his smile returns,
Nor long his dreadful anger burns.

VI.

How far beyond our vile defects,
Is every gift his hand imparts!
High as the bright expanded skies,
His vast unbounded mercies rise.

VII.

As distant as creating power
Has fix'd the east and western shore;
So far our numerous crimes remove,
At the sweet voice of pardoning love.

VIII.

The tenderest yearning nature knows,
A father's love too faintly shows
The ever-kind indulgent care
Which God's own happy children share.

IX.

He knows our fram, surveys our birth,
Compos'd of dust, frails sons of earth;
Man like a fair, but short-liv'd flower,
Springs up and blooms one smiling hour.

X.

But if a noxious blast arise,
Sudden its transient glory flies;
Those charms which made the scene so gay,
Steal from the sight and die away.

XI.

But mercy with unchanging rays
Forever shines, while time decays;
And children's children shall record
The truth and goodness of the Lord.

XII.

To those, who with delightful awe,
Love and obey his sacred law,
Whose hearts with warm devotion glow,
Whose lives their grateful duty show.

XIII.

The Lord is King, his hand alone
Has fix'd in heaven, his radiant throne;
He sends his sovereign laws abroad,
And heaven and earth confess the God.

XIV.

Immortal form'd by power divine,
Attending angels round him shine,
Observant wait his sacred will,
And his commands with joy fulfill.

XV.

Ye heavenly hosts adore the Lord,
Who form'd you to obey his word;
Let everlasting praises rise
Through the bright armies of the skies.

XVI.

While all his works his praise proclaim,
And men and angels bless his name;
O let my heart, my life, my tongue,
Attend and join the blissful song.

PSALM CIV

Awake my soul, but to the hallowed lyre
to thy Creator's name; while all my powers
Low at his feet present their prostrate homage,
and deepest reverence mingles with the praise.
Thou, O Jehovah, art the King supreme,
In robes of awful majesty array'd;
In robes of light, which dazzle angel eyes,
And shade the glories from their fainting view:
While far beneath thy feet, a wide expanse,
A radiant curtain of celestial blue,
Adorn'd with stars and suns, by hand has spread:
that potent hand which in the water restores
Of heaven, hath firmly laid with wondrous skill,
The stable beams of God's imperial seat.
Clouds form his chariot, the impetuous wind,
Rein'd in its full career, obeys his word;
And on its rapid wing he walks serene.
His angels formed of pure ethereal flame,
All spirit, zeal, activity and fire,
Bright ministers fulfill his high command
With swift obedience and unceasing ardour.
  Earth's old foundations by his word were fixed
Immovable, till the almighty word
Commands, and time in nature are no more.
Thy forming word, O God of nature, spread,
Wide o'er the surface of the infant world,
The fluid wave, an universal robe;
And o'er the mountain tops the waters rose.
At thy rebuke they fled, thy awful voice
In thunder spoke, and swift they roll'd away;
Nor hills obstruct their course, nor vales confine.
Obedient to thy word they seek the place

435

Thy hand has form'd, their copious reservoir;
Nor dare presume to rise beyond the bounds
Their Maker set, nor cover earth again.
He sends refreshing springs to bless the vales;
In silver streams among the hills they rove,
Adorn the scene, and share a thousand lives.
Here flocks and herds partake the cooling draught;
And here wild beast their raging thirst allay.
Hither feather'd tribes of various wing
Resort, and on the trees near waving build
Their airy nests, and tune their cheerful songs,
Amid the verdure of leafy shade,
To the soft cadence of the willing rill

By their Creator's hand the thirsty hills,
Are watered from the deep; whose stores in clouds
Exhal'd and shed in softening showers, the earth
Teems with rich fruit the product of his bounty.
For cattle here appears the springing grass,
And there for man the helpful herbage grows;
Earth yields her plenteous stores of food for all.
Here the rich vintage flows and purple streams,
To glad the heart; and there the olive drops
Its shining fatness for the use of man.
Full harvests in extended prospect rise,
Of strength-restoring, life-sustaining bread.
The trees, supplied with sap, confess his care,
And Lebanon's tall cedars own their Lord.
On the tall cedar, and the spiry fir,
The birds erect their nest, and dwell secure.
Accessless hills and craggy rocks afford
To creatures of the weak and timorous kind,
(Whom nature has not arm'd,) a safe retreat.
The changing moon obeys her Maker's word,

As with full orb or waning light she leads
The seasons on, alternate with the sun;
Who knows his task, pursues his radiant course,
And sets obedient at the appointed hour.
Then night ordain'd by thee, kind Lord of all,
Her friendly veil extends; the beast of prey
In search of food, their gloomy coverts leave,
And roaring lions ask their meat from God.
All night they roam, till at the sun's approach
Assembling, they retire and seek their dens.
Then man in safety rises, and pursues
His daily work, protected by thy care,
And labours cheerful till the close of day.

   Lord, how astonishing how vast thy works,
Creation speaks! And providence confirms!
In all the numerous wonders of thy hand,
Infinite power and wisdom shine confest.
Great source of good, from thy all-bounteous hand
The earth is filled with riches, and the sea
Through all her vast dominions, spreads abroad
Thy large munificence; there myriads live
Dependent on the hand; there ships pursue
Amid the countless perils of the deep.
Leviathan, proud tyrant of the main,
Rejoices in thy care, and sportive rolls
His bulk enormous through the troubled wave.
All wait on thee, through the earth and air and seas;
From thee, great Father of the universe,
Thy family expectant ask their food.
With open hand thy sovereign bounty gives,
And all receive a full supply from thee.
Thy care withheld, they droop; the breath of life,
Receiv'd from thee, then animates no more;

They die and mingle with their native dust.
Again thy all-creating spirit breathes,
And creatures live and people earth anew

  Jehovah's boundless glory shall endure,
And shine unchanging through eternal years.
His eye complacent views his numerous works;
For all is fair, and good, and just, and wise.

  When his almighty power appears alone,
Nor mercy softens his tremendous rays;
Earth trembles at his awful glance, the hills
Smoke at his touch, and nature shrinks away.

  To him, all glorious Lord, my song is due;
The praises of my God, shall be my theme;
While he prolongs my life, (that life is his!)
Still let me meditate his wondrous works,
And tracing them, his infinite perfections.
Divine employ, when I can humbly hope
He is my God, and gladness fills my heart!
While sinners, who nor fear, nor love his name,
Consume away, and all their hopes are lost.
Bless thou the Lord, my soul; with sacred awe,
Yet mingled with delight, adore and praise.
Ye saints, who know the wonders of his hand,
Assist the grateful song, and praise the Lord.

PSALM CV

Ye grateful tribes, approach Jehovah's throne,
  Adoring low; his sacred name invoke
To aid song, and spread his praise abroad,
In strains of joy recount his glorious deeds,
And talk with rapture of his wondrous works.
With transport glory in his holy name,
With triumph own his privilege divine,
Near to approach, and worship at his feet.
O seek the Lord, implore his potent aid,
Forever with unwearied ardour seek
The favor of your God, your bliss, your all.
Recall his miracles of power and grace,
The wonders his Almighty arm has wrought,
The sacred truth of his unchanging word.
Ye children of his favorite servant, come,
Ye sons of Jacob, own your father's God,
And speak his wondrous grace fulfill'd to you.
Yes, we assert with joy the glorious claim,
for Jacob's God is ours; his sovereign power
O'er all the world his righteous acts declare.
But his eternal faithfulness and love,
In his own covenant shall forever shine
Inviolate, while ages roll away.
His gracious covenant first with Abraham made,
His sacred, solemn oath, to Isaac given,
Confirm'd to Jacob and eternal law,
Fixed and immovable shall ever stand.
He spoke! "To thee my sovereign hand shall give,
"And to thy race, the sure inheritance,
"And Canaan's fruitful country shall be yours."

While yet their numbers and their strength were small,

A few poor wandering strangers, weak and low.
From land to land, obedient to their God,
Removing still; his kind protecting arm
Preserved from wrongs, the favorites of his care;
And kings, reprov'd, rever'd the awful word,
which said, "Untouch'd by my anointed sons,
"In peace, uninjur'd, let my prophets live."

   Obedient to his word, pale famine came;
The pining nations felt her meager frown,
And sinking life its broken staff deplor'd,
Then his peculiar people to preserve,
And led their steps were cheering plenty smiled,
Was Joseph sent, the messenger of heaven;
Though sold a slave, by his perfidious friends,
Though in a prisons gloomy cell confin'd,
With fetters loaded, and forever still,
With infamy, more cruel that his chains.
Mysterious providence! That try'd his soul
With deep adversity, and thus prepar'd
For future honors his unshaken mind.
The word of God with awful evidence
Appeared, to try his injur'd servants cause,
And prov'd his innocence, and clear'd his fame.
By Egypt's monarch freed, the royal smile
Gave, with the cheerful sweets of liberty,
The envy'd honors of unbounded power:
Lord of his house, and ruler of his stores!
Attendant princes waited on his eye
to read their fate, and listening sentence learn'd
Superior wisdom from his charming tongue.

   To share the pleasures of his happy state,
Now Jacob and his sons rejoicing came;

to them 'er richest pastures Egypt gave;
In Goshen's fair sequester'd vale retir'd,
They unmolested fed their fleecy care.
Favor'd by providence, the people grew
To great increase; their haughty masters saw
Their envied strength superior to their own.
The sovereign power who rules the thoughts of men,
Permitted deadly hate to fill the hearts
Of Egypt's sons, protectors now no more
But jealous enemies and cruel lords.

   Then Moses by divine command was sent,
And Aaron, chosen messengers of God.
Surprising signs their embassy confirm'd,
And dreadful wonders spoke the hand of heaven.
Ham's wretched sons in gloomy darkness mourn'd;
Substantial night around their dwellings spread,
And struck resistless terror to their hearts.
Where healthful waters roll'd their crystal waves,
Now streams of blood (dire prodigy!) appear'd
And gasping fishes on the banks expir'd,
And spread contagion around the frightened shores.

   Then croaking frogs spontaneous rose to life,
A numerous host, infesting every place;
Nor could the humble cot, or stately palace
Exclude the hateful guest! --- The potent word
Again was uttered; and the coast were spread
with noxious vermin; insects now appall'd
The pride of Egypt, and her haughty Lord.
But heaven had greater vengeance yet in store;
Of hail, in flaming fire, and over the land
Wide- wasting death and desolation spread.
Scorched with ethereal flames, no more the vine

441

Her purple cluster boasts; no more the fig
Crowns the luxuriant feast with luscious sweets;
Nor lofty trees, the glory of the plains,
Resist the furious tempest; now they spread
In shatter'd fragments o'er the scene of ruin.

   Again the Almighty gave the dreadful word,
And countless armies of invaders came,
Insatiate locusts, blackening all the plains,
Devouring all the greedy flames had spar'd,
Of herbs, or fruits, or grain; and through the land
Fell devastation triumph'd uncontrol'd.

   At length, to fill the measure of their woes,
The last, the dreadful stroke of heaven descends.
One fatal night the pride of Egypt fell;
The eldest born from Pharaoh's royal house,
Down to the meanest cottage: shrieks of horror
Burst through the midnight silence; and the parent
Was rous'd from his short repose to wild distraction.
   Then crowned with honors and enriched with spoils,
The God of Israel brought his people forth.
Fresh looming health spread through the vigorous tribes,
And welcome liberty exulting smil'd.
While, trembling at her heaven-protected guest,
Pale Egypt felt a gleam of joy revive,
Soon as she saw them from her coasts retire.
In safety Israel journeyed; for their God,
Their guardian, and their God, was ever near.
A wondrous cloud by day proclaim'd his presence,
At once their kind direction and defense.
By night of flaming pillar, beaming far
With heavenly splendor, cheer'd the fabled shades;
and darkness and her gloomy terrors fled.

His bounteous hand was open to their wants;
They ask'd, and all their wishes were supply'd.
He gave them bread from heaven, delicious manna!
And fowls on ready wing commission'd came
to spread their table with a plenteous feast.
They thirsted, and the flinty rock obey'd
Heaven's high command; while from the opening cleft
Pour'd forth a wondrous stream, the desert smil'd,
And rivers flowed amid the sandy waste.

   Thus ever mindful of his sacred word,
The God of truth, his gracious promise (made
Long sense to faithful Abraham,) now accomplish'd
with a wondrous goodness to his happy race.
Thus his almighty arm conducted safe
His chosen tribes to liberty and joy.
To them the forfeit heathen lands he gave,
A fair inheritance! and plenty filled
Their ample stores, unknown, and unacquir'd.
On them, the toil of strangers heaven bestow'd,
that they his favor'd people, might observe

His righteous laws, and grateful on their hearts
Forever keep his precepts deep impress'd,
And own his favors with obedient love.
Oh! Let your hearts and lives adore the Lord,
and ever joyful tongue resound his praise.

ANNE STEELE

PSALM CXVI

I.

I love the Lord, his gracious ear
Inclined to my distressed prayer;
He heard my supplicating voice,
And bade my fainting heart rejoice.

II.

For this, when future sorrows rise,
To him I'll breathe my humble cries,
For this, through all my future days,
Adore his name and sing his praise.

III.

Death spread around his fatal chains,
To drag me to infernal pains;
I felt the agonizing dart,
and horror seiz'd my trembling heart.

IV.

'Twas then in my extreme distress,
I call'd upon the God of grace,
Whose power can death and hell control;
Lord, I beseech thee, save my soul.

V.

Forever gracious is the Lord,
Forever faithful to his word;
By sweet experience now I prove,
His mercy, his unchanging love.

VI.

The Lord preserves, with tender care,
The weak, the humble, and sincere;
Low in the dust my hopes were laid,
But God appear'd with timely aid.

VII.

Return my soul, and sweetly rest
On thy Almighty Father's breast;
The bounties of his grace adore,
And count his wondrous mercies o'er.

VIII.

Thy mercy, Lord, preserv'd my breath,
And snatched my fainting soul from death,
Remov'd my sorrows, dry'd my tears,
And save' me from surrounding snares.

IX.

now will I walk before the Lord,
A living witness to his word;
With faith and prayer I sought his face,
My griefs were great, and great his grace.

X.

No meaner help, no mortal art,
Could ease the anguish of my heart;
My hasty tongue, and rash replies,
Pronounc'd the words of men but lies.

XI.

What shall I render to the Lord?
Or how his wondrous grace record:
To him my grateful voice all raise,
And pour libations to his praise.

XII.

His crowded court shall see me pay
the vows of my distressful day;
In life and death the saints shall find
Their guardian God forever kind.

XIII.

Thy servant, Lord, is wholly thine,
By nature's ties, and bonds divine;
From deep distress and sorrow free,
Anew I give myself to thee.

XIV.

To thee, with sacrifice of praise,
My invocations I will raise;
To thee my vows shall warm ascend,
While crowds the solemn rights attend.

XV.

O Salem, in thy sacred courts,
Where glory dwells in joy resorts,
To notes divine I'll tune the song,
And praise shall flow from every tongue.

PSALM CXXX

I.

From the dark borders of despair
  To thee, my God, I cry;
O wilt thou pitying hear my prayer,
  And every plaintive sigh?

II.

Lord, who shall stand before thy face,
  If thou shouldst mark our faults
With eye severe? what hope of grace
  Could cheer my mournful thoughts?

III.

But sovereign mercy dwells with thee,
  Hope dawns amid my fears;
Divine forgiveness, large and free,
  Shall stay my flowing tears.

IV.

On God alone my soul would wait,
  His sacred word my stay;
His sacred word can light create,
  And turn my night today.

V.

And those who wait with longing eyes
  To see the cheerful morn,
So shall my ardent wishes rise,
  Till thou my God, return.

VI.

Let fainting Israel on the Lord
  With cheerful hope recline,
For power and mercy in his word
  With boundless glory shine.

VII.

Unnumber'd though their sins appear,
   And filled their hearts with pain,
His saving love dispels their fear,
   And cleanses every stain.

PSALM CXXXIII

I.

How pleasing is the scene, how sweet!
   When kindred souls in friendship join;
Whose joys and cares united meet,
in bands of amity divine.

II.

Less fragrant was the ointment pour'd
On Aaron's consecrated head,
When balmy sweets profusely shower'd,
Down to his sacred vesture spread.

III.

Not flowery Hermon e'er display'd,
(Impearl'd with dew,) a fairer sight;
Nor Zion's beauteous hills, array'd
In golden beams of morning light.

IV.

'Tis here the Lord indulgent sheds
His kindest gifts, heavenly store;
With life immortal crowns their heads,
When earth's frail comforts please no more.

PSALM CXXXVII

I.

Where Babel's rivers winding stray,
   A silent, cool retreat we chose;
There lost in thoughtful sadness lay,
And pondering o'er our mighty woes.

II.

Our mighty woes increasing rise,
Revolving Zion's hapless fate;
And louder griefs, and streaming eyes,
Deplore her wretched, ruin'd state.

III.

No more could music soothes our cares
Our hearts neglected and unstrung,
(Vanish'd their once delightful airs,)
All silent, on the willows hung.

IV.

Our barbarous masters mock'd our pains,
While with insulting haughty tongues,
They bade us tune the charming strains,
And give them one of Zion's songs.

V.

Ah, no; shall Zion's sacred airs,
Inspir'd by heaven be thus profaned?
Be sung to please such ears as theirs,
Whose impious arms destroy'd our land?

VI.

Far from our dear lov'd native soil,
Shall we resume the pleasing lay?
Can rugged bondage wear a smile,
Or ever-wasting grief be gay?

VII.

If I forget thy ruin'd state,
Jerusalem, my heart's desire;
Then let my useless hand forget
Her skill to strike the founding lyre.

VIII.

If I indulge a mirthful song,
Or they dear name my memory leave;
All silent, let my faithless tongue
fast to my mouth forever cleave.

IX.

Jerusalem, lamented name!
Shall still my mournful voice employ!
And I the sadly pleasing theme
Prefer to every thought of joy.

X.

Remember, Lord, proud Edom's sons,
who cruel, urged the conquering foe,
To raze her beauteous towers at once,
And lay her lofty structures low.

XI.

Sad ruin, Babel, thou shalt share,
And sure reward awaits thy guilt;
Then shall my heart untaught to spare,
Repay the blood thy hand has spilt.

XII.

Happy the man who then shall rise,
(While heaven the righteous vengeance owns,)
And dash with unrelenting eyes,
Thy bleeding babes against the stones.

PSALM CXXXVIII

I.

To thee, my God, my heart shall bring
    the lively grateful song;
Attending kings shall hear me sing,
    with rapture on my tongue.

II.

Before thy throne with prostrate joy,
    I will adore thy name;
Thy praise shall be my best employ,
    Thy love and truth my theme.

III.

Amid the glories of thy name,
    Thy truth exalted shines!
A faithful God thy words proclaim
    In everlasting lines.

IV.

When in the day of deep distress,
    To thee, my God, I cry'd
With strength divine by powerful grace
    My fainting soul supply'd.

V.

The monarchs of the earth shall hear,
    And join my sacred lays;
Thy glorious name with joy revere,
    And sing thy wondrous praise.

VI.

The eternal God looks kindly down,
    And smiles on humble souls;
But from afar his piercing frown
    The sons of pride controls.

VII.

What though around my painful way
   Continual trouble grows;
Thy saving hand shall be my stay,
   And crush my wrathful foes.

VIII.

Thou, Lord, wilt all my hopes fulfill,
   To thee the work belongs;
Let endless mercy and guide me still,
   and tune my grateful songs.

PSALM CXXXIX

O Lord, thy awful searching eye has trac'd
   My heart through every secret winding fold,
And all its inmost powers to thee are known.
Thou see'st my rising in my resting hours,
And every latent thought within my breast
is paired to the; my path by the surrounded,
My bed encircled; God is ever near.
My steps are all before thee, not a word
Can steal in softest whisper from my tongue,
but thou can'st hear and mark its whole intent.
If I look back, thy awful steps I see;
before me, thou art there; thy potent hand
Restrains and guards, upholds and guides my feet.
Infinite knowledge! My astonish'd mind
Sinks down with awe, and wonders and adores.
Imagination droops her trembling wing,
nor vainly tempts the height and depth stupendons.
To shun thy spirit whither shall I fly?
Where shall I hide me from a present God?

Could I ascend to heaven, thy throne is there,
And thy full rays would meet my dazzled sight.
Or if to hell I forced my desperate way,
Thy dreadful presence there forever frowns.
If mounted on the morning's lightsome wings,
Swift to creation's utmost bounds I fly,
Thy hand alone sustains and guides my flight.
Shall I, to shun the terrors of thine eye,
In midnight's sable mantle wrap me round?
Vain thought! at one tremendous glance of thine,
The midnight shade shall blaze with sudden day.
From thee no darkness hides; at thy command,
Night's deepest gloom shall spread meridian beams;
And light and darkness are alike to thee.

E'er the first dawn of life this frame was thine,
Thy guardian power preserv'd me yet unborn.
My first formation,(work of skill divine!)
Demands my wonder, adoration, praise.
Stupendous are thy works! my conscious soul
With solemn dread, attest the awful power
Whose endless miracles through nature shine.
My substance, when my being first began,
Was thy attentive care; thy sovereign hand
Wrought with Almighty art the growing frame,
In just proportion fashion'd every limb,
(all drawn before unerring and thy book,)
'Till fair and perfect rose the human form.

But oh! How precious, how divinely sweet,
My God, to meditate thy thoughts of love!
Shall I attempt to state their mighty sum!
Impossible; for not the countless sands
Which spread the shore can equal half the number.

453

Whene'er I wake from sleep's inactive bands,
With pleasure I pursue the blest employ;
Still near my God, and wondering at his love.
Yet though thy mercies rise unknown, unnumber'd,
O God of glory, with resistless power
Eternal justice guards thy holy law:
So shall the wretches find, who dare thy sword.
To sure destruction, hence, ye guilty tribes,
Far hence, ye sons of cruelty, depart.
Against my God they speak with impious tongues,
Vile foes to thee, unconscious of thy fear,
and sport profanely with thy awful name.
Do I not view them with abhorrent eye?
Their fixed aversion to the righteous laws
Moves all the painful passions of my soul.
Am I not filled with grief when sinners rise
Rebellious, to dispute thy sacred will?
With perfect hatred I detest their ways,
and count thy enemies my worst of foes.

Search me, O God my inmost heart explore,
And try, O try the secret springs within me:
Should one perverse, rebellious wish remain,
Expel the lurking poison from my heart;
and let thy gracious hand, (unerring guide,)
Conduct me safe to everlasting bliss.

PSALM CXLII

I.

To God the refuge of his saints,
I humbly breathed my ardent prayer,
And poured out all my long complaints,
And spread before him every care.

II.

My spirit overwhelm'd with grief,
Surroundings snares beset my way;
Of thee, O Lord, I sought relief,
whose eyes my devious path survey.

III.

All other helps I find were vain,
And hope, and friends, and comfort fail'd;
to thee alone I told my pain,
While yet my potent fears prevail'd.

IV.

To thee my God, I breathe my cries,
Dear refuge of my fainting heart;
Thou all on whom my hope relies,
I am undone if thou depart.

V.

Thou see'st my wretched, weak and low;
O Lord, attend my plaintive cry,
And save me from my every foe:
My foes how strong! How weak am I!

VI.

O free my soul, dissolve the chain,
Then shall I spread my praise abroad;
Thy saints shall join the cheerful strain,
And speak the bounties of thy God.

ANNE STEELE

PSALM CXLIII

I.

Hear, O my God, with pity hear
My humble supplicating moan;
In mercy answer all my prayer,
And make thy truth and goodness known.

II.

And O let mercy still be nigh;
Should awful justice frown severe,
Before the terrors of thine eye,
What trembling mortal can appear?

III.

My persecuting foes prevail,
Almost I yield my struggling breath;
The cheerful rays of comfort fail,
And sink me to the shades of death.

IV.

While thus oppressive sorrows flow,
Unintermitting o'er my head;
my inmost powers are whelm'd in woe,
And all my hopes and joys are fled.

V.

I call to mind the former days;
Thy ancient works declare thy name,
Thy truth, thy goodness, and thy grace;
and these, O Lord, are still the same.

VI.

To thee, I stretch my suppliant hands,
To thee my longing soul aspires;
As cheering showers to thirsty lands,
Come, Lord, and fill these strong desires.

VII.

Come, Lord, on wings of mercy fly,
My spirit fails at thy delay;
Hide not thy face; I faint, I die,
Without thy blissful healing ray

VIII.

Speak to my heart; the gloomy night
Shall vanish, and sweet morning break;
In thee I trust, my guide, my light,
Teach me the way my feet should take.

IX.

My soul's desires ascend to thee,
O save me from my numerous foes;
To thy kind guardian wing I flee,
For safe defense and sweet repose.

X.

Teach me to do thy sacred will;
Thou art my God, my hope, my stay;
Let thy good spirit lead me still,
And point the safe, the upright way.

XI.

Thy name, thy righteousness I plead,
O Lord, revive my drooping heart;
Let these distressing fears recede,
And bid my troubles all depart.

XII.

Those unrelenting foes destroy,
Which thus against my peace combine;
Then shall my service be my joy,
And all my active powers be thine.

ANNE STEELE

PSALM CXLIV

I.

Blest be the Lord, my strength, my shield,
Amid the dangers of the field;
'Tis he instructs me for the fight,
And arms me with resistless might.

II.

His constant love, his saving power,
 Is my defense, my sacred tower;
Rebellion hears his potent word,
And my glad people own their Lord.

III.

Lord, what is man, that he should share
Thy kind regard, thy constant care?
Can all the weak, the wretched race,
Deserve such condescending grace?

IV.

Man's short existence, frail at best,
Is empty vanity confess'd;
His life, a shadow, fleets away,
and leaves no traces of its stay.

V.

Descend from heaven, almighty Lord,
And earth shall tremble at thy word;
The smoking hills with conscious fear,
Shall own their awful Maker near.

VI.

While thy keen pointed lightenings fly,
Like flaming arrows through the sky,
My foes disperse'd shall rise no more,
Nor dare the terrors of thy power.

VII.

O let thy potent arm control
These threatening waves that round the roll,
These sons of vanity that rise,
With fraudful hands and impious lies.

VIII.

Then shall thy name new songs inspire,
And wake to joy the sounding lyre,
And every tuneful string shall raise
In various notes, my grateful praise.

IX.

'Tis power divine, 'tis God alone,
Whom kings preserv'd in dangers, own;
Who saves, in war's tumultuous strife,
From raging swords his servant's life.

X.

O Lord, thy saving power oppose
To these invading threatening foes;
These strangers to thy sacred laws,
Whose boast is vain, and false their cause.

XI.

Then shall our sons beneath thy care,
Grow up like plants erect and fair;
Our daughters shall like pillars rise,
Where royal buildings charm the eyes.

XII.

Then plenty shall our stores increase,
Plenty, the lovely child of peace;
The fold its fleecy wealth shall yield,
and pour its thousands o'er the field.

XIII.

The well-fed ox shall then afford
His cheerful labours to his lord;
No more shall cruel plunder reign,
Nor want nor misery complain.

XIV

O happy people! favor'd state!
Whom such peculiar blessings wait;
Happy! who on the Lord depend,
Their God, their guardian, and their friend.

PSALM CXLV

I.

My God, my king, to thee I'll raise
My voice, and all my powers;
Unwearied songs of sacred praise
   Shall fill the circling hours.

II.

Thy name shall dwell upon my tongue,
   While suns shall set and rise,
And tune my everlasting song,
   When all creation dies.

III.

Great is the Lord! our souls adore,
   We wonder whilst we praise!
His power what creature can explore,
   Or equal honors raise?

IV.

Yet shall thy works, almighty Lord,
    Our noblest songs adorn;
Thy glorious acts we will record,
    For ages yet unborn.

V.

Thy praise shall be my awful theme,
    The wonders of thy power;
I'll speak the honors of thy name,
    And bid the world adore.

VI.

The men that hear my sacred lyre,
    Shall spread thy praises around;
While thy tremendous deeds inspire
    To notes of solemn sound.

VII.

But sweetly flowing strains shall tell
    The riches of thy grace;
And songs with grateful joy reveal
    Thy spotless righteousness.

VIII.

How full the Lord's compassions flow!
    His wrath, how slow to rise!
Swift pardon smiles upon his brow,
    And every terror dies.

IX.

How large his tender mercies are!
    How wide his power extends!
On his beneficence and care
    The universe depends.

X.

Great God, whilst nature speaks thy praise,
  With all her numerous tongues,
Thy saints shall tune diviner lays,
  And love inspire their songs.

XI.

Thy power and grandeur shall sing,
  The glories of thy reign;
Thy wondrous deeds, Almighty King,
  Shall fill the raptur'd strain.

XII.

Thy kingdom, Lord, forever stands,
  While earthly thrones decay;
And time submits to thy commands,
  While ages roll away.

XIII.

The falling saint, with powerful grace,
  The God of love will raise;
The humble, bending with distress,
  Shall rise and speak his praise.

XIV.

To thee, O Lord, for daily meat,
  Thy creatures lift their eyes;
On thee, their common Father, wait,
  From thee, receive supplies.

XV.

Thy sovereign bounty freely gives
  Its unexhausted store;
And universal nature lives
  On thy sustaining power.

XVI.

Holy and just in all its ways,
    Is providence divine;
In all its works, immortal rays
    Of power and mercy shine.

XVII.

Whoe'er invokes the God of grace,
    Shall find him ever near;
To all that humbly seek his face
    He lends a pitying ear.

XVIII.

His pitying attends the cry
    Of those who fear his name;
Their every want he will supply,
    And raise their sinking frame.

XIX.

How blest in his protecting care,
    The souls who love the Lord!
While impious men his vengeance dare,
    And die beneath the sword.

XX.

The praise of God, delightful theme!
    Shall fill my heart and tongue;
Let all creation bless his name,
    In one eternal song.

PSALM CXLVI

I.

Ye sons of Zion, praise the Lord,
  Come tune your songs in sweet accord,
Awake my soul, awake and join
The sacred hymn, and notes divine.

II.

The praises of my God, my King,
(While I have life or breath to sing,)
Shall fill my heart, and tune my tongue,
'Till heaven improve the blissful song.

III.

No more in princes vainly trust,
Frail sons of earth; man is but dust!
With all his pride, with all his power,
The helpless creature of an hour.

IV.

He breathes, he thinks, but ah, he dies
No more the potent, or the wife;
The scheme his morning thoughts begun,
Sinks down before the setting sun.

V.

Happy the man, whose hopes divine
On Israel's guardian God recline!
Who can with sacred transport say,
This God is mine, my help, my stay.

VI.

Heaven, earth and sea declare his name;
He built and fill'd their spacious frame;
But o'er creation's fairest lines
His steadfast truth unchanging shines.

VII.

His justice favors those who mourn,
Beneath the proud oppressor's scorn;
The hungry poor his hand sustains,
And breaks the wretched captive's chains.

VIII.

To sightless eyes, long clos'd in night
His touch restores the joys of light;
Poor mourners rais'd confess his care,
He loves the humble and sincere.

IX.

If wandering strangers friendless roam,
Divine protection is their home;
The Lord relieves the widow's care,
And dries the weeping orphan's tears.

X.

But vengeance awaits the impious race
Who hate his laws, and scorn his grace;
Their ways to sure destruction tend,
And all their hopes in ruin end.

XI.

The Lord shall reign forever king,
And age to age his glory sing;
Thy God, O happy Zion, reigns,
Resound his praise in joyful strains.

PSALM CXLVII

I.

Praise ye the Lord: Oh, blissful theme,
　To sing the honors of his name!
'Tis pleasure, 'tis divine delight,
And praise is lovely in his sight!

II.

His Salem now the Lord restores;
No more her ruin she deplores;
Again the scatter'd tribes return,
And Israel's sons no longer mourn.

III.

No more than breaking hearts despair,
He binds their wounds with tender care;
His healing hand removes their pain,
And cheerful comfort smiles again.

IV.

He counts the host of starry flames,
Knows all their natures and their names;
Great is our God! his wondrous power,
And boundless wisdom we adore.

V.

How gracious is the Lord! how kind!
To raise the meek dejected mind;
But awful tears in his frown,
Shall cast rebellious sinners down.

VI.

Sing to the Lord, let praise inspire
The grateful voice, the tuneful lyre;
In strains of joy, proclaim abroad
The endless glories of our God.

VII.

He veils the sky with treasured showers;
On earth the plenteous blessings pours;
The mountains smile in lively green,
And fairer blooms the flowery scene.

VIII.

His bounteous hand, (great spring of good!)
Provides the brute creation food;
He feeds the ravens when they cry;
All nature lives beneath his eye.

IX.

In nature what can him delight,
Most lovely in its Maker's sight?
Not active strength his favor moves,
Nor comely form he best approves.

X.

Dear to the Lord, forever dear,
The heart where he implants his fear;
The souls who on his grace rely,
These, these are lovely in his eye.

XI.

Jerusalem, his honors raise;
Thy God, O Zion, claims thy praise;
His mighty arm defends thy gates,
His blessing on thy children waits.

XII.

Sweet peace, to crown the happy scene,
O'er thy fair border smiles serene;
The finest wheat luxuriant grows,
And joyful plenty round thee flows.

XIII.

He speaks! and swiftly from the skies
To earth the sovereign mandate flies;
Observant nature hears his word,
And bows obedient to her Lord.

XIV.

Now thick descending flakes of snow,
O'er earth a fleecy mantle throw;
Now glittering frost o'er all the plains
Extends its universal chains.

XV.

At his fierce storms of icy hail
The shivering powers of nature fail;
Before his cold what life can stand,
Unshelter'd by his guardian hand?

XVI.

He speaks! the ice and snows obey,
And nature's fetters melt away;
Now vernal gales soft rising blow,
And murmuring waters gently flow.

XVII.

But nobler works his grace record,
To Israel he reveals his word;
To Jacob's happy sons alone
He makes his sacred precepts known.

XVIII.

Such bliss no other nation shares,
The laws of heaven are only theirs;
Ye favor'd tribes your voices raise,
And bless your God in songs of praise.

PSALM CXLVIII

Jehovah's praise, in high immortal strains
  Resound, ye heavens, through all your blissful plains.
Bright with the splendor of his dazzling rays,
Exalted realms of joy reflect his praise,
Through the fair mansions of eternal day;
His praise let all your shining ranks proclaim,
And teach the distant worlds your Maker's name.
His glorious power, O radiant sun, display,
Far as thy vital beams diffuse the day.
Thou silver moon, array'd in softer light,
Recount his wonders to the listening night:
Let all thy glittering train attendant weight,
And every star his Maker's name repeat.

  Ye heavens supreme, where his full glories shine,
Declare his praise, with eloquence divine.
Ye watery clouds, as round the skies you move,
Convey his wondrous name where'er you rove.
His power, ye fair expanded skies, proclaim,
Whose word produc'd the vast stupendous frame.
On his decree the heavenly orbs depend,
Nor change their course 'till time in nature end.
  Let earth and seas their Maker's honor raise,
And monsters shout his name in dreadful praise.

  Ethereal fires which blaze along the skies,
Convey his name to earth, and swift surprise.

  Let changeful vapour rise his power to show,
And in soft praise decsend the fleecy snow.
Let hail impetuous rattling on the ground,
In rougher cadence spread his wonders round.

Whilst stormy winds that bear his awful word,
Compel the trembling world to own her Lord.

Ye rocky mountains, sound his praise on high;
In joyful notes, verdant hills, reply.
Ye fruitful trees, your Maker's bounty show,
And smile his praise on every loaded bough:
While stately cedars, with the cluster'd vine,
And lowly plants the silent worship join.

Ye beasts of prey, who wild in forest roam,
Ye gentle herds, who know your peaceful home,
Declare his praise, whose ample stores maintain
The countless tenants of his wide domain.

Ye birds, that high in trackless ether rove,
Or with soft music charm the vocal grove,
In every note your Maker's praise resound,
While humble reptiles whisper from the ground.

Ye monarchs of the earth, your Lord adore;
From him you hold your delegated power.

Ye judges, his impartial laws revere,
Be every sentence guided by his fear:
let senate, prince and people join, to raise
The grateful tribute of obedient praise.

In life's unfolding bloom, ye young and gay,
While flowery pleasures strew your verdant way.
Adore the bounteous hand, which largely pours
Its sweetest blessings on your vernal hours;
In your Creator's praise, with duteous joy,
Your bloom of life, your active powers employ.

Let age declining to the gates of death,
In praise respire their feebly panting breath:
And infants in their dawn of reason join,
Their lisping voice, and learn the song divine.

   Let heaven, and earth, and time, and nature sing
The glorious name of their Almighty King:
But equal honors, earth nor heaven can raise,
His glory far transcends creation's praise.
Yet while creation owns his guardian care,
Superior bliss his happy children share;
To him they gain a near access, and prove
The wonders of his condescending love.
Let Israel with peculiar joy proclaim
The boundless glories of Jehovah's name.

PSALM CXLIX

I.

Come praise the Lord, ye tuneful bands,
Ye saints assembled in his name;
New strains of joy your God demands,
New mercies all your praises claim.

II.

Let Israel's tribes, with blessings crown'd,
Their God, their mighty Maker sing;
And Zion's sons with joy resound
The endless glories of their king.

III.

His name the measur'd dance shall guide,
And joy and sacred mirth inspire;
His name shall o'er the song preside,
And tune the sweet, the charming lyre.

IV.

He bends complacent to your praise,
Your God approves the blest employ;
The thankful meek, his love will raise
To crowns of everlasting joy.

V.

O let the saints aloud rejoice,
And sounds of glory fill the song;
All day let rapture to their voice,
And night the blissful strain prolong.

VI.

Let every mouth be fill'd with praise,
The God of heaven their awful theme;
Whilst his resistless sword displays,
In heaven-taught hands, his dreadful name.

VII.

Bright terrors wait his high commands,
When justice waves the flaming sword,
Vindictive o'er the heathen lands,
Which hate his saints and scorn his word.

VIII.

While haughty princes bound in chains,
Confess the just, the powerful God;
Let awful joy in warlike strains,
Proclaim his glorious acts abroad.

IX.

His hand, thus righteously severe,
Fulfills the threatenings of his word;
Thus honored shall the saints appear;
Adore the great, the glorious Lord.

PSALM CL

I.

Praise ye the Lord; let praise employ,
In his own courts, your songs of joy;
The spacious firmament around,
Shall echo back the joyful sound.

II.

Recount his works in strains divine;
His wondrous works how bright they shine;
Praise him for his almighty deeds,
Whose greatness all your praise exceeds.

III.

Awake the trumpet's piercing sound,
To spread your sacred pleasures round;
While sweeter music tends the lute,
The warbling heart, and breathing flute.

IV.

Ye virgin train with joy advance
To praise him in the graceful dance;
To praise awake each tuneful string,
And to the solemn organ sing.

V.

Let the loud cymbal sounding high,
To softer deeper notes reply;
Harmonious let the concert rise,
And bear the rapture to the skies.

VI.

Let all whom life and breath inspire,
Attend, and join the blissful choir;
But chiefly you who know his word,
Adore, and love, and praise the Lord.

Made in United States
Orlando, FL
13 January 2024

42469834R00300